Contents

List of Figures

The Corporate Environment

David Farnham is principal lecturer in industrial relations at Portsmouth Polytechnic. In addition to teaching, industrial and consultancy experience, he has written widely in a range of academic and professional journals. He is author of *Personnel in context* and co-author of *Public administration in the United Kingdom* (with Malcolm McVicar) and *Understanding industrial relations* (with John Pimlott).

Management Studies Series
Series Editors: Michael Armstrong and David Farnham

Today's business environment demands that managers possess a wide range of knowledge, skills and competencies. The Professional Management Foundation Programme is a major initiative developed by a group of forward-looking professional institutes to help them meet these needs. This series of practical, introductory texts, while ideally suited to students on the Programme, will be equally useful for anyone wishing to enhance their understanding of contemporary management techniques and methods.

Other titles in the series:

Managing Human Resources
Jane Weightman

Finance and Accounting for Managers
David Davies

Management Information Systems and Statistics
Roland and Frances Bee

Management Processes and Functions
Michael Armstrong

MANAGEMENT STUDIES

The Corporate Environment

David Farnham

Institute of Personnel Management

First published in 1990
Reprinted 1990
Reprinted 1992

© David Farnham, 1990

Phototypeset by Input Typesetting Ltd, London
and printed in Great Britain by Short Run Press, Exeter.

British Library Cataloguing in Publication Data
Farnham, David
    The corporate environment.
    1. Great Britain.   Companies.   Management
    I. Title   II. Series
    658.00941

    ISBN 0–85292–439–9

List of Tables

viii *The Corporate Environment*

Editors' Foreword

Today's business environment demands that managers possess a wide range of knowledge, skills and competencies. As well as a sound understanding of management processes and functions, managers need to be able to make the best use of their time and talents, and of other people's, and to work with and through others to achieve corporate objectives. They also need to demonstrate a full understanding of the business environment and of their organization's key resources: its people, finance and information.

Management education in Britain has at last begun to take full account of these business realities. In particular, the Professional Management Foundation Programme is a major initiative developed by a group of forward-looking professional institutes to meet these needs. They recognize that a synthesis of knowledge and skills, and theory and practice, is vital for all managers and those aspiring to management positions.

For many years, the Institute of Personnel Management has been strongly committed to developing professional excellence. This major new series reflects this ideal. It covers five key areas: management processes and functions; the corporate environment; managing human resources; management information systems and statistics; and finance and accounting for managers. In drawing on the expertise of experienced teachers and managers, this series provides all students of management with an invaluable set of practical, introductory and informed texts on contemporary management studies.

MICHAEL ARMSTRONG
DAVID FARNHAM
April 1990

Acknowledgements

A number of people have contributed to the completion of this book. They include Jim Basker, Anne Cordwent, Felicity Farnham, Frances Farnham, Terry Hanson, Ron Hodrien and Matthew Reisz, who assisted in a variety of ways. I wish to acknowledge and thank them all. I would also like to thank Sylvia Horton, who read, commented on and suggested amendments to the draft manuscript. Without her contribution this book would not have been completed on time. Any remaining inaccuracies, errors or omissions are, of course, entirely my responsibility.

D.F.

Introduction

This book focuses on the external environment in which organizations and managements operate. Broadly defined, management consists of those generalist and specialist staff in all types of organizations who are responsible for organizational effectiveness and enterprise efficiency. Management as a group also exerts control over the resources employed by organizations and the activities conducted within them. According to Drucker, management is fast emerging as the central resource of the developed countries and the basic need of the developing ones. In the modern world 'management and managers are becoming the generic, the distinctive, the constitutive organs of developed society'.[1] More recently Drucker (1989) has claimed that 'rarely in human history has any institution emerged as quickly as management or had an impact so fast'. Indeed, 'in less than 150 years, management has transformed the social and economic fabric of the world's developed countries'.[2]

During the past several years much research and many books have been published on management. These have covered management as the activity of running things, managerial specialisms, managerial work and how management tasks are organized. Some studies have examined the elite status of management in society and the concept of managerialism in the modern world. Those supporting the managerialist thesis have proposed that in the advanced economies economic power has passed away from the owners of productive capital to the owners of technical and managerial expertise. According to writers such as Galbraith (1967), it is the managerial 'technostructure' that dominates modern enterprises, and it no longer finds profit-maximizing its main aim but rather survival, security and the elimination of risk.

Whilst much has been written on management in its various aspects, there is no up-to-date study of the wider corporate environment, or the external factors impinging on complex

1

business organizations, whether manufacturing, service or welfare ones, and the managerial tasks being conducted within them. This book, in meeting the syllabus requirements of Module 2 of the Consultative Council of Professional Management Organizations' foundation management programme, attempts to fill that gap in the literature. It should also prove useful to students on other courses˙ where the corporate environment is studied, such as the Diploma in Management Studies, business studies programmes and national diploma courses.

The book examines the corporate environment within which business and public sector organizations operate in the United Kingdom and has three main aims. First, it analyses and describes the environmental setting of modern business activity in both the private and public sectors. Second, it examines the main environmental factors affecting organizations and managerial policy making within them. Third, it outlines how management has to take account of these external environmental factors and influences in its corporate operations and decisions.

An introductory book of this nature must of necessity be selective in the topics identified, examined and discussed. And it is not intended to provide definitive and generic explanations of the impact of these complex socio-economic phenomena on private and public enterprises, since these are contingent on organizational circumstances. The book seeks instead to inform and sensitize its managerial readers to the wider environmental factors impinging on their organizations and to introduce students of management to the concepts, literature and ideas underpinning their studies of management and the corporate environment. It needs to be recognized too that even if managements can better understand the external environment in which their enterprises operate, and even partially manage it, they cannot effectively control it. The corporate environment is continuously changing and is, by definition, external to the individual and collective influences of management as decision-takers and executives of corporate policies.

Figure 1 provides an analytical framework for examining the corporate environment in which modern business corporations and public-sector organizations operate. In one sense the corporate sector, whether private or public, is the prime means whereby society's limited economic resources are converted and transfor-

Figure 1 The corporate environment: an analytical framework

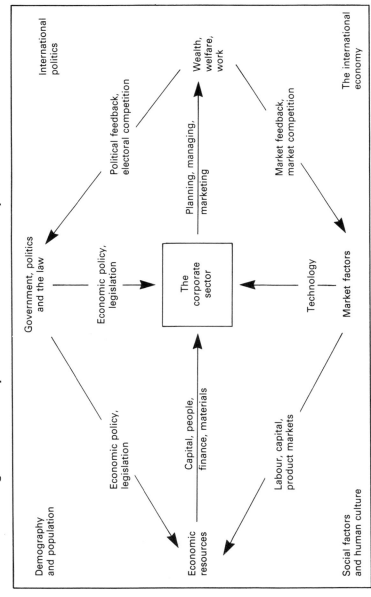

International politics

Demography and population

Wealth, welfare, work

The international economy

Political feedback, electoral competition

Market feedback, market competition

Government, politics and the law

Planning, managing, marketing

Economic policy, legislation

The corporate sector

Technology

Market factors

Economic policy, legislation

Capital, people, finance, materials

Labour, capital, product markets

Economic resources

Social factors and human culture

med, through planning, managing and marketing, into the creation of new resources which can loosely be described as 'wealth' and 'welfare'. In another sense, the corporate sector is in crucial juxtaposition between the market factors which, to varying degrees, determine the ways in which wealth, welfare and work are created and distributed in society and the political and legal forces regulating the collective activities of business corporations as producers, consumers and employers of society's, and increasingly the world's, scarce resources. The corporate sector not only uses, converts and creates resources for economic, political and social ends. More significantly, it also provides the interface between market demands for economic efficiency and the accumulation of private capital, on the one side, and political demands for public welfare provision and citizen rights on the other. Herein lie the roots of the tensions between the ideas of the enterprise culture of recent times and those of the Welfare State which was created in the early post-war period.

Another feature of the corporate environment highlighted in figure 1 is the multiplicity of external contexts in which organizational activity takes place. They include demography and population trends, social structure, human culture, the international economy and international politics. They all affect the corporate sector and are forces exogenous to organizations which have to be taken into account in planning, policy-making and managing within them. Moreover, the corporate environment is not static. A further feature is its dynamic and transitory nature. It is not stability which characterizes the modern world but constant and continuous change, whether economic, social, political or technological. One of management's tasks is to identify, predict and react to changes in the organizational environment and manage them effectively.

Within this framework, chapter 1 examines the contexts in which capitalist business organization and corporate ownership take place. Chapter 2 provides the background to the corporate sector and describes the basic elements making up the wealth-producing and welfare-providing organizations. Chapters 3 and 4 examine the demographic and social structures of the UK, the changes taking place within them and their impact on private and public-sector organizations. In chapters 5 and 6 the economic and market background of business operations is considered, as well as the macro-economic context in which government economic policy choices are made. The political framework within which public policy decisions are determined and implemented is discussed in chapters 7 and 8, together with the role of elections and political groupings in a liberal democracy such as the UK. Chapters 9 and 10 analyse and outline the nature, sources and administration of the law and the legal context within which business corporations are required to operate. Finally, the epilogue summarizes the changing global, geo-political and socio-technical contexts within which organizations trade and operate, and some of their implications for managers.

References

1 DRUCKER P. *Technology, management and society*. London, Heinemann, 1970. p 36.
2 DRUCKER P. *The new realities*. London, Heinemann, 1989. p 213.

1

Capitalism, Corporate Ownership and Corporate Culture

This chapter describes the institutional setting within which modern business organizations operate. It starts from the assumption that the United Kingdom, like all Western economies, is both an industrial society and a capitalist one. An industrial society is one where large-scale enterprises are the characteristic form of business organization and where, traditionally, large numbers of workers, advanced technology and costly resources are brought together in a corporate system.

These large business enterprises are characterized by high degrees of role and functional specialization. The organizational division of labour, for example, takes place both horizontally and vertically. Horizontally, job tasks and work roles are differentiated according to their operational, functional or departmental responsibilities, with professional managers directing organizational sub-units. There is also a separation of decision-taking from action-taking so that vertical jobs are distinguished by the amount of discretion that each role has. This provides a hierarchy of managerial direction and control, enabling managerial role holders to operate within a defined structure of corporate power and authority.

The prime economic goal of the modern business corporation is operational efficiency, as measured by its productivity, or output per unit of inputs employed, and its profitability, or its surplus of revenue over costs. It is through the economies of scale of mass production, or mass provision, that substantial reductions in the average costs of products or services are achieved and increasing levels of cost-effective output or throughput are attained.

Capitalism exists where society's capital resources, or human-made aids to production, are predominantly privately owned, though not necessarily by individuals. Indeed, every capitalist society has its own distinct forms of capital ownership and control. Under capitalism, society's economic resources, including labour, are allocated primarily by market forces or the price mechanism, with the continual search for profit or surplus value acting as the economic dynamism. What distinguish the exact form of capitalism in a particular country are the extent to which the market system is used, the degree of competition in its markets and the level of government intervention in the economy.

Industrial Capitalism

There are two theories explaining the development of industrial capitalism. One is the theory of industrial society, the other is the theory of capitalist society. The theory of industrial society draws on the works of mainstream liberal writers such as Dahrendorf (1959), Kerr (1973), Aron (1961) and Galbraith (1967). The theory of capitalist society is drawn from Marxist writings.

Those supporting the theory of industrial society place more emphasis on the industrial than on the capitalist nature of modern societies. They identify the major characteristics of industrial society as the dominance of industry over agriculture, the growth of large, complex organizations and the application of sophisticated technologies in the provision of goods and services. The extension of industrial society is accompanied by high density of population, urbanization, secularization, political democracy and continuous change.

Dahrendorf argues that capitalist society, which was typical of nineteenth-century Britain, has given way to industrial society because both the capitalist class and the working class have disintegrated and there is no longer social conflict between them. Further, because of the complexity of their economic systems, industrial societies become highly specialized, with an increasingly fragmented division of labour. This is accompanied by the emergence of a managerial technostructure, the separation of corporate ownership from managerial control and an increasingly fragmented labour force, with a plurality of skills, statuses and interests. The new managerial class, it is argued, is more socially responsible than was the former capitalist class and, because of its acknowledged expertise and professional skills, is also more technically competent.

Kerr argues that all industrial societies, whether Western

capitalist countries or State socialist ones, are converging and becoming similar in their institutional and cultural features. This is because the same industrial technologies produce corresponding occupational structures and stratification systems. As countries develop they all require higher levels of managerial, technical and human resource skills. Kerr also provides a theory of development. It predicts increasing wealth and leisure and therefore an end to political and social conflict. Rising affluence and increased welfare provision, it is suggested, remove the causes of protest based on class. Bell (1973) links the development of industrial society with the extension of political democracy and the end of ideology in politics. He argues that industrial societies are characterized by a basic consensus about values, the efficacy of compromise and the ability of science and technology to find solutions to all human problems.

The theory of industrial society is both optimistic and idealistic. However, its implicit ideology of the beneficence of industrialism and technocracy has been criticized not only by Marxists. Other writers have pointed out that some people are increasingly alienated in industrial societies. They claim that social *anomie*, or normlessness, develops as traditional bases of authority and social integration are undermined by social change and modernization. The process of industrialization is not problem-free. Moreover, welfare economists, such as Mishan (1977), Hirsch (1976) and Pacey (1983), question whether economic growth and technological development can be equated with economic welfare and social progress. The economic costs of continuous growth do not take into account the social costs associated with damage to the environment, the depletion of finite resources and the impact on personal well-being.

The theory of capitalist society, in contrast, is based on Marxist analysis. It suggests that the essence of capitalism is its division of society into two classes related to the means of production. Those owning the means of production constitute a ruling class, the bourgeoisie; those owning only their labour power are the working class, or proletariat. It is the move away from agrarian feudal society to a capitalist industrial one that provides the opportunity for transferring power from the land-owning class to the owners of society's capital resources such as its factories, machinery and money.

In its continual search for profit, either to reinvest or to invest elsewhere, the capitalist class needs to maintain demand for its goods and services. This requires ever larger units and scales of production and results in monopoly capitalism as smaller, inefficient production units are swallowed up by larger, successful ones. Historically the pursuit of success in the marketplace demanded the expansion not only of internal markets but also of protected external ones. Hence governments were enlisted to support imperialist policies, justifying the economic development of the non-industrial world. In this way, empires, colonies and protectorates became both sources of raw materials and markets for capitalist manufactured goods.

The theory of capitalist society also argues that conflict between the capitalist class and the wage-earning class is endemic. Since those owning productive capital want the highest return on their investment, they need to keep wage costs down. This creates continuous tensions and antagonisms between the two opposing classes, which are constantly trying to maintain or increase their own share of the national product. Changes in society come about as a result of this conflict, with the relative power of organized capital and organized labour able to determine the distribution of the wealth and resources of capitalism between them. However, as wealth accumulates in the form of money, that money becomes a form of capital—finance capital. A separation of productive capital and finance capital takes place, with finance capital becoming the dominant element as capitalism matures.

Inherent in advanced capitalism are problems which necessitate the involvement of the State, either to support private industry or to provide those goods or services which capitalists are unwilling to supply. These include education, welfare services, research and development, defence, and the provision of State-run monopoly industries. In this way, Marxists argue, capitalism and the State become inextricably linked, with the latter always serving the interests of the former. Whilst supporters of capitalism praise its efficiency, wealth-producing potential and compatibility with individual human freedoms, Marxists claim that it is characterized by exploitation, class struggle and personal alienation.

Given the twin theories of industrial society and capitalist society, and in order to understand the nature of modern industrial capitalism, to what extent are these two apparently differing approaches to modern Western economies compatible? In this writer's view they are complementary. Indeed, it is more useful and realistic to accept that 'it is only through the synthesis of aspects of each of the contending theories that an adequate interpretation of the available empirical material can be made'.[1] In practice, Western industrial societies such as that of the UK are diverse, complex and dynamic societies rooted in capitalist social relations. They are also technologically advanced, and within them the corporate sector, whether privately or publicly owned, is a focal source of wealth formation, welfare provision, capital investment and work creation.

Corporate Ownership and Control

Some idea of the vast economic power and financial resources possessed by large capitalist organizations in the UK is indicated by the fact that the total financial capital employed in its top 1,000 companies, in 1987–88, was about £348,043 million, with an average return on capital of about 6 per cent. Their turnover was estimated at £555,054 million, ranging from the largest, that of British Petroleum, with sales of £34,942 million, to James Longley (Holdings), building contractors, with sales of £59 million. The pre-tax profits of these 1,000 companies totalled £55,799 million, providing an average profit per company of about 10 per cent on sales.[2]

The classic model of corporate ownership and control in the business sector is that of the small to medium-sized firm, owned and controlled by the second or third generation of the founding family which created it in the heyday of early capitalism. Such firms continue to exist but they are becoming fewer and are now the exception rather than the rule. In general, family-owned and family-controlled enterprises have long ago succumbed to the massive economic and social changes which have transformed British society and industrial capitalism in the twentieth century.

The modern business enterprise is the large, sometimes multinational corporation that is impersonally owned and controlled. The former system of personal corporate ownership, with individuals and families controlling their own companies, is being replaced by a system of impersonal ownership and corporate control. Whilst modern business enterprises are just as much owner-controlled as were their predecessors, the identity of the owners has changed. In the UK of the late twentieth century 'the owners of the largest modern enterprises are other enterprises, which are, in turn, owned by yet other enterprises'. These enterprises are linked to one another 'through chains of control which do not originate in the personal wealth and power of individuals and families . . . [but] by interweaving chains of intercorporate relations'.[3]

Table 1
Percentage distribution of shareholdings in British PLCs, 1963–81

Shareholders	1963	1969	1975	1981
Individuals	54·0	47·2	37·5	28·2
Charities	2·1	2·1	2·3	2·2
Banks	1·3	1·7	0·7	0·3
Insurance companies	10·0	12·0	15·9	20·5
Pension funds	6·4	9·0	16·8	26·7
Investment trusts	11·3	10·5	10·5	6·8
Unit trusts	1·3	2·9	4·1	3·6
Companies	5·1	5·4	3·0	5·1
Public sector	1·5	2·6	3·6	3·0
Overseas	7·0	6·6	5·6	3·6
Total	100·0	100·0	100·0	100·0

Source: *The Observer*, 13 November 1983.

Some indication of the growth of corporate ownership of UK companies in recent years is provided in table 1. It shows a significant decrease in the percentage shareholdings held by private individuals between 1963 and 1981 and a steady rise of corporate shareholdings. Although banks and investment trusts appear to have marginally diminished their direct percentage shareholdings during these years, insurance companies and pension funds dramatically increased theirs. An examination of total corporate and institutional shareholdings for these years of banks, insurance companies, pension funds, unit trusts and companies collectively shows that they rose from some 35 per cent of the total in 1963 to 42 per cent in 1969, 51 per cent in 1975 and 63 per cent in 1981. These trends continued during the past decade.

Scott (1986) provides a detailed analysis of corporate ownership and control for the mid-1970s. Using the methods and techniques pioneered by early corporate ownership researchers such as Florence (1961) and Moyle (1971), he presents a systematic and comprehensive analysis of the structure and corporate control of Britain's main large companies. He focuses on the top 250 companies of 1976. His final classification of corporate control is presented in table 2. He uses the concepts of 'majority control', 'minority control' and control through a 'constellation of interests' as the main categories for analysing contemporary corporate structure.

Majority control of a company may be 'simple majority', 'wholly owned' or 'shared majority'. Simple majority control describes situations where those holding a straight majority of shares in a company can act in much the same way as did traditional capitalist entrepreneurs. Wholly owned control is a form of majority control where *all* the relevant shares are held by the company's controllers, whether as individuals or corporate bodies. Shared majority control involves co-operation between the dominant shareholders, collectively having majority ownership.

Minority control takes three forms: 'secure minority'; 'limited minority'; and 'shared minority'. Examination of minority control focuses on the twenty largest shareholders. This 'will disclose the dominant shareholding interest, if such an interest exists, or will show the composition of the controlling constellation'.[4] Secure minority control is where the largest single shareholder cannot be outvoted by any coalition drawn from the remaining nineteen of the twenty largest shareholders in an enterprise. Limited minority control is where dominant shareholders have rather less than the percentage required for secure minority control. Shared minority control involves two or more associated but independent shareholders co-operating with one another.

Mutual control operates in the building and friendly society sector, where 'policy-holders or depositors are the voting members, and voting rights do not vary with the size of the policy or deposit'.[5] In enterprises where financial intermediaries, such as insurance companies, pension funds and the commercial banks, are the dominant shareholders but none is able to exercise minority control individually, control is exercised through a constellation of interests.

In table 2 it is notable that the single largest category of corpor-

Table 2

Corporate control in Britain: classification 1976

Type of Controller

Mode of control	Personal	Corporate			State	Mixed	Other	Total
		British	*Foreign*	*Mixed*				
Public corporations	–	–	–	–	13	–	–	13
Wholly owned	7	1	28	0	2	0	0	38
Majority	15	2	9	0	2	0	0	28
Shared majority	0	7	1	3	0	1	0	12
Secure minority	13	9	3	0	1	3	0	29
Limited minority	11	4	2	0	0	1	0	18
Shared minority	0	2	0	0	0	2	0	4
Mutual	–	–	–	–	–	–	8	8
Constellation of interests	–	–	–	–	–	100	–	100
Total	46	25	43	3	18	107	8	250

Source: J. Scott, *Capitalist property and financial power*, Brighton, Wheatsheaf, 1986.

ate control is through 'a constellation of interests'. This occurs
when there is no dominant shareholding. In other words, 100 of
Britain's top 250 companies in 1976, or 40 per cent of them, were
controlled in this way, with a further eight subject to mutual
control. The next largest category was those companies with some
kind of majority control; there were seventy-eight of these, almost
a third of the total. Forty-four companies, or under 20 per cent
of the total, had some kind of minority control. Thirteen enterprises which were publicly controlled made up the rest.

Out of all 250 enterprises taken together, seventy-nine, or about
a third of them, appeared to have a single controlling interest.
These comprised thirteen public corporations, thirty-eight wholly
owned enterprises and twenty-eight majority-owned ones. Of
these, the State had a controlling interest in seventeen, personal
shareholders in twenty-two, with the remaining forty being controlled by corporate interests. Those controlled by corporate interests were predominantly foreign-owned, with the largest single
group being wholly owned foreign subsidiaries. British and foreign
corporate interests were also important in 'shared control' enterprises. Overall it can be seen that in 1976 107 enterprises were
controlled by 'mixed' interests, seventy-one by British, foreign
or other corporate interests, forty-six by personal interests and
eighteen by the State. According to Scott, corporate capital, entrepreneurial capital and State capital 'make up the controlling
groups in those enterprises having a dominant interest, and they
also comprise the main participants in the controlling constellation
of the remaining enterprises'.[6]

Corporate Culture

Whilst industrial capitalism provides an economic framework and
a macro-culture within which business decisions and market
relations are determined, each business enterprise, whether privately or publicly owned, is unique. Industrial capitalism is characterized by a number of features. The main ones are:

- The economic means of production are privately owned.
- Economic activity is geared to making profit for the owners
  of private capital.

- Workers sell their skills for money wages.
- The buying and selling of goods are organized into markets, where economic decisions are 'commodified'.

Each capitalist organization, however, has its own corporate culture. Some managerial leaders of organizations deliberately foster a distinctive culture. Others have no concept of corporate culture. In these cases it emerges and changes by accident and exception rather than by design.

Although it is a difficult term to define with precision, Handy (1985) describes corporate culture as 'deep-set beliefs about the way work should be organized, the way authority should be exercised, people rewarded, people controlled'.[7] Thus all organizations have corporate cultures, or groups of subcultures, which may be 'strong' or 'weak'. Strong cultures are deliberately fostered by management and are readily acknowledged, if not always accepted, by those working in such organizations and by their customers and clients. Weak cultures are more heterogeneous than strong ones and they are less central to corporate performance and identity. Examples of strong cultures are 'patient care' in the National Health Service and 'IBM means service'.

Managing corporate culture

There are various ways of analysing corporate culture. A useful one is provided by Deal and Kennedy (1982). They claim that corporate cultures differ but each is seen to have three general characteristics: 'Is the company's way of doing things consciously planned or not? . . . Has the company made its culture explicit, or has it been left implicit? . . . Finally, is the company's culture managed or not?' Deal and Kennedy suggest that though it is not yet the norm, 'the concept of an explicit, conscious, managed culture as a guide to behavior is spreading among managers at all levels'. Consequently, actively managing corporate culture is increasingly recognized as making an important contribution to employee effectiveness and corporate performance.[8]

Since each company has different markets, products, customers and competitors, Deal and Kennedy argue that it is the business environment which acts as the greatest single influence shaping corporate culture. They believe that strong cultures are powerful levers for guiding employee behaviour, by helping them perform better. They provide systems of informal rules spelling out how people are expected to behave and they enable people to feel better about what they do, so that they are more likely to work harder. 'By and large, the most successful managers we know are . . . those who strive to make a mark through creating a guiding vision, shaping shared values, and otherwise providing leadership for the people with whom they work.'[9]

Deal and Kennedy use the term 'strong culture' to describe the driving force behind American business success and 'corporate tribes' to classify corporate cultures. In analysing the components of corporate cultures, they identify 'values', 'heroes', 'rites and rituals' and the 'cultural network' as their essential elements. Values are the bedrock of corporate cultures, since they provide 'a sense of common direction for all employees and guidelines for their day-to-day behavior'. In successful businesses, emphasizing explicit corporate values, these values stand for something, are known by those working in the company and involve managers shaping and developing them in response to changes in the business environment. Companies guided by strong shared values tend to reflect them in their organizational design. 'Shared values and beliefs also play an important role in communicating to the outside world what to expect of a company.'[10]

If values are the core of corporate cultures, heroes personify them and provide role models for employees to follow. This is because 'heroism is a leadership component that is all but forgotten by modern management'. Whether corporate heroes are born or made, it is argued, they reinforce the basic values of corporate cultures. Besides supplying role models, corporate heroes make success attainable and human, symbolize the company to the outside world, preserve what makes the company special, set standards of performance, and motivate employees. It is suggested that organizations need to recognize the potential of corporate heroes as the 'stuff and hope of culture'. It is only when companies 'make heroes out of bosses and workers—that is, when we all accept the responsibility of playing to a world stage—will we banish the sterility of modern organization'.[11]

Rites and rituals, according to Deal and Kennedy, are the systematic and routine programmes of daily corporate life. 'In their mundane manifestations—which we call rituals—they show employees the kind of behavior that is expected of them.' Further, 'in their extravaganzas—which we call ceremonies—they provide visible and potent examples of what the company stands for'. Rites and rituals, in other words, are corporate cultures in action. A variety of rituals exist. They include social rituals, work rituals, management rituals and 'recognition' rituals, such as 'rites of passage' when people get promoted or retired. Through their corporate rituals strong cultures teach people how to behave.

It is through the cultural network that corporate values are promoted and communicated. A range of characters or role players in the cultural network is identified, such as 'storytellers', 'spies', 'priests', 'cabals' and 'whisperers'. These provide a hidden hierarchy of power within organizations, enabling those working them effectively to get things done and to understand what is going on around them. 'Culture networkers rely on the network to work for the bulk of their communications with the people in the organization.'[12]

The Deal and Kennedy cultural typology identifies four categories of generic corporate cultures. They stress, however, that no single company known today precisely fits into any one of these categories. In fact, within any single real-world organization, a mix of all four types of culture will be found. Indeed, some companies with very strong cultures are claimed to blend the best of all four elements. This is done 'in ways that allow these companies to perform well when the environment around them changes', as it inevitably does. The four categories are 'macho', 'worker/player', 'better' and 'process' cultures. Each is determined primarily by two features of the marketplace: the degree of risk associated with corporate activities and the speed at which companies and employees get feedback on whether their decisions or strategies are successful.

Table 3 indicates how different corporate cultures relate to marketplace features. Macho cultures, for example, consist of corporate individualists taking high risks with quick feedback on whether their actions are right or wrong. They enable companies to do what needs to be done in high-risk, quick-return situations. Building strong, cohesive cultures in macho climates is difficult. Worker/player cultures operate best where activity is everything, risks are few and market feedback is quick. They tend to have short-term perspectives but provide young people with

Table 3

Corporate cultures and marketplace features

Type of culture	Marketplace feedback	
	Degree of risk	Speed of feature
'Tough-guy macho'	High	Quick
'Work hard/play hard'	Low	Quick
'Better your company'	High	Slow
'Process'	Low	Little

Source: T. E. Deal and A. A. Kennedy, *Corporate cultures*, Reading, Mass. Addison-Wesley, 1982.

opportunities for making their mark. Better cultures involve 'big-stake decisions' involving high risks and slow feedback. They are vulnerable to short-term economic fluctuations and cash flow problems. Process cultures are low-risk, slow-feedback environments where the financial stakes are low. Protectiveness and caution by employees are typical responses to slow feedback and people are valued where they protect the system's integrity more than their own.[13]

Power, role, task and person cultures

Handy provides a different classification of corporate cultures. He identifies them as 'power', 'role', 'task' and 'person' cultures. He argues that a single culture should not be allowed to swamp an organization but any one organization 'will find itself pushed towards at least two and perhaps three of these cultures'. In his view organizations which are differentiated in their cultures, but which control that differentiation by integration, are likely to be more successful than those which do not. In managing corporate activities, managers are recommended to ensure that, 'if the appropriate culture prevails where that set of activities prevails, then that part of the organization will be more effective'.

Handy identifies four sets of activities: 'steady-state', 'innovative/developmental', 'breakdown/crises' and 'policy direction'. Role cultures are most appropriate for steady-state or routine activities and task cultures for innovative/developmental ones. Where unexpected breakdown/crises occur; and for policy direction activites, power cultures are to be preferred, since the 'management of crisis should override committees, rules and procedures, and rely on political support for initiative'.[14]

Role cultures emphasize job descriptions, communication procedures for settling disputes, with co-ordination provided by a small group of senior managers. Rules and procedures are the main source of influence. Role cultures are slow to react to change but offer security and predictability to individuals. They are frustrating for people wanting control over their work or for anyone 'who is eagerly ambitious or more interested in results than method'. Such individuals will only be content at the top of their organizations.

Task cultures, in contrast, are extremely adaptable, emphasize getting the job done and integrate individuals with the organization's objectives. 'The task culture thrives where speed of reaction, integration, sensitivity and creativity are more important than depth of specialization.' Further, it is in tune with 'ideologies of change and adaptation, individual freedom and low status differentials'.

Power cultures exist where there are few rules or procedures and there is little bureaucracy. They place a lot of faith in individuals, little in committees, and judge by results. 'It is a political organization in that decisions are taken very largely on the outcome of a balance of influence rather than on procedural or purely logical grounds.'

Person cultures, where individuals are the focal point, rarely exist in practice. This is because 'organizations tend to have objectives over and above the collective objectives of those who comprise them'. Communes and producer co-operatives seek to achieve person cultures but, once created, they exert their own rules on individuals. They then become task cultures 'but often a power or a role culture' as well.[15]

The Implications for Management

Industrial capitalism provides the dominant economic, social and ideological framework within which modern business organizations operate. Managerial activity has not only helped in the emergence and growth of industrial capitalism. It has also developed out of industrial capitalism, with its advanced technologies, large-scale enterprises, complex division of labour, concentrated patterns of capital ownership and the largely market allocation of society's scarce resources. Under industrial capital-ism, it is the responsibility of each organization's corporate leaders and their managerial executives to ensure that the objectives for which the enterprise has been created are achieved. They also have to ensure that the resources consumed in the work process are utilized in the most efficient manner, given the enterprise's substantive, productivity and profit goals.

It needs to be recognized by the members of the managerial teams that whilst management's commitment to enterprise policies and the tasks associated with them is normally unconditional, under industrial capitalism non-managerial employees are not always as firmly committed. They bring to organizations their own values and beliefs about the nature of work, and its place in their lives, which are not always congruent with those of their managerial leaders. For many of them work is merely instrumen-tal, a means to non-work ends; it is not an end in itself. It is one of the skills of management to provide an organizational climate which encourages and motivates employee commitment to enter-prise goals. In this way, the personal needs of individual employees may be integrated with organizational needs for success.

With the growing power and concentration of finance capital, monopoly capital and multinational capital, many business enter-prises are operating in a turbulent environment. Thus the fortunes and even survival of some companies are outside their own immediate control. Even effectively managed enterprises are unable to cope in these circumstances with the consequences of large-scale capital movements affecting their product markets or financial stability. Further, with the growing scale of business organizations, combined periodically with depressed market con-ditions, some medium-sized companies and some large ones are subject to speculative take-over and merger bids which would normally be avoidable. It is not only corporate board members who are vulnerable in these situations. Senior and middle man-agers are even more threatened at such times, with managerial redundancy the likely result.

Given the complexities of managing modern large-scale business corporations, in recent years growing interest has been shown in the concept of corporate culture. In essence, the identification of an organization's corporate culture has become an important element in managing change in leading organizations in both the private and the public sectors. Managers need to understand the predominant organizational culture within which managerial and workforce actions take place. They also need to understand how existing culture can act as a constraint on organizational change. Where managers seek to effect change, they have a greater likelihood of achieving it by changing corporate culture than by using structural or procedural methods alone. Although more difficult to carry out in practice, it is by modifying the values, beliefs and ideas held by people about their employing organization, its objectives and its ways of achieving them that real and substantive change can be most effectively managed.

References

1 SCOTT J. *Corporations, classes and capitalism*. London, Hutchinson, 1979. p 29.
2 ALLEN M (ed). *The Times 1000, 1988–89*. London, Times Books, 1989. p 7.
3 SCOTT J. *Capitalist property and financial power*. Brighton, Wheatsheaf, 1986. p 1.
4 *ibid*. p 80.
5 *ibid*. p 99.
6 *ibid*. p 80.
7 HANDY C. *Understanding organizations*. Harmondsworth, Penguin, 1985. p 177.
8 DEAL T E *and* KENNEDY A A. *Corporate cultures*. Reading, Mass. Addison-Wesley, 1982. pp 15–18.
9 *ibid*. pp 272f and 275.
10 *ibid*. pp 21, 31 and 32.
11 *ibid*. pp 37, 39, 41 and 57.
12 *ibid*. pp 14, 67–74, 87–98 and 103.
13 *ibid*. pp 107–123.
14 HANDY. *op. cit.* pp 199f and 210.
15 *ibid*. pp 183–84.

2

The Corporate Sector

The UK is a corporate society, operating in a capitalist economic framework. Large-scale private and public enterprises dominate the economy and are pre-eminent in the social structure. Modern business corporations, which take a variety of forms, have a number of economic functions. They include:

- Producing and selling the goods and services demanded by individuals and organizations.
- Employing and rewarding the owners of the vast capital and skilled human resources used in the economic process.
- Trading with one another, nationally and internationally.
- Setting the economic pace of the nation.

If the nineteenth century was the age of individualism, the twentieth century may be contrasted as the age of organizations. Throughout modern society, it is organized and directed activity which is the common form of enterprise. This applies across all sectors of the economy and includes not only manufacturing and commerce but also governmental and political bodies, social and welfare services, the education and training sectors, communications and entertainment, and all parts of the economic infrastructure. Modern enterprise is essentially organized enterprise.

Corporate Society

Various attempts have been made to classify complex, formal organizations. One well known functional typology is provided by Blau and Scott (1963). Their classification is based on the criterion of who is the 'prime beneficiary' of the organization. They identify four basic categories of person involved in relationships in any

organization. These are: '(1) the workers or rank-and-file participants; (2) the owners or managers of the organization; (3) the
clients or, more generally, the "public-in-contact" . . . and (4)
the public-at-large, that is, the members of the society in which
the organization operates'. On this basis four types of organization
are identified. These are: mutual benefit concerns; business concerns; service organizations and 'commonweal organizations'. The
prime beneficiaries in each case are the membership, owners,
client groups and public at large respectively.[1]

Etzioni (1975) provides a regulatory typology of organizations.
He uses the concept of 'compliance' to provide a comparative
analysis of modern organizations. For Etzioni compliance consists
of two elements: the *power* applied by the organization to lower-
level participants and the *involvement* in the organization
developed by lower participants. He identifies three kinds of
organizational power and three kinds of participant involvement.
'Coercive' power, for example, rests on the application, or the
threat of application, of physical sanctions against lower participants. 'Remunerative' power is based on control over material
resources and rewards and 'normative' power rests on the allocation and manipulation of symbolic rewards and deprivations,
such as esteem and prestige. The three kinds of involvement
outlined by Etzioni are 'alienative', 'calculative' and 'moral'. Alienative involvement occurs where lower participants are involved
in an organization against their wishes; this commonly induces
intense negative feelings against it. Calculative involvement is
where attachment to the organization is instituted by extrinsic
rewards, generating either negative or positive feelings of low
intensity. Moral involvement, which reflects high positive orientation to the organization, is based on the identification of lower
participants with the values and purposes of the organization.[2]

Etzioni argues that although there are nine possible types of
compliance, 'three of these types (congruent types) are more
effective than the other six; they are also empirically more fre-
quent'. These are: coercive power with alienative involvement,
remunerative power with calculative involvement and normative
power with moral involvement. He hypothesizes that organizations tend to shift their compliance structures from incongruent
to congruent ones, with those having congruent structures tending
to resist factors pushing them towards incongruency.[3]

Technological typologies of organizations are suggested by writers such as Blauner (1964) and Woodward (1965 and 1970), whilst structural typologies are advance by Ackoff (1970) and Vickers (1970). But organizations can also be classified by their orientation and ownership. Corporate orientation, for example, is demonstrated by the basic goals they seek to achieve. For Thomason (1981), the basic goals or purposes of private-sector businesses are to satisfy consumer demand in the marketplace. The goals of public service organizations, in contrast, are to satisfy citizen needs—'regardless of whether the citizen can translate that need into effective demand or of whether any means can be found of charging directly for that service'. Thus private-sector and public-sector organizations have essentially different goals. They are distinguishable, says Thomason, 'by the terms demand and need, and their derivative objectives are characterized differently'.[4]

The relationship between corporate orientation and corporate ownership is shown in figure 2. Organizations may be directed towards either profit and revenue goals or towards welfare and

Figure 2   Corporate typologies, by orientation and ownership

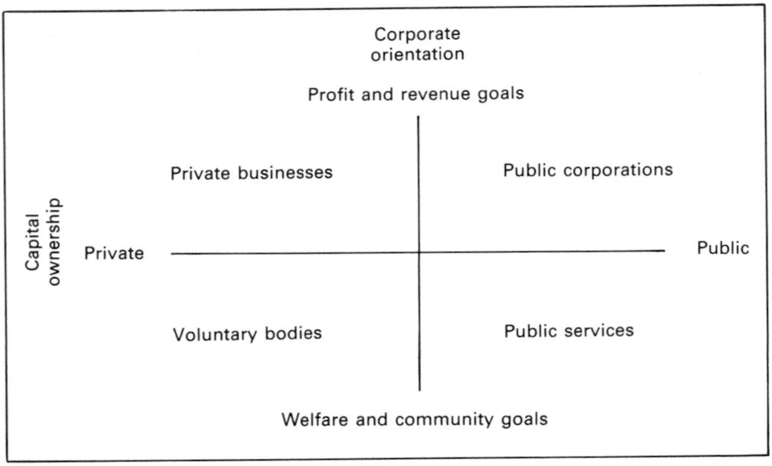

Source. D. Farnham, *Personnel in context*, London, IPM, 1986

community ones, whilst corporate ownership may be either private or public. By this typology there are four categories of corporate enterprise:

- Private businesses.
- Public corporations.
- Public services.
- Voluntary bodies.

Private businesses dominate agriculture, manufacturing, distribution, many service enterprises and the financial sector such as the banks, insurance companies, pension funds and the Stock Exchange. They are profit-oriented and privately owned. Public corporations are public trading bodies which have a substantial degree of financial independence from central government. Although a number of public corporations were privatized during the 1980s when the government sold them off to private shareholders, including British Telecom, British Gas and the water authorities, there were about fifty public corporations still operating at the beginning of the 1990s.

The public services, such as education, health care and social services, as well as central government activities, have welfare and community goals and are owned by the State or by State agencies. In most cases the financial resources for public service organizations are provided from tax revenues rather than from direct charges on individuals. They are generally goods and services provided by the community collectively for personal consumption as citizen rights, not according to the ability of individual households to pay.

The last category of corporate body is voluntary associations. These include professional bodies, trade unions, pressure groups, political parties, employers' associations, charitable trusts, the Churches and non-Christian religious organizations. In general they tend to be relatively small organizations and normally employ far fewer resources than do private businesses, the public corporations and the public services. Their goals tend to be welfare and community-oriented, with their assets privately owned. In some cases they are democratically controlled bodies, run by their members on collegiate and participatory lines.

Private Businesses

Individuals wishing to set up a business, with a view to making a profit, may do so without any legal formality, provided they trade under their own name. Where individuals trade under another name they are required to register their business under the Registration of Business Names Act, 1916. Sole traders may or may not employ others in their business operations but their personal liability for any trading debts is unlimited. This means that any part of a sole trader's property or assets may be used to pay off debts incurred in the course of the proprietor's trading activities. Because a sole trader's access to financial capital is strictly limited, most such businesses tend to be small. They are typically found in taxi services, retail shopkeeping, small hotels, catering and jobbing building.

Amongst professional workers, such as accountants, architects, dentists, doctors and solicitors, partnerships are fairly common. Partnerships are defined in law by the Partnership Act, 1890. They are associations of persons carrying on a business in common with a view to making a profit. A partnership is required to register its business name, unless it consists only of the names of the partners, and in most cases is limited to a maximum of twenty persons. Partnerships generally employ people, and all partners have a duty to take part in managing the undertaking. As with sole traders, the financial liability of partnerships is usually unlimited, except under the provisions of the Limited Partnership Act, 1907. This enables limited liability to be extended to some partners, confined to the amount initially invested or agreed to be invested in the partnership. They have no right, however, to take part in managing the business. Limited partnerships are also required to register with the Registrar of Companies. As with sole traders, partnerships do not continue in perpetuity. When key partners die or retire the partnership ends.

The most common form of private business is the registered company or business corporation. It is the large-scale business corporation, and its public-sector counterparts, which are the main focus of this text. By the early 1990s there were over 900,000 registered companies in Britain. This figure compares with some 700,000 in 1979 and about 500,000 in 1970. The various Companies Acts provide the basic legal regulation of these enterprises.

The Acts facilitate the legal incorporation of private businesses by creating a legal entity, or corporate body, which is separate and distinct from the personality and existence of any individual who is a member of the organization. As Thomason (1975) writes, it is 'this legal fictional body which employs people, or which holds and owns property or enters into commercial contracts'.[5] The Companies Acts lay down rules for the constitution, management and dissolution of such organizations, though they leave their internal management largely to a company's directors, subject to specific safeguards for shareholders. The Registrars of Companies for England and Wales and for Scotland issue certificates of incorporation and record changes of name. They are also responsible for company registrations and for the safe custody of documents required by statute.

Table 4

Number of registered British companies, 1982–88   *(000s)*

Year	Public	Private	Total
1982	3·2	804·6	807·8
1983	3·4	858·7	862·1
1984	3·7	891·2	894·9
1985	4·3	863·8	868·1
1986	5·1	848·8	853·9
1987	5·2	871·4	876·6
1988	6·6	914·0	920·6

Source: *Companies in 1987–88*, London, HMSO, 1988.

There are two types of registered company, as shown in table 4: the private limited company (Ltd) and the public limited company (PLC). There are many more private limited companies than PLCs. In 1989, for example, Britain had some 6,000 PLCs and 914,000 private companies, with PLCs representing about 7 per cent of total corporate registrations, compared with only 4 per cent in 1982. There are major differences between these two types of business corporation. PLCs, for example, have far larger financial resources per company than do private companies and their shares are bought and sold on the Stock Exchange. PLCs are sometimes multinational corporations, private companies rarely so. PLCs are normally employers of large numbers of human resources, whilst private companies employ far fewer people per enterprise.

More generally, both types of joint-stock or limited company have a number of commercial advantages:

- Incorporation makes financial capital available for such businesses, normally in the form of shares, from a variety of sources, where each contributor need only provide a small proportion of the total paid-up money capital.

- Transfer of this capital ownership is possible, through the buying and selling of shares.

- Further financial capital can be raised, if the business is successful.

- Limited liability is provided for corporate shareholders. This means that if a company is wound up and goes out of business, the financial liability of each shareholder is limited to the amount of the original shareholding.

Normally shareholders receive a financial return on their shares from corporate profits, called 'dividends'.

One reason for the growth in the number of PLCs registered in the UK during the 1980s was the increase in company flotations at the time. This was accompanied by significant take-over activity in the UK stock market, where some of the biggest deals ever seen were successfully concluded. During 1987–88, for example, the British Petroleum Company's bid for Britoil was by far the largest, costing some £2,520 million. This was three times the amount which the Trustee Savings Bank paid for the Hill Samuel group, at £777 million. It is estimated that in 1987–88 'as many as 27 bids were worth over £100 million, ten times more than in the previous period [1986–87]'. The bidders for major concerns were not always British. 'Interest in taking over British companies is increasing, particularly from European Community companies and other western European countries as harmonization year 1992 draws near.'[6]

Some indication of the vast financial capital resources employed in the UK's top business corporations, as well as their impressive financial power, is provided in table 5. This shows the financial capital and gross profits of the ten largest business corporations

Table 5

*Capital employed in the UK's top ten business corporations,
and their profits, 1987–88* (£000s)

Company	Capital employed	Profits
Electricity Council[a]	38,777,600	803,500
British Petroleum Company	18,477,000	3,883,000
Shell Transport and Trading	14,579,000	2,576,000
British Telecom	12,064,000	2,661,000
British Gas	7,392,000	1,398,000
BAT Industries	6,396,000	1,542,000
Imperial Chemical Industries	6,154,000	1,574,000
Hanson Group	4,871,000	1,041,000
British Coal	4,370,000	352,000
General Electric Company	3,795,000	683,000

Note
a Nationalized industry.
Source: *The Times 1,000, 1987–88*, London, Times Books, 1988.

in 1988. Their financial capital alone exceeded £100,000 million, with the top four companies accounting for £83,900 million of this, or some 70 per cent of the total. Their corporate profits in turn exceeded £15,000 million. Such data reinforce the claim of Hannah and Kay (1977) that 'Britain, which combines a highly developed securities market with negligible restrictions on merger, has achieved increases in and levels of concentration which are the highest among developed countries with large and diversified economies'.[7]

Public Corporations

It is often assumed that public corporations are identical with the nationalized industries. But this is not the case. Although relatively few nationalized industries remain after the privatizations of the 1980s, certainly compared with the period 1945–79, all nationalized industries are public corporations—but not all public corporations, such as the Bank of England and the Royal Mint, are nationalized industries. Even if the public corporation is the dominant structure for the nationalized industries and other public authorities, the concept is much older. The Port of London Authority was created in 1908, for example, 'the Forestry Commission in 1919, the BBC in 1926, the Central Electricity Board in 1927 and the London Passenger Transport Board in 1933'.[8]

Public corporations have a number of features:

- They are publicly owned and publicly accountable bodies which are treated identically in public expenditure White Papers, even though many of them are not revenue-earning organizations.

- They are separate legal bodies created by statute, or royal charter, which can enter into contracts, sue and be sued.

- They are managed by boards, appointed by Ministers, which are accountable to Parliament for the efficient running of their corporation.

- They are financed either directly by central government or by the revenue they obtain from sales of the goods or services they provide. Capital expenditure is financed by borrowing from the Treasury or the general public, or by using their own reserves.

- They are exempt from the normal parliamentary control exercised over government departments.

- Their employees are not civil servants.

The independent legal status of public corporations was originally designed to give them a degree of commercial flexibility not possible in government departments. In practice, government control over the activities of public corporations is ultimately ensured by the statutory powers conferred on their responsible Ministers. Ministers appoint their boards, for example, and determine their terms of appointment. It is Ministers too who authorize the raising of financial capital from external sources. Most important, Ministers are empowered, after appropriate consultation with their boards, to direct them in ways considered to be necessary in the public interest.

As can be seen in table 6, there were over thirty public corporations which were not nationalized bodies in 1990. The earliest ones, the BBC and the Scottish Special Housing Association, were created before the Second World War. Eleven more were set up during the 1940s, 1950s and 1960s, with ten others being estab-

Table 6

Public corporations, other than nationalized industries, 1990

Corporation	Vesting year
Audit Commission	1983
Bank of England	1946
British Broadcasting Corporation	1926
British Technology Group[a]	1981
Commonwealth Development Corporation	1948
Covent Garden Market Authority	1961
Crown Suppliers[a]	1976
Development Board for Rural Wales	1977
English Industrial Estates Corporation	1986
General Practice Finance Corporation	1966
Highlands and Islands Development Board	1965
Independent Broadcasting Authority[a]	1972
Land Authority for Wales	1976
Local Authority Airport Companies	1987
Local Authority Bus Companies	1986
New Town Development Corporations	1946
Northern Ireland Housing Executive[a]	1971
Northern Ireland Transport Holding Company[a]	1968
Oil and Pipeline Agency	1985
Passenger Transport Executives	1975
Pilotage Commission	1979
Royal Mint	1975
Scottish Development Agency	1975
Scottish Special Housing Association	1937
Trust Ports (Northern Ireland)	1974
UK Atomic Energy Authority	1986
Urban Development Corporations	1981
Welsh Development Agency	1976
Welsh Fourth Channel Authority	1981

Note
a Succeeded previous corporations.
Source: Central Statistical Office, *Economic trends*, London, HMSO, various years.

lished in the 1970s. Another eleven public corporations were created in the 1980s, including the Audit Commission, the Oil and Pipeline Agency and the Welsh Fourth Channel Authority. This was despite the apparent hostility of government policy to public enterprise at the time. The situation was offset, however, by the transfer of other bodies such as the Housing Corporation and the Royal Ordnance Factories to the private sector.

Most of UK's nationalized industries were formed between 1946 and 1950. They included airlines, coal, electricity, gas, railways and road transport. The iron and steel industry, also nationalized then, was denationalized in 1953 and then taken back into public ownership in 1967. Further nationalization took place in the 1970s when, in response to the UK's continued industrial decline, another group of private organizations came into public ownership during the Wilson and Callaghan Labour administrations. These included British Aerospace, British Leyland, British Shipbuilders and the British National Oil Corporation. In general, Labour governments have tended to favour nationalization, Conservative ones to oppose it.

It would be wrong, however, to view the expansion of the nationalized industries in the post-war period—a process which has only recently been reversed—in purely ideological terms. As Curwen (1986) argues: 'at the end of the day there are a number of sound economic reasons which can be used to justify nationalization'. They include: to rationalize what had previously been a random imposition of centralized control on certain industries; to prevent the potential abuse of monopoly economic power; to enforce an economically co-ordinated structure on certain industries; to centralize key industries for strategic economic purposes; to provide an opportunity for investing in a co-ordinated modernization programme; and to use some industries as instruments of government economic policy. The main social reasons for nationalization include: enhancing the welfare of the community at large; facilitating the transfer of wealth and power from elite groups to the community at large; and holding down the prices of goods and services to protect the poor, 'since no private sector industry can be expected to pursue such a policy voluntarily'.[9]

Table 7 shows the UK's nationalized industries in 1990, with their financial capital and the number of employees. Although they provide a variety of essential goods and services to the public, only ten remained out of some twenty industries which had been nationalized bodies in 1979. Between 1981 and 1990 the nationalized industries that were privatized included British Aerospace (1981), the National Freight Corporation (1982), Britoil (1982), Associated British Ports (1983), Enterprise Oil (1984), British

Table 7
The nationalized industries, 1990: capital and employees

Corporation	Capital employed (£000s)	No. of employees
British Coal	4,370,000	162,800
British Railways Board	1,701,300	166,989
British Shipbuilders	41,847	8,642
British Steel Corporation	3,638,000	54,650
British Waterways Board	N/A	2,455
Civil Aviation Authority	N/A	6,700
London Regional Transport	1,791,100	54,785
Post Office	1,954,100	188,732
Scottish Transport Group	167,200	10,732

Note. Excludes industries privatized subsequently, such as the Electricity Council, area electricity boards, the English regional water authorities, Scottish electricity boards and the Welsh Water Authority.
Source: The Times 1,000, 1987–88, London, Times Books, 1989.

Telecom (1984), the warship yards of British Shipbuilders (1984 onwards), British Gas (1986), British Airways (1987), the regional water authorities (1990), the Central Electricity Generating Board and the area electricity boards (1990).

Other public corporations passing from public to private ownership during this time included Cable and Wireless in 1981 and British Trust Ports in 1985. Bodies which were dissolved included the National Ports Council, whose functions were transferred to the Department of Transport in 1981, the Northern Ireland Development Agency in 1983 and the National Film Finance Corporation (NFFC) in 1985. The NFFC was replaced by the private-sector British Screen Finance Consortium.

The transfer of ownership of public corporations to private shareholders has both its supporters and its critics. The arguments in favour are political and commercial. The political arguments include:

● Reducing the role of the State in economic activity.

● Diminishing political regulation of the economy.

● Fostering a share-owning democracy by expanding personal share ownership.

- Facilitating workers' share-holding in their own companies to improve industrial relations.
- Reducing the public-sector borrowing requirement (the amount which the government borrows yearly to balance its income and expenditure).
- Removing civil service interference from the corporations to enable management to manage.

The commercial arguments include:

- Promoting new business opportunities for investment and expansion.
- Meeting international competition.
- Facilitating efficiency and productivity improvements.
- Cutting unit costs.
- Adopting a market orientation to customers and clients.

Opponents of privatization argue that the selling of public assets result in lost revenue to government and the public authorities, as well as weakening government influence in economic and industrial affairs. More substantively, it is argued, since the nationalized industries are often monopolies, they need to be controlled centrally by political means rather than by private-sector monopolist suppliers with commercial aims. Another argument is that because they are public utilities they should meet citizen need rather than market demand based solely on the ability to pay. Further, as commanding heights of the economy, public utilities of this sort need to be planned by a central authority to ensure that efficiency, investment, and research and development are not simply profit-led.

It is also argued that there is a tendency to sell public assets to private share-holders too cheaply. The Labour Research Department, for example, which examined the cases of Cable and Wireless, Amersham International and Associated British Ports, argues that after selling 49·9 per cent of Cable and Wireless for 168p a share in October 1981, and raising £224 million for itself, the government returned £35 million to the company to fund investment. Two and a half years later, at the end of March 1983, the shares were worth 413p each. This put a value of £553 million on the stake which the government had sold. In the case of Amersham International the offer price was 142p a share before privatization, rising to 249p at the end of March 1983. In Associated British Ports 'shares sold by the government at 112p in February 1983 were worth 164p six weeks later at the end of March'. This put a value of £32 million on the stake sold by the government, '£10m more than the government received'.[10]

The Public Services

Public services are provided by central government and the local authorities. They employ about 5 million people, or about a fifth of the employed labour force, and supply individual citizens and organizations with a wide range of services and facilities. These services, whilst funded collectively through National Insurance and taxes, are often consumed personally by millions of ordinary women and men and their families. The services include: national defence, the agencies of law enforcement, fire protection, environmental health, health care, personal social services, education, public transport and roads, recreational facilities and consumer protection.

Central government

Central government encompasses all those bodies, for whose activities a Minister of the Crown is directly or indirectly responsible to Parliament. It includes the armed services, government departments, departmental agencies and non-departmental agencies (NDAs), such as the Arts Council, the Meat and Livestock Committee, and the Botanic Gardens at Kew, which are not headed by a government Minister. There are some twenty major government departments such as Defence, Education and Science, the Treasury, Employment, Agriculture, and the Scottish Office. The most important departments are headed by Ministers of State, usually called Secretaries of State. Each departmental Minister, in turn, is assisted by second-ranking or Junior Ministers of State and by third-ranking Parliamentary Secretaries. Collectively they form a ministerial team. Each department has a hierarchy of civil servants, headed by a Permanent Secretary. Departmental work is allocated between smaller units or divisions, some of which have line management functions, others staff or service functions. Departmental agencies, such as the Defence Procurement Agency in the Ministry of Defence, are units which administer bodies of self-contained work. They enjoy a degree of autonomy within their departments.

In 1988 the Efficiency Unit of the Cabinet Office published a radical report entitled *Improving Management in Government: the Next Steps*. It is widely known as the Ibbs report and pointed to the improvement in the managing of government business which it claimed had been achieved since 1979. The Ibbs report proposed further changes in the structure and management of the civil service so as to secure better value for money for the taxpayer and improved services to clients. It stated that the civil service was too large an organization and too diverse to be managed as a single entity. 'With 600,000 employees it is an enormous organization compared with any private sector company and most public sector organizations . . . At present the freedom of an individual manager to manage effectively . . . is severely circumscribed.'[11]

The report went on to recommend that free-standing agencies should be created to carry out the executive functions of government. This was to be done within a policy and resource framework set by a small core of policy-makers in central departments. These agencies might remain within the public sector or outside it. The government broadly accepted the Ibbs proposals and within months some twenty-nine areas of government work were being considered for agency status. They covered about 170,000 civil servants. The first agencies to be established were the Vehicle Inspectorate and Her Majesty's Stationery Office, in summer 1988. It is possible that the 'next steps' initiative will result in some three-quarters of all civil servants being employed in agencies. This would leave a small core of about 20,000 elite civil servants in ministerially headed government departments, responsible for policy-making and advice.

Other public constituted bodies, which are not government departments but are financially dependent upon and subject to varying degrees of control by departments, include the National Health Service (NHS), the national research councils and the Polytechnics and Colleges Funding Council. NDAs, such as the Advisory Conciliation and Arbitration Service, the Equal Opportunities Commission and the Commission for Racial Equality, are outside the traditional framework of the civil service. Their work is normally regarded as unsuitable for the typical government department. Subject to fulfilling their statutory duties, they are autonomous and independent of government control and have some insulation from parliamentary scrutiny. Currently, there are some 1,600 NDAs, comprising about 400 executive, 1,000 advisory, 60 tribunal and 100 other such bodies.

The NHS was created by the National Health Service Act, 1946. It was based on the principle that medical care and comprehensive health services should be readily available and supplied, largely free of charge, to anyone normally resident in the UK. Although nominally under the control of a central Department of Health, until 1974 hospitals were administered through regional hospital boards; the family doctor, dental and optical services through local executive councils; and all other health services through the county and county borough councils. In 1974 the tripartite health services in England and Wales were unified by the creation of fourteen regional health authorities (RHAs), ninety area health authorities (AHAs) and 192 district management teams. The executive councils were replaced by family practitioner committees, although they continued to retain a semi-autonomous position in the service. In 1982 further reorganization saw the abolition of the AHAs, and a two-tier structure of fourteen RHAs and 191 local district health authorities was installed.

The Royal Commission on the National Health Service in 1979 restated the objectives of the NHS. These were that the NHS should:

> encourage and assist individuals to remain healthy;
> provide equality of treatment to health services;
> provide a broad range of services to a high standard;
> provide equality of access to these services;
> provide a service free at the time of use;
> satisfy the reasonable expectations of its users;
> remain a national service responsive to local needs.[12]

The Commission conceded that these objectives were sometimes in conflict and that there were problems of choice amongst the objectives, given the rising costs of the service and the limited resources available to most patients' needs.

In 1989 the government published a White Paper, *Working for Patients*, proposing radical reforms of the NHS. The proposals were designed to enable 'a higher quality of patient care to be obtained from the resources which the nation is able to devote to the NHS'. In presenting its programme of action the government aimed 'to give patients, wherever they live in the UK, better health care and greater choice of the services available'.[13]

The government proposals included:

- Delegating as much decision-making as possible to where patient care is delivered,
- Giving some hospitals self-governing status to manage their own budgets and determine patient care policies,
- Introducing an internal market, encouraging hospitals to compete for patients. General practitioners would be encouragedto manage their own budgets and provide better patient care at lower cost.

The general thrust of the White Paper was to encourage greater economic efficiency and effectiveness by using internal market mechanisms and private-sector business methods. These initiatives reflected similar changes in other parts of the public sector which emphasized market values rather than welfare ones.

In seeking the more efficient management of NHS resources the government wanted better use made of staff, better management information systems and greater involvement of doctors and nurses in the management of the service. The government also sought greater pay flexibility 'in order to allow managers to relate pay rates to local markets and to reward individual performance'. This, combined with local rather than national conditions of service, would enable managers 'to devise employment packages that are most suited to local needs' and assist the 'aim of achieving better value for money.'[14]

The local authorities

In 1990 there were 448 local authorities in England and Wales and sixty-five in Scotland. They consisted of forty-seven top-tier or non-metropolitan county authorities in England and Wales and

401 lower-tier district or borough authorities. Since the abolition of the Greater London Council and the six metropolitan councils of Greater Manchester, Merseyside, South Yorkshire, Tyne and Wear, West Midlands and West Yorkshire in 1986, area-wide local authority services in these conurbations are co-ordinated through a series of joint boards. In Scotland there are nine top-tier authorities or regional councils and three all-purpose island councils: Orkney, Shetland and the Western Isles. The nine regions, in turn, are divided into fifty-three lower-tier district councils. Local councils of these sorts consist of elected councillors working in co-operation with the professional officers employed by the authorities. Their joint task is to ensure the efficient provision of the wide range of services, laid down by law, which the authorities are required or choose to provide for their local communities.

Those local authority services which are planned over a wide geographical area are generally the responsibility of county authorities. These include consumer protection, the fire services, roads and traffic, and strategic planning. Personal services, such as education, libraries and social services, are provided either by shire county councils or by metropolitan district councils. Local services, including cemeteries, development control, environmental health and housing, are usually allocated to district authorities. Other local government services, such as art galleries, museums and provision for physical recreation, are provided through district councils or county authorities. In these cases the authorities decide the respective allocation of services between themselves.

Managing local authorities is a dual function shared between elected councillors and professional chief officers. Effective working relationships are normally established between majority political groups and management teams of chief officers, despite sometimes highly charged political environments. This relationship varies from authority to authority and is often shaped by the personalities and preferences of council leaders and their chief executives. Effective working relationships between politicians and officers are necessary, some would claim, since the fundamental purpose of local government is the attainment of political objectives to a predetermined standard of performance with the minimum use of resources and the pursuit of value for money through efficiency, economy and effectiveness.

Like the rest of the public sector, local government since 1979 has undergone continuous and radical change. The metropolitan county authorities have been abolished, many local authority powers have been removed or reduced and new central government controls have been imposed upon local government. In the field of economic development, new development corporations have been created, enterprise zones established and partnerships between central and local government, and between local authorities and local business communities, have been forged.

In the new climate in which local authorities are operating, their professional officers are having to acquire a wide knowledge of market forces, of how the private sector works, and an appreciable change in the local authority ethos is emerging. This means that the authorities are acting as enablers rather than direct providers of services. Under the Local Government Act, 1988, for example, local authorities are becoming increasingly involved with the phased implementation of compulsory competitive tendering for services. This includes drawing up specifications, defining standards, soliciting tenders and selecting the most favourable one. Where in-house bids are successful, departmental heads have to play the part of contractors to their client council, bringing a new slant to the member-officer relationship. Where the outcome is 'contracting out' of delivering services, officers act in a representative role as client, with monitoring of performance a vital element in their activities.

Local authorities are also facing the predominantly administrative problems of implementing the Community Charge, of effecting the transfer of budgetary management to schools, and of coping with the consequences of far-reaching housing reform. This all means that the character of local government is rapidly changing, with officers having to manage change in the interests of the communities they serve, the staff they employ and the people for whom they provide services. Whilst there appears to be increasing flexibility in local government, there is also a need to ensure cohesion in the managing of its affairs. Since the legislative measures of the 1980s require different types of response from those of the past, there is a risk that corporate unity, in those authorities where it had been established, could easily become fragmented and diffused.

The Implications for Management

The large, complex business corporations which dominate the modern economy have to adapt continually to the dynamic external forces impinging on them. These business corporations, whether privately or publicly owned, depend on the effective use of the material resources, human resources and expertise of their managerial teams to satisfy the organizational purposes for which they were created. Increasingly it is the pressures of the marketplace which impinge on the managerial leaders of each business corporation in its search for success and economic efficiency. This has always been the case for private enterprise. Recently it has become an increasingly important factor in determining managerial policy and decision-making in public enterprise organizations too.

In a sense, then, managing in both major sectors of the economy has converged rather than diverged in recent years. Although the convergence must not be overstated, the problems facing management in all large-scale business corporations have more in common than in the past. And the managerial techniques and styles of management used in both the private and the public sectors are more similar than previously. This is because managements in the two sectors each face analogous problems and constraints in their policy-making and executive roles. One such area is their budgeting, financial managing and accounting procedures. There appears to be, for example, more emphasis in all large enterprises on efficient resource management programmes. These include the use of sophisticated budget and financial planning processes, computer-based management information systems and value-for-money auditing operations.

Given the market and financial factors confronting most business corporations today, another area where many managements are re-assessing their approaches and policies is in managing their human resources. Some managements are using increasingly sophisticated methods of human resource management. Here the emphasis is being placed on employee co-operation rather than confrontation, individual rewards rather than collective ones and union collaboration rather than workplace conflict. Employees are also being required to work more flexibly, be appraised more regularly and demonstrate high performance levels. Line managers, in turn, are being expected to take greater responsibility for the personnel management activities of their jobs. This means demonstrating effectiveness in recruiting, rewarding, motivating and developing employees, thus enabling the workforce to contribute ever more efficiently to corporate goals and activities. As one leading industrialist has commented, to get the competitive edge, managements are having to improve the quality of their people resources. In particular, he says, it is the quality of the business corporation's managers which makes the crucial difference. 'Increasingly competition is between workforces, not just between products.'[15]

References

1 BLAU P. *and* SCOTT W R. *Formal organizations*. London, Routledge & Kegan Paul, 1963. p 42f.
2 ETZIONI A. *A comparative analysis of complex organizations*. New York, Free Press, 1975. pp 5, 10 and 12.
3 *ibid*. pp 14 and 22.
4 THOMASON G. *A textbook of personnel management*. London, Institute of Personnel Management, 1981. p 9.
5 THOMASON G. *A textbook of personnel management*. London, Institute of Personnel Management, 1975. p 87.
6 ALLEN M. (ed). *The Times 1000, 1987–88*. London, Times Books, 1989. p 12.
7 HANNAH L. *and* KAY J A. *Concentration in modern industry: theory and the UK experience*. London, Macmillan, 1977. p 1.
8 CURWEN P. *Public enterprise*. Brighton, Wheatsheaf, 1986. p 25f.
9 *ibid*.
10 LABOUR RESEARCH DEPARTMENT. *Labour research*. 44, 1987. p 198.
11 JENKINS K., CAINES K. *and* JACKSON A. *Improving management in government: the next steps*. London, HMSO, 1988.
12 ROYAL COMMISSION ON THE NATIONAL HEALTH SERVICE. *Report*. London, HMSO, 1979. p 16.
13 DEPARTMENT OF HEALTH. *Working for patients*. London, HMSO, 1989. pp 4 and 101.
14 *ibid*. pp 17 and 20.
15 ARMSTRONG G. 'Commitment through employee relations'. Paper presented to Institute of Personnel Management National Conference, 22 October 1987.

3

Population and Demography

Demography is the statistical study of populations through census returns, records of births, deaths and marriages, and other means. In outline, demography is concerned with the size, composition and distribution of populations, typically for a country but also for geographical regions or on a world basis. It also focuses on changes in the features of population over time and their causes. The demographic structure of a country's population clearly has implications for the demand for its goods and services and for the ways in which they are produced and distributed. The size and age structure of a population, for example, critically affect the actual and potential labour supply and the availability of appropriate skills and aptitudes in the labour market. It also affects public policy issues such as in the provision of educational, welfare, social and other services.

The Elements of Demography

The size of a population is the number of people living in a given geographical area—locally, regionally, nationally or globally—at any one time. Clearly, population is a dynamic feature of social life, since it is constantly changing. Movements in population distribution, and variations in the numbers of those entering and leaving a given population over a given period, ensure that claimed population sizes are only approximations or a demographic 'snapshot', precise only at the moment when they are counted. Further, given the sheer scope and complexity of modern population statistics, the figures and numbers provided by official sources are normally historical, and sometimes questionable, although projections and trends are used for social planning and other purposes.

The total population of the UK in mid-1987 was calculated to

be some 57 million persons. However, as suggested, the accuracy
of such data requires careful definition of persons, places and
time. For most analytical purposes it is insufficient to know how
many people are in a particular place at a given time. It is also
necessary to know about changes in population over time and
their causes. In accounting for population changes, demographers
identify the immediate causes in the relationships of births, deaths
and migration. The relationship between the composition of a
population and its fertility, mortality and migratory features is, of
course, reciprocal. Composition affects demography but demography, in turn, affects demographic composition which reflects the
age and sex structure of a whole population.

The total population of a country such as the UK comprises
two elements: natural change and migration change. The natural
change component consists of total births plus or minus total
deaths, whilst the migration change component consists of total
immigrants plus or minus total emigrants. Where both components change positively, or one does while the other remains
constant, total population rises. Where both components change
negatively, or one does, with the other constant, total population
falls. Where the natural change and the migration components
are both relatively static, or a rise in one is complemented by a
fall in the other, total population tends to stabilize.

The composition of a population can be analysed by a number
of characteristics. These include: its age, sex, race, geographical
distribution, marital status, occupation, education and religion.
Each of these characteristics is related to the number of births
and deaths, and to those migrating in and out of the population,
over time. Other things being equal, populations with larger proportions of men and women in the early reproductive years have
a high crude birth rate. This measures the number of live births
per thousand of the population per year. Similarly, populations
with larger proportions of elderly people have a high crude death
rate. Given common levels of technological provision, it is arguable that populations with a large proportion of people aged
between sixteen and sixty-five have distinct economic advantages
in terms of their productive human resources.

In addition to absolute numbers, demographers use relative
numbers. These include demographic ratios, proportions, percentages and rates. Relative numbers in demography contribute to

the understanding of demographic facts and changes, because they summarize data and relationships between data. In the UK, for example, there were 27·7 million males and 29·2 million females in 1987. The sex ratio is the number of males divided by the number of females. Hence the UK sex ratio in 1987 was 0·95. Similarly, proportions are ratios showing one part of a population relative to the whole of it. Their value always falls between zero and one. In 1987 the proportion of males to females in the UK was 0·51, i.e. 49 per cent of the UK population were male in 1987 and 51 per cent were female.

Demographic rates are calculated in the same ways as other ratios. Their additional feature is that they express what has happened in a unit of time, normally a year. Two of the most commonly used demographic rates are crude birth rates and crude death rates. With 776,000 live births amongst the UK's 57 million population in 1987, the crude birth rate for that year was 13·6 per thousand of the population. Similarly, with just over 644,000 deaths, the crude death rate was 11·3 per thousand. And with 318,000 male deaths out of 27·7 million males in 1987, and 326,000 female deaths out of 29·2 million females, the crude death rates for males and females were 11·5 and 11·2 per thousand respectively. The major weakness of crude demographic rates, measuring birth and death rates for example, is that they do not take into account the age distribution of the society or population being described.

Population Structure and Demographic Change

Table 8 outlines population changes and projections of population growth in the UK for the period 1951–2006. Between 1951 and 1986 the population increased by some 6·5 million persons, or by about 13 per cent. During those years the number of live births peaked in the 1960s but fell off substantially during the 1970s and 1980s. Similarly, the 1950s, 1960s and 1970s were years of net emigration, with the early 1980s a period of marginal net immigration. By the turn of the twenty-first century, it is estimated, the total UK population will be on a slowly rising plateau of some 59 million inhabitants, with the number of live births falling and a marginal rise in net emigration.

Table 8

UK population changes and projections, 1951–2006

Period	(000s) Resident population at start of period	Annual average change					(000s)
		Live births	Deaths	Net natural change	Net migration	Other adjustments	Overall annual change
1951–61	50,290	839	593	246	− 9	+15	252
1961–71	52,807	963	639	324	−32	+20	312
1971–81	55,928	736	666	70	−44	+17	42
1981–86	56,352	732	662	70	+ 9	+ 3	82
1986–87	56,736	764	634	129	+31	+ 4	167
1987–91[a]	56,891	804	647	157	−17	0	140
1991–96[b]	57,452	834	645	190	−17	0	172
1996–2001[b]	58,312	795	648	146	−17	0	129
2001–2006	58,957	732	654	78	−17	0	61

Notes
a Changes in numbers of armed services plus adjustments to reconcile differences between estimated population change
   and the figures for natural change and net civilian migration.
b Projection.
Source: Central Statistical Office, *Social trends* 19, London, HMSO, 1989.

Table 9 shows the number of live births and female fertility rates in the UK for selected years. In the post-war period total live births peaked in the mid-1960s and reached over a million in 1964. This represented a crude birth rate of almost 19 per thousand women, a general fertility rate of 94 per thousand women aged fifteen to forty four, and a total fertility rate of almost three children per woman for that period. In 1977, by contrast, live births, at 657,000, were the lowest in the period since 1950, with crude birth rates, general fertility rates and total fertility rates falling to 11·7, 58·9 and 1·69 respectively. By the mid-1980s live births were rising once again, but much more slowly than in the 1950s and 1960s. It is expected that further falls in the numbers of live births will occur during the 1990s. By 2001, it is projected, the crude birth rate will be about 13 per thousand and the total fertility rate about two children per woman. Since the trough in births during the mid-1970s, birth rates amongst women over twenty-five years of age have generally risen and are projected to continue rising into the next century. Birth rates amongst women aged twenty to twenty-four are projected to remain stable, whilst those amongst the under-twenties will decrease slightly.

Table 9
Live births in the UK: totals and rates for selected years

Year	Total live births (000s)	Crude birth rate	General fertility rate[a]	Mean age of mothers at birth	Total period fertility rate[b]
1956	825	16·1	78·8	28·0	2·36
1964	1,015	18·8	94·1	27·2	2·95
1977	657	11·7	58·9	26·8	1·69
1987	776	13·6	62·3	27·1	1·32
2001[c]	759	12·9	64·3	28·4	1·99

Notes
a Total births per 1,000 women aged fifteen to forty-four.
b Average number of children born per woman.
c Projections.
Source: Central Statistical Office, *Social trends*, 19, London, HMSO, 1989.

Deaths in the UK have averaged between 600,000 and 660,000 annually in the period since 1950. Within these overall limits, crude death rates have steadily fallen from over 12 per thousand of the population in the 1960s to just over 11 per thousand in the 1980s. Death rates vary by age and sex. Thus whilst death rates for females have declined marginally over the past two or three decades, those for men have declined more impressively. They fell from 12·6 per thousand males in 1961 to 11·5 in 1987. In the 1960s death rates for males aged over eighty-five were about 260 per thousand and 216 per thousand for females. By 1987 these had declined to 194 per thousand for males over eighty-five and 160 per thousand for females.[1]

Death rates for perinatal mortality and infant mortality have also drastically reduced in recent decades, even if they compare unfavourably with most parts of western Europe. In England and Wales in 1987, for example, the number of still births and deaths in the first week of life declined to its lowest ever ratio of 8·9 per thousand total births. Similarly, the infant mortality rate for England and Wales in 1987 was 9·2 per thousand. This continues the downward trend, interrupted only in 1986, of the past two decades.[2]

Another feature of the population structure in the post-war period is the emergence and growth of a significant number of ethnic minority groups. These are defined as groups sharing a distinct awareness of a common cultural identity which separates them from other groups around them. As can be seen in table 10, it is estimated that during the period 1985–87 the ethnic minority populations numbered about 2·5 million, some 400,000 more than in 1981, when the corresponding figure was about 2·1 million. This was equivalent to an annual average increase of just under 80,000 per year and made up 4·5 per cent of the British population. This compares 'with 3·9 per cent in 1981 and 2·3 per cent in 1971.'[3] The largest ethnic group was Indian, comprising 30 per cent of the total, followed by West Indians at 21 per cent and Pakistanis at 16 per cent. Those of Arab, African and Bangladeshi ethnic origins, in contrast, each accounted for less than 5 per cent of the total population of all ethnic minority groups at that time.

According to the Department of Employment's Labour Force Surveys, almost half the ethnic minority populations have been born in New Commonwealth countries and Pakistan (NCWP), about 43 per cent in the UK and 8 per cent elsewhere. These proportions differ according to ethnic group. Relatively large numbers of those of Indian, Pakistani and Bangladeshi ethnic

Table 10
UK population, by ethnic group, 1981–87

Ethnic group	% 1981	Estimated population (000s)				1985–87	% (Average)
		1981	1985	1986	1987		
White	–	51,000	51,222	51,204	51,573	–	94·4
All ethnic minority groups	100	2,092	2,376	2,559	2,484	100	4·6
West Indian	25	528	547	526	489	22	1·0
African	4	80	102	98	116	4	0·2
Indian	35	727	689	784	761	30	1·4
Pakistani	14	284	406	413	392	16	0·7
Bangladeshi	2	52	99	117	116	4	0·2
Chinese	4	92	122	113	126	5	0·2
Arab	3	53	61	73	79	3	0·1
Mixed	10	217	232	269	263	10	0·5
Other	3	60	117	164	141	6	0·3
Not stated	–	608	637	607	467	–	1·0
All ethnic groups	–	53,700	56,610	56,927	57,007	–	100·0

Source: Department of Employment, Labour force survey, London, HMSO, various years.

origins were born in NCWP, whilst relatively large proportions of those of Arab or Chinese ethnic origin were born in the rest of the world. On the other hand, the proportions of the different ethnic minority populations born in the UK reflect historical patterns of immigration. Thus over a half those of West Indian origin, for example, were born in the UK. This reflects the fact that West Indians were one of the earliest groups to settle in the UK. When the duration of residence of different minority groups in the UK is examined, it is known that only 3 per cent of the total ethnic minority population born overseas had entered the UK before 1955. Approximately 25 per cent had entered by 1965 and 66 per cent by 1975. Further, 'approximately three-quarters of overseas-born West Indians and Africans entered the United Kingdom before 1970, but the corresponding proportion for those from the Indian sub-continent was only about 40 per cent'.[4]

Age and Geographical Structure

Table 11 shows the age structure of the population from 1951, with projections to 2001. Those aged under fourteen showed a steady rise in numbers till the early 1970s. This trend declined in the 1980s but is expected to rise again in the 1990s. Whilst the under-fourteens provided about 23 per cent of the total population between 1951 and 1971, the proportion fell to around 21 per cent

Table 11
Age structure of the UK population 1951–2001   *(millions)*

Mid-year estimate	0–14	15–44	45–64	65–74	75–84	85+	All ages
1951	11·3	21·4	12·0	3·7	1·6	0·2	50·2
1961	12·4	20·8	13·4	4·0	1·9	0·3	52·8
1971	13·4	21·6	13·4	4·8	3·3	0·5	55·9
1981	11·6	23·8	12·4	5·2	2·7	0·6	56·3
1987	10·8	25·1	12·2	5·0	3·0	0·8	56·8
1991[a]	11·0	25·0	12·4	5·0	3·1	0·9	56·9
1996[a]	11·7	24·2	13·2	5·0	3·1	1·1	58·3
2001[a]	12·0	24·0	13·8	4·8	3·2	1·2	59·0

Note
a Projection.
Source: Central Statistical Office, *Social trends* 19, London, HMSO, 1989.

in 1981 and 19 per cent in the late 1980s. As a proportion of the whole population, this group is not expected to increase again until the mid-1990s; it is likely to constitute some 20 per cent of the total population by the year 2000.

Those aged between fifteen and sixty-four, the group from which the labour force is drawn, rose steadily from some 33 million persons in 1951 to just over 37 million in the late 1980s. This is unlikely to change much in the 1990s. As a proportion of the population, the fifteen to sixty-four group comprised some two-thirds (67 per cent) in 1951. After then it steadily declined to around 63 per cent by 1971, rising to 66 per cent by the late 1980s. It is expected to fall to about 64 per cent of the total in the 1990s. The age group which has shown the most significant changes both absolutely and relatively since the 1950s is that over seventy-five. Whilst there were about 1·5 million people aged between seventy-five and eighty-four in 1951, the number had risen to 3 million by the late 1980s. The number is expected to rise marginally in the 1990s. This group made up 3 per cent of the total population in 1951, 5 per cent in the late 1980s, and is expected to rise to about 5·5 per cent by the year 2000. Similarly, those aged over eighty-five increased from some 200,000 in 1951 to about 800,000 by the late 1980s, with projections of over a million people in this age group by the turn of the century. This represents a rise in the population of those over eighty-five from under 0·5 per cent in 1951 to almost 1·5 per cent in the late 1980s and over 2 per cent by 2001.

This analysis indicates that the age structure of the population is undergoing substantial and complex change. A low birth rate and increased longevity account for some but not all of the changes. On the one side, the ageing of the population is very much in the public eye. Nevertheless, 'the scale of the increase over the near future in the numbers of the very old in particular seems not to have been widely recognised'. On the other hand, during the next two decades the population of conventional working age will be of an older age profile. On the present projections its size may subsequently shrink. This means, other things being equal, that 'the size of the labour force would also shrink, with important implications for the economy.'[5]

It is also apparent that the age and sex profiles of each of the ethnic minority populations are different from those of the white

The Corporate Environment

population. The Bangladeshi and Pakistani groups are the youngest, with around half the male and female populations aged under
sixteen. The age distribution of those of West Indian, African and
Indian ethnic origin, however, is more like those of the total
population. Relatively few of the ethnic minority populations are
forty-five or over. This compares with about one in three of the
white population. Also, whilst there are ninety-five males to every
hundred females in the total population, there are more males to
females in the ethnic minority populations, with 103 males to 100
females. In most of the ethnic minority populations men outnumber women, especially amongst the Arab, African and Bangladeshi groups. The exception is the West Indian community, where
women outnumber men.

Table 12
Population growth rate in the UK regions, 1977–87

Region	Growth rate per thousand			Population mid-1987 (000s)
	1977–81	*1981–84*	*1984–87*	
Scotland	−2	−2	−2	5,112
Clydeside	−8	−8	−8	1,658
Rest	1	0	0	3,455
Wales	1	−1	3	2,836
Northern Ireland	2	3	5	1,575
England	1	1	3	47,407
North	−3	−3	−2	3,077
Yorkshire	0	−1	0	4,900
East Midlands	4	2	6	3,942
East Anglia	9	8	13	2,014
Greater London	−7	−2	1	6,770
South-east	1	2	4	10,548
South-west	5	6	9	4,588
West Midlands	1	−1	1	5,198
North-west	−3	−3	−1	6,370

Source: *Population trends* 54, London, HMSO, 1988.

Table 12 outlines UK population growth rates by geographical
region for the years 1977–87. Whilst England, Wales and Northern
Ireland experienced positive population growth rates for this
period, Scotland experienced absolute and relative losses,
especially from Clydeside. Within England, population growth
rates increased in the southern, eastern and Midland regions but

decreased in the northern and north-western regions. All the metropolitan areas, such as Greater Manchester, South Yorkshire, Merseyside, West Midlands, Tyne and Wear, and West Yorkshire, lost population. Greater London also lost population from 1977 till the mid-1980s. After that Greater London's population stabilized and then its growth rate increased slightly, especially in some inner London boroughs. Overall, the geographical pattern of population distribution appears to display the following characteristics: inner cities are in decline; smaller urban areas continue to grow; retirement and resort areas are experiencing increases in population as the retired move out from the cities and towns.

The Working Population

The working population consists of the employed labour force, including the armed services, plus the unemployed. In 1990 the employed labour force was about 25 million persons, with the number of unemployed, including non-claimants, standing at about 3 million. This made a total working population of about 28 million. This section focuses on the civilian working population and omits any analysis of those relatively small numbers working for the military authorities and the armed services.

The civilian labour force

The civilian labour force can be classified in a number of ways: by sector, full-time or part-time employment, industry, sex, age, and participation or activity rates. Table 13, for example, analyses the UK labour force by employment sector for selected years in the 1980s. Of an estimated labour force of 24·9 million in 1987, some 18·5 million, or about 75 per cent, were employed in the private sector and 6·4 million, or about 25 per cent, in the public sector. This contrasts with the early 1980s, when 71 per cent of the labour force of 24 million was employed in the private sector and 29 per cent in the public sector. Between 1981 and 1987 employment in the public sector fell by over 800,000, or by some 11 per cent, whilst employment in the private sector increased by about 1·4 million, or 8 per cent. Most of the decline in the public-

The Corporate Environment

Table 13

UK labour force by sector, 1981, 1986 and 1987 (000s)

Sector	1981	1986	1987	% change 1981–87
Private	17,159	17,996	18,539	+ 8·0
Public	7,185	6,546	6,370	−11·3
Public corporations	1,867	1,199	996	−46·7
Government	2,419	2,337	2,312	− 4·4
Local authorities	2,899	3,010	3,062	+ 5·6
Total employed labour force	24,344	24,542	24,909	+ 2·3

Source: Adapted from Central Statistical Office, *Economic Trends* 410, London, HMSO, 1987.

sector labour force occurred in the public corporations. As noted in chapter 2, several of these bodies were privatized, resulting in a fall in employment from almost 2 million public corporation employees in 1981 to just under a million in 1987.

A detailed analysis of people in full-time equivalent (FTE) employment in the public sector for the years 1977–87, rather than a head count, shows a decline from some 6·5 million FTEs in the late 1970s to about 6 million in the mid-1980s. The number had fallen further, to some 5·5 million, by the late 1980s. The decline of total employment in the public corporations in recent years has already been noted. As can be seen from table 14, the number of FTEs employed in the public corporations fell from over 2 million in 1977 to under a million in 1987. This represents a percentage fall of some 52 per cent for those years.

In central government, FTE employment in the National Health Service peaked in the early 1980s and declined slightly subsequently. Civil service FTEs declined from 740,000 in 1977 to 540,000 in 1987, a decrease of over 20 per cent. This was only partly offset by an increase of FTEs in other central government agencies, such as the former Training Commission, of some 46,000, or 36 per cent, during the same period. The decline in civil service FTE employment can be accounted for in three ways. First, there was a steady decline in the number of industrial or manual civil servants during this period. Second, some civil service work was hived off into what in effect were 'new' public agencies such as Her Majesty's Stationery Office and the Crown Agents.

Table 14

UK public-sector employment, 1977–87: full-time equivalents

(000s)

Sector	1977	1978	1979	1980	1981	1982	1983	1984	1985	1986	1987
Public corporations	2,058	2,060	2,034	2,007	1,862	1,736	1,641	1,589	1,247	1,182	980
Central government											
HM forces	327	318	314	323	334	324	322	326	326	322	319
NHS	947	957	975	999	1,036	1,045	1,045	1,030	1,026	1,021	1,018
Civil service	740	731	724	700	684	659	643	619	596	597	584
Other	126	134	173	172	169	168	169	168	192	179	172
Total	2,140	2,140	2,186	2,194	2,223	2,196	2,179	2,143	2,140	2,119	2,093
Local authorities											
Education	1,099	1,105	1,110	1,087	1,058	1,041	1,034	1,027	1,021	1,029	1,043
Social services	222	228	235	235	240	241	246	251	256	263	271
Construction	152	152	150	146	136	131	130	126	125	125	128
Police	168	165	172	176	180	180	182	182	182	184	186
Other	683	675	701	699	692	681	709	734	741	751	749
Total	2,324	2,325	2,368	2,343	2,306	2,274	2,301	2,320	2,325	2,352	2,377
Total public sector	6,522	6,525	6,588	6,544	6,391	6,206	6,121	6,052	5,712	5,653	5,450

Source: Adapted from Central Statistical Office, *Economic trends* 410, London, HMSO, 1987.

Third. there was a deliberate policy by government of reducing civil service manpower. This was achieved by streamlining, privatizing, deregulating and contracting out.

In the local authority sector, education has the largest proportion of FTEs and provided between 44 and 47 per cent of local authority employment for this period. FTEs peaked in education in 1979 but levelled out in the 1980s. In the social services, in contrast, they rose from some 222,000 in 1977 to about 271,000 in 1987, an increase of 22 per cent. In the police service FTEs increased between 1977 and 1987 from 168,000 to 186,000. This represents an absolute rise of 18,000, or some 11 per cent in the ten-year period. FTEs employed in local authority construction, on the other hand, fell by 24,000 during these years, or by almost 16 per cent. The figures reflect the changes of emphasis in public policy. They involved more resources for maintaining law and order, and for coping with the community and social problems arising from an ageing population, and poverty and unemployment amongst the growing 'underclass', with a correspondingly decreased provision of resources for public-sector housing.

The structure of civilian employment by industry for 1982 and 1987 is outlined in table 15. During this period the total numbers employed in agriculture, energy and water, and manufacturing fell by an estimated 840,000, or 11 per cent. The total employed in construction and in other services, in contrast, rose by almost 2 million, or 14 per cent. With total employment in transport and communications relatively stable, the result was an increase of just over a million in the civilian labour force during the period. Another feature of the labour force in these years was the growth in the number of self-employed from just over 2 million to 2·7 million. The self-employed represented 9·2 per cent of the civilian labour force in 1982 but 11·1 per cent in 1987. In all sectors of industry the highest proportions of the self-employed were in agriculture and construction, with 46 per cent and 33 per cent respectively. All sectors increased their proportion of self-employed workers in 1982–87, though some only marginally.

During the 1970s the civilian labour force grew at an average of 140,000 per year. By the late 1980s it had reached some 28 million. This resulted in part from the relatively high birth rate of the 1960s. One effect was to increase the number of sixteen-year-old entrants to the labour market during the second half of

Table 15

UK civilian employment by industry, 1982 and 1987

(000s)

	1982			1987		
	Employees	Self-employed	Total employed	Employees	Self-employed	Total employed
Agriculture	358	274	632	320	273	593
Forestry, fishing, energy and water	680	1	681	500	1	501
Manufacturing	5,863	150	6,013	5,171	224	5,394
Construction	1,067	407	1,474	1,013	515	1,528
Transport, communications	1,380	97	1,477	1,354	115	1,469
Other services	12,066	1,241	13,307	13,504	1,601	15,106
Total	21,414	2,170	23,584	21,862	2,729	24,591

Source: Adapted from Central Statistical Office, Economic trends 410, London, HMSO, 1987.

the 1970s, reaching a peak in the early 1980s. After that the number of sixteen-year-old entrants fell. This trend is projected to continue until the 1990s. Between the late 1980s and mid-1990s, it is estimated, the civilian labour force will grow by nearly a million. A rise of over 2 million is projected in the age group twenty to fifty five, with a fall of over a million amongst sixteen to twenty-four-year-olds.[6]

Table 16

UK civilian labour force activity rates, by sex and age, for selected years   *(%)*

Year	16–19		20–24		25–44		45–59[a]		60–64[b]		65+[c]		Over 16	
	M	F	M	F	M	F	M	F	M	F	M	F	M	F
1971	69	65	80	60	95	52	95	62	83	51	19	12	81	44
1981	72	70	85	69	96	62	93	68	69	53	10	8	77	48
1985	74	71	85	69	94	66	89	69	54	52	18	7	74	48
1988	75	74	86	70	94	70	88	71	57	54	7	7	74	51
1991[d]	76	75	86	71	94	72	88	72	56	55	6	6	74	52
1995[d]	76	77	86	72	94	75	88	72	55	56	5	6	73	53

Notes
a Forty-five to fifty-four for females.
b Fifty-five to fifty-nine for females.
c Over sixty for females.
d Projection.
Source: Adapted from Central Statistical Office, *Social Trends* 19, London, HMSO, 1989.

Table 16 provides an analysis of civilian labour force participation rates, by age and sex, for selected years since 1971 and projections into the 1990s. The civilian labour force participation rate (CLFPR) is defined as the percentage of the population in a given age group which is employed. In 1971 the CLFPR was 81 per cent for all males over sixteen years of age and 44 per cent for females. By the late 1980s the percentage had decreased to 74 for males and increased to 51 for females. Clearly the CLFPR varies widely amongst age groups, between the sexes and over time.

In general, male participation rates have fallen in all age groups in recent years, with the exception of sixteen-to-nineteen-year-olds, but especially in older groups. Amongst females, the numbers in employment have risen and female participation rates for all age groups have increased, except for those aged sixty and over. The increase in female participation rates has been due partly to the growth in the availability of part-time jobs and other social and economic changes encouraging women into the labour market. Demographic factors have also influenced female participation rates. Thus women with children are less likely to be economically active than are those who remain childless. Also, lower birth rates in the 1970s, compared with the 1960s, and a rise in the average age when women had children have increased female participation rates and will continue to do so in the 1990s.

The unemployed

The other element in the working population, the unemployed, is defined as those who are not in paid work and are either moving to a job or cannot find work at the prevailing wage rate. Various methods are used to analyse unemployment and to categorize the unemployed. One way is to distinguish between unemployed claimants and non-claimants. Unemployed non-claimants, for example, are those not entitled to unemployment benefits, normally because they have not paid enough National Insurance contributions to qualify. There are also people who do not register as unemployed because they do not believe there are any jobs for them, as in areas of high unemployment. Finally, there are those beyond statutory retirement age who may be seeking work but do not qualify for unemployment benefit. Clearly, official unemployment statistics covering only the registered unemployed, or unemployed claimants, considerably underestimate the real level of unemployment at any one time.

Unemployed claimants are individuals who are entitled to unemployment benefit. In the early 1980s the number claiming benefit rose sharply, with recorded unemployment around or in excess of 3 million for most of the period. It was not until May 1987 that the number of claimants fell below the 3 million mark, the lowest it had been for four years. Table 17 shows the fall in unemployed claimants since 1984. The figures must be treated with some caution, since the government changed the method of calculating unemployment twenty-four times in the period 1979–88.

In outline, unemployment rates for both males and females rose very sharply in 1980 and 1981. The upward trend continued subsequently, though the rate of increase slowed down in the

Table 17
*Unemployed claimants in the UK: annual averages, 1984,
1986 and 1988*   *(000s)*

Type of claimant	1984	1986	1988
Males			
Under twenty-five	753	727	558
Twenty-five and over	1,445	1,539	1,335
Females			
Under twenty-five	479	461	340
Twenty-five and over	481	585	497
All claimants	3,158	3,312	2,730

Source: Adapted from Central Statistical Office, *Social Trends* 19, London,
HMSO, 1988.

period up to 1986. After that date there was a steady fall, although male unemployment was consistently higher than the female rate. In 1979 the annual average unemployment rate was only 5 per cent. By 1983 it had risen to almost 13 per cent, but fell slowly to around 8 per cent by 1988.[7] Indeed, after 1984 unemployment fell. The reason was continued exits from the labour market and a decline of new entrants. Since 1986 there has been a proportionally larger fall in unemployed claimants for both sexes in the under-twenty-five age groups. It arose partly from the introduction of youth training programmes by the government which were designed to deal with the long-term unemployed. These job creation programmes, however, sometimes only removed people temporarily from the unemployed register.

After 1979 the long-term unemployed—claimants who had been unemployed for over a year—accounted for an increasing proportion of all claimants. In July 1979, for example, they accounted for some 25 per cent of the total, whilst by July 1988 they comprised nearly 41 per cent. The growth in long-term unemployment has been concentrated in the longest duration groups. The proportion of all claimants unemployed for more than five years, for example, increased from 2 per cent in July 1983 to 11 per cent in July 1988. Moreover the proportion of claimants who are long-term unemployed increases with age. In July 1988 two-thirds of unemployed males over fifty had been unemployed for over a year, whilst for males aged sixteen to nineteen the corresponding figure was 17 per cent. The duration of unemployment for females also shows relatively high proportions of older women who are long-term unemployed.

Employment trends

As indicated earlier, in the period from the early 1980s to the late 1980s the employed labour force rose by about 1·7 million, from 23·6 million to 25·3 million, which was what it had been in the late 1970s. The public sector had employed about 30 per cent of the labour force in 1983 but the figure had fallen to 25 per cent by 1987. Most of the decrease in public-sector employment in the 1980s is accounted for by privatization. The selling of British Telecom and British Gas alone resulted in 300,000 employees being transferred from the public to the private sector between 1984 and 1986. In the private sector, the number of employees fell from over 23 million in the late 1970s to just over 22 million by the late 1980s. Within this sector, manufacturing employment fell by over 2 million jobs, or some 30 per cent, over the same period, whilst in private services employment increased by over 1·6 million, or 12 per cent. The number of employees in banking, finance, insurance, business services and leasing grew steadily in these years, accounting for nearly half the increase in all service industries between 1979 and 1988.

From the early 1980s to the late 1980s the number of employees in employment rose by over a million. Virtually all the rise was accounted for by females, both full-time and part-time. The increase in male part-time employees only marginally exceeded the decrease in full-time male employees. Amongst the self-employed, over 50 per cent of the growth was due to full-time males. The overall trend in self-employment was complementary to that for employees. Between the late 1970s and late 1980s the number of self-employed rose from just under 2 million to over 3 million. Whereas in the late 1970s only 19 per cent of the self-employed were women, ten years later they constituted 25 per cent of the self-employed. Manufacturing continues to account for only some 9 per cent of total self-employment, whilst the service industries account for almost two-thirds.[8]

Table 18 shows full-time employees as a percentage of all employment in Britain by industry for 1983 and 1987. Between 1981 and 1987 the number of full-time employees fell by about

Table 18

Full-time employees as a percentage of all employment in Britain, by industry, 1983 and 1987   *(%)*

Industry sector	1983	1987
Agriculture, forestry, fishing	43·1	38·8
Energy and water supply	96·1	95·5
Extractive industries	92·7	91·2
Metal goods	92·3	90·2
Other manufacturing	83·3	80·5
Construction	67·9	58·3
Distribution	57·9	48·1
Transport and communications	87·5	82·1
Financial services	75·1	72·4
Other services	65·4	59·6
All industries ('000)	16,264	16,050

Source: Adapted from Central Statistical Office, *Social Trends* 19, London, HMSO, 1988.

one per cent. Although there were differences in the proportions of full-time employees amongst various sectors for each of these years, it was only in energy and water supply that the proportion was the same in 1987 as it was in 1983. In all other industries the proportion of part-time employees increased. 'This implies that between 1983 and 1987 the industries which were contracting and relinquishing a higher proportion of full-time employees and those which were expanding were employing a higher proportion of part-time employees.'[9]

Of the public sector's 6·4 million employees in 1987, some 1·7 million, or 27 per cent, were part-timers. Of these only 170,000 were male and 1·5 million were female. The public corporations had the largest proportion of full-time employees, some 960,000 out of a million. The National Health Service and local authorities had the highest proportions of part-time employees, with 38 per cent and 37 per cent respectively. In these two sectors part-time employment accounted for only 8 per cent and 11 per cent of all male employment respectively, but 46 per cent and 45 per cent of all female employment. Part-time female employment was particularly noticeable in education and the social services, at 55 per cent and 63 per cent respectively.

The Implications for Management

The composition and structure of a country's population, such as that of the UK, have considerable implications for all business organizations and for the managers running them, in the short term and in the medium and long terms. As producers of goods and services, organizations need to plan and operationalize their marketing and production strategies. In doing so, managements have to take account of a number of basic demographic factors. These include the distributional and structural features of its targeted population, such as age profiles and projections, sex ratio, ethnic composition, family size, geographical dispersion, life expectancies, and other demographic trends. Private-sector business corporations, for example, are likely to base their planning on the expected economic consequences of these and related demographic factors. As population changes work through into the economy they create opportunities for developing new markets and products, whilst old ones decline.

Managements in the public corporations and public services, by contrast, are more likely to take account of the expected social and welfare consequences of population structure and change. Changes in the age distribution of the population, for example, lead to new demands on the education, health and social services. In practice, however, they can only be met within the economic and financial constraints set by the country's political leaders.

As employers of human resources business corporations also have to adapt their personnel strategies in line with population structure and demographic change. The composition and structure of the working population from which they draw their human resources are themselves a function of demographic factors. The age structure of the population, for example, is an important determinant of the availability of the immediate and longer-term labour skills employers demand. With a static economy, and a reasonably balanced age structure, as in the inter-war period 1920–39, there is likely to be an excess of labour supply. With a growing economy, and an unbalanced age structure, with many old and relatively few young people, as in the mid-1990s, there is likely to be an excess of labour demand.

In the latter circumstances, employers have to adopt proactive human resource policies to deal with actual and potential labour shortages. Such policies need to be aimed at:

- Recruiting effectively with attractive employment packages.
- Retaining existing employees with appropriate motivational incentives.
- Utilizing the maximum potential and personal contribution of all employees.
- Training their workforces to be adaptable and flexible, thus enabling individuals to meet the changing operational demands made on them, according to market conditions.

These are skilled managerial tasks and have clear cost implications for employers and managers. Such issues have to be addressed by management if rising employer demand and specific labour shortages are to be adequately faced.

Another area where managements are adapting their personnel policies in response to increasing labour shortages, and changing patterns of demography, is in satisfying the needs of the growing proportion of women entering the labour market. Because of family commitments, or other reasons, some women are prepared to work only part-time. This requires employers to provide flexible patterns of working for such individuals, new forms of employment contract and creche facilities for young children. At the other end of the employment spectrum, employers are becoming increasingly conscious of the legal and moral need to provide job opportunities, and conditions of employment, that do not discriminate against professional women or women managers who want a progressive career and career development. Women as well as other social groups are increasingly expecting equality of opportunity at work. This puts more responsibility on managers to provide the right conditions. The changing sex distribution of the labour force appears to be facilitating it. Managements are also required not to discriminate on grounds of race. They need to develop effective personnel policies which cater for the differing cultural, religious and social characteristics of ethnic minorities.

References

1 CENTRAL STATISTICAL OFFICE. *Social trends 19*. London, HMSO, 1989. p 30.
2 HASKEY J. 'The ethnic minority population of Great Britain', *Population trends*. 54, winter, 1988, p 5.
3 *ibid*. p 30.
4 *ibid*.
5 *Population trends*. 50, winter, 1987, p 22.
6 CENTRAL STATISTICAL OFFICE. *op. cit*. p 69.
7 ORGANIZATION FOR ECONOMIC CO-OPERATION AND DEVELOPMENT. *Quarterly labour force statistics*. Paris, OECD, 1989.
8 CENTRAL STATISTICAL OFFICE. *op. cit*. p 74.
9 *ibid*. p 75f.

4

Social Structure and Social Change

Like all societies, the UK comprises a varied population of individuals and groups with differing structural features and social characteristics. People live in a particular territory, or geopolitical area, are subject to a common system of government and claim a unique national identity, even though there are regional variations. All these features differ in turn from those of other societies and go to make up the country's distinctive social culture and patterns of social relations. The social culture consists of the dominant values and behavioural norms according to which people act out their social roles as individuals and as members of groups. Such roles include their gender role, their role as members of families, of work and non-work organizations, and their role as citizens and actors within the political system.

The social structure reflects the distribution of power in society. Power is the ability of individuals, or members of specific groups, to further their own goals and interests, sometimes at the expense of others'. It is a pervasive characteristic of all human societies and relationships. In all human structures and groupings some factions and some individuals have more power and authority than others, with power and control over resources tending to be closely linked, as are lack of power and inequality. Normally those who are rich, powerful and members of elite groups are able to accumulate society's valued resources, such as property, wealth and status, and to control access to them by others. Similarly, those who are poor, politically weak and constitute excluded groups are frequently deprived of society's valued resources and any control over them. Nevertheless, the social structure is neither static nor fixed. Social change, or any alteration in the basic structures of society and social groupings, is a continuous phenomenon and is particularly intense in the modern world.

Class, Status and Inequality

All societies are unequal in the distribution of resources, property, power and rights. These economic and social features of human activity are attributes of people's position in society rather than of their personal qualities as individuals. It is clear from observation that some individuals and some social groups have more resources, wealth and positional power than others. Obviously, individuals are unequally endowed in terms of their size, height, strength, health, intelligence, and so on. But it is not these differences which provide the basis from which social stratification, or the existence of structured inequalities of society's material and symbolic rewards, emerges. As Littlejohn (1972) points out, a society is socially stratified when it shows 'significant breaks or discontinuities in the distribution of one of the several attributes mentioned above, as a result of which are formed collectivities or groups which we call strata'.[1]

Sociologists distinguish between two main types of social stratification. The first is based on differences between one stratum and another. These are 'expressed in terms of legal rights or of established customs which have the essential binding character of law'. They are relatively closed or immobile societies consisting of systems of 'estates' or 'castes'. Estates were part of European feudalism and are strata distinguished from one another through differential immunities defined by law. In medieval Europe, for example, there were three estates: the aristocracy and gentry, the clergy, and the commoners, including peasants, merchants and artisans. Caste denotes the social stratification most conspicuously associated with Hinduism. Here differences between strata are defined largely by religion in terms of degrees of 'purity' or 'impurity' between social groups.[2]

The second type of social stratification is found largely in industrial capitalist societies. In this case, strata emerge from 'the interplay of a variety of factors related to the institutions of property and education and the structure of the national economy'.[3] Since the study of stratification focuses on the distributive processes within societies, the question of who gets what and why is a controversial one. Compared with estate or caste societies, however, industrial capitalist societies are relatively open and allow of greater mobility between classes. Within them 'there is considerable mobility for a minority both upwards and downwards in the social hierarchy. Nevertheless, their main feature remains the continuity of family position between generations.'[4]

According to Halsey (1986), the structure of social inequality derives from the differential distribution of power and advantage in society between individuals and groups. Power is the resources which people command, individually and collectively, to achieve their economic and social objectives, whilst advantage is their control over the things which are scarce and thus valued. The latter include property, wealth, human skills, education, social recognition, and so on. 'Power and advantage are controvertible. Together they define the character of strata and the relations between them in a stratification system.' Modern social stratification of this sort has three dimensions: class, status and power. Class arises largely out of the social division of labour and comprises those occupational groups and families sharing like work and a similar market position in society. Status is created out of the tendency to attach positive and negative values to certain human attributes such as personal worth, social position and patterns of behaviour. Power is concerned with the organized pursuit of economic and social goals through parties and political means. 'In short, classes belong to the economic, status groups to the social, and parties to the political structure of society.'[5]

The anatomy of class composition under industrial capitalism is displayed essentially in the occupational structure. Its foundation lies in the marketplace, not in tradition and not in the law. Class structures have four general features:

- Membership of a class is not dependent on an individual's inherited position.

- Classes are relatively more open than are other systems of social stratification, with the boundaries between classes never clear-cut.

- Classes institutionalize economic differences amongst groups, reflecting inequalities in the distribution of income, wealth and control of resources.

- Since class membership is partly achieved, rather then being merely ascribed, social mobility up, down or across the class

structure is far more common than in the relatively closed
stratification systems associated with estates and castes.

A class, then, is a 'large-scale social grouping of people who share
common economic resources, which strongly influence the types
of life-style they are able to lead', with 'ownership of wealth,
together with occupation [being] the chief bases of class differences'.[6]

Table 19

*UK socio-economic groups, by occupational category, 1981:
10 per cent employment sample*

	Socio-economic group	Total	%
1	Employers and managers (large establishments)	103,344	4·5
2	Employers and managers (small establishments)	170,083	7·4
3	Professional workers (self-employed)	15,536	0·7
4	Professional workers (employees)	76,547	3·4
5·1	Ancilliary workers and artists	224,234	9·8
5·2	Foremen and supervisors (non-manual)	23,349	1·0
6	Junior non-manual workers	492,621	21·5
7	Personal service workers	130,069	5·7
8	Foremen and supervisors (manual)	58,798	2·6
9	Skilled manual workers	399,887	17·4
10	Semi-skilled manual workers	277,990	12·1
11	Unskilled manual workers	133,129	5·8
12	Own-account workers (other than professional)	93,629	4·1
13	Farmers: employers and managers	11,568	0·5
14	Farmers (own account)	11,523	0·5
15	Agricultural workers	22,684	1·0
16	Armed forces	24,870	1·1
17	Other	20,518	0·9
	Total	2,290,379	100·0

Source: Office of Population Censuses and Surveys, *Census, 1981. National
report. Great Britain*, part 2, London, HMSO, 1983.

There are a number of methods of classifying and describing the
contemporary class structure of the UK. Given the importance
of occupation as a determinant of class composition, one useful
categorization is the Registrar General's classification of socio-
economic groups, introduced in 1951. It comprises groups of

unranked occupations, each of which incorporates people with similar social, cultural and recreational standards. The classification is built up from non-manual and manual occupational groups, separating out workers in agriculture and the armed services, and uses employment status as a differentiating factor. The socio-economic groupings for the early 1980s, based on a 10 per cent employment sample at the last census of population, are shown in table 19. Its main feature is the relative growth of middle-class white-collar occupations in recent years. Indeed, according to some observers the majority of the population now fall into this class, because of the relative decline of manual 'blue-collar' employment since the 1960s. This also means that the occupational structure, when ranked according to social status, is now diamond-shaped, or narrow at the top and bottom but broad in the middle. This contrasts with the early twentieth-century position, when it was more like a pyramid—narrow at the top and broad at the base.

Dahrendorf (1982) provides a useful conceptual analysis of contemporary class structure in the UK. He views it as 'a layer cake in which clear distinctions can be drawn between the bottom of the cake, the jam in the middle, and the chocolate on the top (if such a concoction holds together)'. He divides the country into a very old, an old and a more recent upper class; an upper middle, middle middle and lower middle class; and a skilled, semi-skilled and unskilled working class. He argues that the relative distribution of the population amongst these classes has changed with time, especially since the 1960s. 'The working class has shrunk, and the upper class has diminished in importance. By sheer weight of numbers, the middle class has gained ground.'[7] It is not a homogeneous middle class, because it is fundamentally divided, he argues, between what may be described as the radical egalitarians on the political left, and the radical market liberals of the right. In Dahrendorf's view, if there are any signs of something approaching class conflict in the UK, its origins lie in the new middle classes, left and right, not in the working class.

However it is measured, the upper class is made up of a very small number of individuals and families owning a disproportionate share of property and wealth, probably the top 5 per cent of wealth holders. Nevertheless, there would appear to be distinct status differences between those who draw their wealth from 'old' money and those with 'new' money. The influence of the upper class as a whole derives from the control and ownership of substantial proportions of industrial and finance capital and access to leading positions in the business, political and cultural elites.

The upper middle class consists of those holding senior managerial, professional and technical positions, equivalent to Galbraith's technostructure, and has grown significantly in number in the post-war period. The middle middle class is a more heterogeneous grouping comprising not only middle-ranking professionals and technocrats but also what may be described as the 'old' middle class. This incorporates the proprietors of small businesses, local shops and small farms. The lower middle class is equally heterogeneous and includes the minor and para-professions, self-employed individual proprietors and white-collar workers employed in routine operational tasks. It is because of their intermediate position in the class structure that:

> Middle-class people find themselves in 'contradictory' situations of 'dual closure' in the sense that they are caught between conflicting pressures and influences. Many lower-middle-class people, for example, identify with the same values as those in more remunerative positions, but may find themselves living on incomes below those of the better-paid manual workers.[8]

The skilled working class or 'labour aristocracy' has higher incomes, better working conditions and more job security than other members of the working class. The semi-skilled working class, in contrast, does jobs which need little or no training, while its jobs are less secure, owing to technological, product market or occupational change. The unskilled working class is even less secure in its job and employment prospects. Indeed, this group borders on the 'underclass' of society. The underclass includes the long-term unemployed, single parents without regular full-time paid employment or family support, and the elderly living alone without an adequate pension. In the UK the ethnic minorities are disproportionally represented in the underclass. It is in this group that the disparities associated with the vast economic and social inequalities which exist in most industrial capitalist societies are most apparent.

Up to the First World War an integrated inequality was,

according to Halsey, a central principle of British social policy. At
that time, he argues, the class system was fully congruent with the
status system which supported it. Slowly and imperceptibly during
the twentieth century a new form of status – citizenship – emerged.
It was achieved by the redistribution of goods and services through
the agency of the State, based on the criterion of need rather than
on purchasing power. Whilst a class society uses the marketplace
as a distributive mechanism, citizenship, according to Halsey, 'is
a special form of status which looks to the state and seeks a
different type of distribution which . . . is essentially levelling'.[9]
Hence, just as the old bonds of social class weaken, so new social
groups come to the fore, with the old status structure weakening
too. The UK remains a class-based society, however, and in the
1980s there was a significant movement away from the citizenship
principle back to the market place for allocating society's limited
economic and social resources. To what extent this is a permanent
shift in social values and behaviour remains to be determined.

Gender Issues

Sex differences are the anatomical and biological characteristics
distinguishing females from males and vice versa. Gender differences, in contrast, are the social expectations which members of
society hold about what is regarded as appropriate behaviour
for individuals of each sex. Gender behaviour, therefore, reflects
socially determined traits of masculinity and femininity. Gender
issues and social relations between the sexes, in the home, at
work and in society generally have become matters of significant
public debate and social change since the 1960s. One manifestation of this was the Sex Discrimination Act, 1975, which established the Equal Opportunities Commission (EOC) in 1975. The
EOC's duties include:

- Working towards the elimination of sex discrimination in the
  UK.
- Promoting equality of opportunity between men and women
  generally.
- Keeping the Equal Pay Act, 1970, and Sex Discrimination
  Act, 1975, under review.

• Proposing changes in the law affecting equal opportunity.

Although there are wide variations in the roles and activities of women and men in different societies, in no known society are females collectively more powerful than men. This is despite the fact that, overall, women generally outnumber men in most populations because of their greater longevity. It is men who tend to hold the most powerful positions in economic, political, educational and military institutions. It is women, on the other hand, who are largely responsible for child-rearing, housework and caring for the sick and elderly. This dominance of men over women in the economic and social orders of society is known as patriarchy. One of the main objectives of women's movements is to modify if not replace patriarchal institutions. Feminism, which dates from the eighteenth century, takes a variety of forms and provides a political focus for those advocating and supporting the basic human right of women to equality with men in all areas of social and economic activity.

Patriarchy in the economic sphere is demonstrated by the fact that women tend to have the least secure, lowest-status and worst-paid jobs. This remains the case even though women's importance in the labour force has increased since the early 1970s and will continue to do so into the 1990s. According to the Department of Employment, the civilian labour force grew by about 2·3 million between 1971 and 1987, although the figure dipped between 1981 and 1983, and is projected to continue to increase gradually until the mid-1990s. Within this trend, the proportion of women in the labour force rose steadily from 37 per cent in 1971 to 42 per cent by the late 1980s, whilst it is projected to rise further to 44 per cent in the mid-1990s.[10] Women's economic activity rates, at all ages, rose steadily throughout the 1980s and will continue to do so, except for those nearing retirement. Conversely, activity rates for men are continuing to fall. The UK has one of the highest percentages of women in paid employment in Europe.

The changing structure of employment is characterized by the continuing growth in female employment, part-time employment, temporary employment and self-employment. A major feature of female employment in the UK is the relatively high number of part-time women workers, certainly compared with its European neighbours. In 1987, for example, the British labour force consisted of some 11·6 million males and 9·7 million females. Of the females, only 5·4 million had full-time jobs, whilst 4·3 million had part-time ones. This compares with 5·5 million female full-timers and 2·8 million part-timers in 1971 and 5·3 million and 3·8 million in 1981.

Part-time employees are likely to be married women. Only 2 per cent of men and 8 per cent of non-married women were in part-time jobs in the mid-1980s. But 24 per cent of married women were part-timers and only 20 per cent of married women were in full-time employment. Amongst women workers there is a significant difference between women with dependent children and the rest. According to the Department of Employment's Labour Force Surveys in the late 1980s, about 66 per cent of married women with dependent children work part-time, compared with 40 per cent of married women without children and some 10 per cent of unmarried women without children. It is the age of their youngest child and family size which largely influence the participation rates of mothers in the labour force.

Women also constitute a large proportion of temporary workers. These are in jobs which are seasonal, casual, on a fixed-term contract, or in some way non-permanent. In the period 1983 to 1985, for example, women represented 70 per cent of temporary part-time and 40 per cent of temporary full-time workers. It was the growth in demand for business services, subcontracting and personal services which led to this increase in temporary work, and to self-employment, in the 1980s.

The employment patterns of lone mothers, a growing statistic, differ from those of mothers in two-parent families. Although lone mothers are more likely to work full-time than part-time, their activity rate declined during the 1980s. One reason was the difficulty they face in making satisfactory child care arrangements in the absence of a partner. Another is the 'poverty trap' created by the social security system. Under its arrangements, supplementary benefit or income support is lost pound for pound above a fairly low level of earnings. Financially it is not worth while for a woman to take paid work unless it is below this threshold or substantially above it. Because widows' benefits are not means-tested, employment rates amongst them are very similar to those of married mothers. Divorced mothers have a higher level of full-time employment, and a lower level of part-time employment, than married mothers. The lowest levels of employment are amongst single mothers. It is this group which is most likely to be entirely dependent on means-tested benefits.

Research also shows that women workers are concentrated in a relatively narrow range of occupations and industries. Generally, these are occupations and industries with part-time labour, less skilled work and a service function. Occupationally women are concentrated in selling, catering, cleaning, hairdressing, clerical work, education, nursing and welfare. Industrially they are concentrated in retail distribution, hotels and catering, public administration and the caring services. Nearly 80 per cent of working women are employed in these four areas. It has also been demonstrated that both the occupational and the industrial distribution of employment are more influenced by gender than by ethnic origin.

The economic inequality of women is further evidenced by the earnings gap which persists between women and men, as indicated in table 20. Women's gross hourly earnings peaked at 75·5 per cent of men's in 1977. Since then they have remained just below 75 per cent of men's. The earnings gap is even greater when weekly earnings are considered, rather than hourly pay rates alone. As can be seen from table 21, even when men's greater opportunities for overtime payments are discounted, the earnings gap is greater for weekly than for hourly earnings because of men's longer working hours. The evidence shows, however, that the earnings of women in full-time employment improved relative to men's earnings until the early 1980s. Subsequently an earnings gap of just over a third has persisted between female and male full-time earnings. The ratio between women's and men's earnings is only partially explained by occupational segregation and the fact that the occupations in which women work are generally poorly paid. Nor is there a general relationship between the earnings differential and the proportion of women in the occupation or the rate of pay. Even in occupations where the majority of workers are female, male earnings remain higher than those of females. This reflects the tendency for men to be concentrated in higher-paid grades, compared with women.

Evidence from the New Earnings Surveys indicates that the earnings gap between female and male manual workers is smaller than that between those in non-manual employment. Male

Table 20

Average gross hourly earnings in Britain, excluding the effects of overtime: full-time employees on adult rates, 1970–87

(pence per hour)

Employee	1970	1973	1975	1977	1979	1981	1983	1985	1987
Women	42·5	60·3	98·3	133·9	165·7	241·2	287·5	329·9	383·8
Men	67·4	93·7	136·3	177·4	226·9	322·5	387·6	445·3	521·3
Differential	24·9	33·4	38·0	43·5	61·2	81·3	100·1	115·4	137·5
Women's earnings as % of men's	63·1	64·4	72·1	75·5	73·0	74·8	74·2	74·0	73·6

Source: New earnings survey, London, HMSO, various years.

77

Table 21

Average gross earnings in Britain, excluding the effects of overtime: full-time employees on adult rates, 1970–87

(£ per week)

Employee	1970	1973	1975	1977	1979	1981	1983	1985	1987
Women	16·2	22·6	37·4	51·0	63·0	91·4	108·8	125·5	147·2
Men	29·7	37·5	60·8	78·6	99·0	137·0	163·3	190·4	222·1
Differential	13·5	14·9	23·4	27·6	36·0	45·6	54·5	64·9	74·9
Women's earnings as % of men's	54·5	60·3	61·5	64·9	63·6	66·7	66·6	65·9	66·3

Source: New earnings survey, London, HMSO, various years.

workers are divided almost equally between manual and non-manual occupations, but almost 75 per cent of female workers are in non-manual employment. Despite the greater earnings gap, the concentration of women in non-manual employment pulls overall female earnings up as a proportion of male earnings. This is because of the higher modal earnings of non-manual workers. In turning to earnings profiles over working lives, we observe that women manual workers reach their maximum earnings in the age band twenty-five to thirty, with those of older women decreasing slightly. The earnings of non-manual workers of both sexes increase more with age than those of manual workers, as a wider earnings gap opens up. Average earnings peak later or non-manual workers, around thirty-five to forty for women and forty-five for men.

This inequality of earnings is due to a number of related factors. One is the widespread job segregation between women and men, with women concentrated in lower-paid work. A second is the impact of child-bearing and child-rearing, when women spend a period out of the labour market, followed by a return to part-time employment. This is often associated with occupational downgrading, poor working conditions, limited promotion prospects and again low pay. A third reason for the earnings gap is that women are concentrated in the lower positions in organizations. Gender segregation is both vertical and horizontal. For example, whilst women occupy nearly 75 per cent of clerical and related occupations, they hold less than 20 per cent of office management posts. Most of the latter are concentrated in first-level posts as supervisors and first-line managers.

In 1977 only 8 per cent of general managers were women, and this situation did not change significantly over the next decade. Most women managers are found in the four areas identified as primarily 'women's' occupations and industries – public administration, the retail trade, hotel and catering, and hairdressing. Nor are women more successful in getting to the top of the professions than they are in industry and commerce. In 1977 only 5 per cent of employed women were professional people, employers or managers, compared with 21 per cent of men. In spite of equal opportunities legislation since the mid-1970s, there are still few women to be found in corporate board rooms or holding chief executive appointments, as indicated by Scase (1987).

The presence of so few women in management prompted research by the former Manpower Services Commission. Its investigation by Davidson and Cooper (1983) showed that whilst it was easy for women to gain employment at the lower levels of organizations, it was much more difficult for them to reach upper middle and senior positions. The results indicated that women were subject to far more pressures at work and at home than their male counterparts. They also faced prejudice and discrimination due to organizational and corporate policy and from people at work. They were disadvantaged too in terms of salary, career development and promotion. Other studies, such as Schein (1973), Davidson and Cooper (1987) and Spencer and Podmore (1987), demonstrate that sexual stereotyping, the dual role of career woman and mother, and the fact that women operate in a man's world are all impediments to any real gender equality in the economic sphere.

Gender inequality is not confined to the economic sphere. It is similarly evident in politics. Women are much less likely than men to become Members of Parliament (MPs), government Ministers or top civil servants. Very few are leading trade unionists, spokespersons of industrial and social interests or local councillors. Women made up 13 per cent of the candidates in the general election of 1987, double the proportion of 1970, but formed only 6·5 per cent of MPs after the election. The forty-one women MPs elected in 1987 were a record number, more than double those elected in 1979, but still a significant underrepresentation of more than 50 per cent of the population. Since 1964 there have been only five women Cabinet Ministers, and only two women have ever held the post of permanent secretary in the civil service.

The differences between the numbers of women and men in top political positions and with access to political power cannot be ascribed to lack of interest in politics. As Rose (1989) says, 'the proportion of women who are interested in politics is similar to that of men according to the British Election Survey'.[11] He considers the underrepresentation of women in politics is in part a reflection of their historic underrepresentation in society. He identifies two specific reasons inhibiting their entry into politics. The first is the need for an aspiring politician to spend time cultivating a party position between the ages of twenty-one and forty, just when a woman is likely to be child-rearing. The second is that success in politics depends increasingly on a good education and a degree. Until recently women have been less likely than men to qualify in that respect.

Since 1944 all females have received compulsory education from five to sixteen along with males, but gender equality stops there. Gender differences in education result in girls concentrating on arts and humanities, with boys tending to specialize in the sciences. Academically girls tend to perform better than boys in primary and secondary school but fall behind afterwards. Females are underrepresented in mathematics, engineering and science courses in higher education. There are fewer women students in higher education and fewer women higher education teachers, especially in senior posts. In school teaching, too, where they constitute 70 per cent of all staff, women occupy relatively few head teacher posts, except at primary school level.

Given the gender inequalities which exist in the UK and other societies, how can they be explained? Why is it that women generally have less than equal access to society's positional goods and resources than men? All social theorists accept that women and men are socialized from birth into stereotypical gender roles. The process starts in the family but is reinforced by the education system, by the media and by other institutions of mass communication. Stratification theorists argue that gender inequality is irrelevant, since a woman's position in society is determined by the status of the family in which she lives, and that is a function of the male breadwinner's earning capacity and social class. Functionalists, in contrast, suggest that gender relations merely reflect a sexual division of labour, with women taking on an expressive and nurturing role in the family and men an instrumental one in earning wages. For functionalists the family unit is a haven of consensus and fulfilment which is necessary for carrying out essential social functions. Relations between the sexes, they claim, are different but equal.

These conservative analyses of gender relations and the roles of women and men have been increasingly challenged by more radical writers. Marxist feminist writers, such as Barrett (1980), argue that the family exists not for the benefit of its members but in the interests of the capitalist class. It is women who provide free labour in the reproduction of future wage labourers and in sustaining existing ones. Capitalists pay the male worker less than if he had to buy these domestic services in the open market, whilst women's domestic role place them in a weak market position when competing for jobs and wage-earning opportunities.

Radical feminist writers such as Spender (1981 and 1989) argue even more strongly than the Marxists against the traditional role of women in society and orthodox gender relations. They see the oppression of women by men as the most significant feature of social inequality. Men's exploitation of women, they argue, is not a by-product of any other form of inequality; it is deliberately institutionalized to ensure the dominance of men in all aspects of social and economic life and gender relations.

Whatever the explanation, gender discrimination and inequality exist. Women generally have more limited access to wealth, status and power than men, and this renders them less able to influence the laws and decisions society makes. Their growing importance in the labour market and their political challenges to patriarchy are important facets of contemporary society.

Race Relations

In the period after 1945 millions of people migrated to all parts of western Europe. They came from the less developed areas of southern Europe, Asia, Africa and the Caribbean. One estimate claims that there were about 16 million people of 'migrant origins' living in western Europe, including the UK, by the early 1980s. These people's families had originated from a variety of countries, including Algeria, Morocco, Indonesia, Turkey, Spain, Italy, Yugoslavia, India, Pakistan, Bangladesh and the West Indies. The underlying reason for these migrations to western Europe was post-war reconstruction and the subsequent expansion of the Western economies. This factor, combined with a fall in the economically active population, because of death or injury in war, 'and an increase in the number of the old and retired, created a shortage of labour in Western Europe. Migrant labour was needed.'[12]

Immigration into the UK in the immediate post-war period was not a new phenomenon. Successive waves of immigrants had been entering the country since the seventeenth century. After the Reformation, Huguenots fled from persecution in France and settled in East Anglia and the Midlands. Jews and other traders came from the Netherlands in the seventeenth century and settled in London. There had also been a thriving Irish community in London since the seventeenth century. Between 1830 and 1847 some 300,000 Irish landed in Liverpool alone. By 1851, it is claimed, 500,000 Irish people had settled in England and Wales. Later, between the early 1930s and mid-1940s, about 150,000 refugees entered the UK from Europe to escape from Nazi persecution, a large proportion of whom were Jews. The factor distinguishing the large-scale immigration which took place into the UK in the years after the Second World War was that most of the newcomers came from what were to be called the New Commonwealth countries and Pakistan. They arrived in response to job opportunities amid the labour shortages of the emerging post-war economy.

Such groups are often referred to as ethnic minorities. According to Giddens (1989), an ethnic minority group has the following characteristics:

1 Its members are disadvantaged, as a result of discrimination against them by others. Discrimination exists when rights and opportunities open to one set of people are denied to another group. For instance, a landlord may refuse to rent a room to someone because she or he is of West Indian background.
2 Members of the minority group have some sense of group solidarity, of 'belonging together'. Experience of being the subject of prejudice and discrimination usually heightens feelings of common loyalty and interests. Members of minority groups often tend to see themselves as 'a people apart' from the majority.
3 Minority groups are usually to some degree physically and socially isolated from the larger community. They tend to be concentrated in certain neighbourhoods, cities, or regions of the country. There is little intermarriage between those in the majority and members of the minority group. People in the minority group might actively promote endogamy (marriage within the group) in order to keep alive their cultural distinctiveness.[13]

Because of these and related factors, the integration and assimilation of ethnic minority groups into their wider communities are problematic and difficult to achieve in practice. This is the case not only in the UK but in other parts of western Europe where ethnic minorities have settled, as well as in the United States, where the struggle for black civil rights and equal opportunity continues today.

The pattern of settlement of the new ethnic minorities in the post-war UK took two paths. First, by the end of the 1940s, migrant workers and their families began to settle from what were at that time British colonies in the Caribbean. They were British citizens, Christians, English-speaking but non-whites. They were encouraged by government to enter the UK because of labour shortages in public transport and the health services and to take on jobs that the indigenous population was not prepared to do. 'But these immigrants suffered from colour prejudice and discrimination, especially in employment, housing and in social life — public houses and working men's clubs.'[14]

Second, in the 1950s, Asian immigrants began to arrive from the former empire in India and Pakistan. They too were British citizens and non-whites but they were not Christians and not English-speaking. They settled in the poorest areas of the inner cities, especially in London, the Midlands and the declining northern textile towns. As Lester (1987) indicates, these immigrants were usually men who came alone, lived in cheap hostels and worked long hours for low wages. When they had saved enough they were joined by their wives, children and families. 'Like the West Indians from the Caribbean, most of these Asian newcomers were victims of a vicious circle of discrimination: low-grade and low-paid jobs, poor housing, [and] inadequate education for their children.'[15] They tend to live in the inner cities and are employed in the textile industries, public services and small retailing units. Many work in the sweated trades, such as the clothing workshops of the East End of London, are low-paid and are vulnerable to fluctuations in trade.

Through these two waves of immigration the pattern was set for the emergence of the non-white ethnic minority groups that have settled here in the past forty years. Despite the attempts of successive governments since the 1960s to facilitate the full integration of the new communities into British society, and to promote equality of opportunity for them, the ethnic minorities generally remain both disadvantaged, compared with the white population, and discriminated against in many respects. Indeed, the increase in unemployment during the 1980s was concentrated especially amongst the ethnic groups. This resulted in rising racial tensions in some of the inner-city areas of London, Liverpool and Bristol. Three times as many young blacks were unemployed at this time, compared with whites, reaching 60 per cent in the inner cities.

There are also strong racist undertones amongst sections of the white population which attribute characteristics of inferiority and stereotyping to non-white minority groups. This stereotyping is based simply on observations about an individual's physically inherited features, such as colour of skin and appearance alone. In this sense, racism is one form of personal prejudice, focusing on physical variations between people. Whilst racist attitudes became entrenched amongst whites during the period of Western colonial expansion in the seventeenth, eighteenth and nineteenth centuries, they also seem to rest on psychological and 'in-group' mechanisms of prejudice and discrimination held by individuals. These are found in many contexts of human societies and are not limited to any one country. As the experience of one British male of West Indian origin indicates:

> Ever since I can remember, and this is going way back, to the early sixties, from being very small I was always aware of being dark—black—and for a 6-year-old it wasn't very pleasant being called 'darkie' and 'monkey', not just by other kids and other people, but by your brothers and sisters as well. Because if you're dark then you're stupid—a fool—and I wasn't a fool, but I was quiet and different. I remember wanting to be white when I grew up because being black was something bad and awful and in all my dreams I was white. . . . I remember the first day I went to school . . . this white kid came up and started to pick on me.[16]

A survey conducted by Jowell and his associates (1986) reported that nine out of ten British whites believed that there was prejudice against blacks and Asians in Britain. The association between age and this perception of Britain as a racially prejudiced society was fairly strong. The younger people were the more likely to see Britain as prejudiced. The survey also reveals that over a third of whites admitted to being racially prejudiced themselves, which is much higher a proportion than similar surveys show in the USA. The groups most likely to admit their prejudice were men, in comparison with women, the old, the unemployed and those in manual occupations. Conservative Party supporters were also more likely to describe themselves as prejudiced, compared with those supporting other political parties. Those surveyed even believed that racial prejudice is more likely to grow in Britain than to diminish.

After 1960 the political responses of governments to the growth in the numbers of the ethnic minority population were twofold. First, after the Commonwealth Immigration Act, 1962, they sought to control the numbers of new immigrants coming into the UK to appease increasing popular hostility to non-white immigration. Second, Parliament enacted its first anti-discrimination law, the Race Relations Act, 1965. It was passed because of acts of racial violence towards people of West Indian origin and to counterbalance some well publicized racist speeches made in the early 1960s. The 1965 Act was very limited in its scope. It created the criminal offence of incitement to racial hatred and made it unlawful to discriminate on racial grounds in places of public resort. It was also short-lived because it failed to touch the real problems of discrimination in employment, housing and education.

The Race Relations Act, 1968, was far more ambitious in scope. It made it unlawful to discriminate on racial grounds in employment, housing, education or the provision of goods. It covered almost everything that could be covered by legislation of this kind but it was feebly enforced. The emphasis was upon conciliation and mutual settlement rather than on the legal rights of those affected, and on enforcement of the law through the courts. Only the Race Relations Board could bring legal proceedings and then only after elaborate conciliation procedures had been exhausted.

In 1974 the second Wilson government was returned to power, promising to legislate against both racial and sex discrimination. The Sex Discrimination Act, 1975, was passed first and was to be a pacesetter for the subsequent Race Relations Act, 1976. Like the 1975 Act, the Race Relations Act of 1976 made it unlawful to discriminate on the grounds of race and ethnic origin in almost all aspects of employment, whether by employers, trade unions, professional bodies, trade associations or business partnerships. The only exception is where a person's race is a genuine occupational qualification, such as requiring a person of a particular racial group to do a job for reasons of authenticity. The Act also covers private and State education in schools, colleges, universities and vocational training organizations. Other parts of the Act relate to housing and the provision of a very wide range of goods, facilities and services to the public. The 1976 Act also provides protection against discrimination on the grounds of a person's nationality.

The Commission for Racial Equality (CRE) was established under the 1976 Act. Its duties are to work towards the elimination of racial discrimination, to promote equality of opportunity and good relations between persons of different racial groups and to keep the working of the Act under review. In relation to enforcement the CRE has four functions:

- It conducts formal investigations into any discriminatory matter and, where it discovers conduct contravening the Act, it issues non-discrimination notices.

- It is empowered to institute legal proceedings in cases of persistent discrimination.

- It has the sole right to institute legal proceedings regarding discriminatory practices and advertisements and instructions and pressures to discriminate.

- It also has certain powers to assist individual complainants, such as in taking their complaint to an industrial tribunal, where special considerations justify the assistance.

Under the Act direct racial discrimination and indirect racial discrimination are distinguished. Direct discrimination arises when a person treats another person less favourably on the grounds of colour, race, ethnic origin or nationality. It is not necessary to show that a person openly expressed an intention to treat someone else less favourably. It is possible to infer a discriminatory motive from all the circumstances in which the treatment was given. Indirect discrimination covers what is notionally equal treatment but has an unequal and unfair effect on those to whom it applies. It arises where some condition or requirement is applied equally to everyone but has a disproportionately adverse impact upon a particular racial group and cannot be justified. The fact that the person concerned did not intend to discriminate is no defence.

The enforcement of race relations legislation is through individual cases and administrative investigations. Most discrimination cases are in employment. They are dealt with by industrial tribunals which are able to declare the rights of the parties, make recommendations and award damages, with the right of appeal to higher courts. Outside the field of employment, cases are dealt with by the county courts in the first instance, supported by legal aid grants provided to applicants by the CRE. Nevertheless, there are formidable practical problems about winning individual cases. Victims of racial discrimination do not normally relish the publicity which such cases receive. Also it is usually very difficult to prove discrimination. In direct discrimination cases the burden of proof is upon the applicant. Proof of discrimination often depends on statistical evidence, and the legal system is not well equipped to evaluate such material.

Despite the race relations legislation of the past twenty-five years, and the removal of the most blatant forms of racial discrimination, distinct patterns of racial disadvantage persist. As Hepple (1987) concludes:

> judged in terms of the aims expressed in the White Paper on Racial Discrimination—to reduce discrimination and by so doing to help break the 'familiar cycle of cumulative disadvantage'—the ineffectiveness of the Race Relations Act 1976 is irrefutable.[17]

Successive surveys show a continued gap between unemployment rates, job levels, career opportunities, earnings, household income, quality of housing and educational opportunity and achievement between the ethnic minority populations and white people. Seventeen years after the second Race Relations Act, 1968, the Policy Studies Institute found, even on a conservative estimate, that there were still 'tens of thousands of acts of racial discrimination in job recruitment every year'.[18] If social research highlights anything, Hepple argues, 'it is that law is more likely to be effective in facilitating action which people want to take than in creating new rights protecting weaker parties'.[19]

Changing Attitudes and Social Trends

One way in which social change can be assessed is by examining people's attitudes over time at the micro level, using an appropriate sampling frame. This can be done by monitoring public attitudes towards a range of political, economic, social and moral issues over a period of years. Another way is to identify what are perceived to be distinctive macro-social indicators, such as intrafamilial relationships, economic data and public policy statistics, and to examine these using a time series analysis. Fortunately there are sources for both these sorts of data sets in the UK. In the first case, there is the British Social Attitudes Series (BSAS) of Social and Community Planning Research (SCPR). This is an independent series of social data whose collection and analysis are funded by the Sainsbury Family Charitable Trusts, supplemented by financial contributions from governmental and voluntary sources. In the second place, there are the social and economic data collected by the government statistical service for social policy and related purposes.

The BSAS started in 1983. Its primary source of data is an hour-long annual interview, with a self-completion supplement, amongst a probability sample of about 3,000 people. The independence of the series is ensured by the SCPR's control over the content of each survey and the publication of its results. According to its authors, 'the focus of the BSAS is on people's underlying attitudes, not on their opinions about topical issues or personalities'. The latter is the role of the opinion polls commissioned by the mass media, the results of which are regularly published and communicated in the press and on television. Opinion polls identify relatively transitory fluctuations in public opinion and do not reveal longer-term changes in national social values. The SCPR's studies, in contrast, provide accumulated data sets which 'form a sort of moving picture, portraying how British people see their world and themselves and, through their eyes, how society itself is changing'.[20] They are therefore important sources of data about current social attitudes and attitudinal change.

Four specific areas were identified by the BSAS as illustrating changes in people's social attitudes in the late 1980s. These concerned economic expectations, public spending, the domestic division of labour and the moral climate. In the SCPR's first survey in 1983 it was clear that those surveyed were fairly pessimistic about Britain's economic prospects, especially regarding inflation and unemployment. By the time of its fifth report in 1987, SCPR concluded that the public were generally more optimistic about the country's economic prospects as compared with the early 1980s. In 1987, for example, for the first time in the BSAS, 'a majority of the sample (57 per cent) predicted that unemployment would not rise, and a further quarter thought it would fall'. Public attitudes towards personal economic prosperity, however, varied with the person's economic position, the prosperous being more confident that prosperity would continue for them, the less prosperous less so. Indeed, despite a clear overall public optimism about the economy, the picture was somewhat patchy. People continued to see inflation and unemployment as threats 'and a sizeable minority of the population, largely concentrated in the lowest income groups, [seemed] to be sceptical that any general improvements in the economy [would] actually benefit them'.[21]

Turning to public spending, SCPR observed that although public attitudes continued to be slightly ambivalent about it, the proportion of respondents favouring higher taxes to pay for increased social provision grew annually in the late 1980s, from just under a third in 1983 to half in 1987. In fact around 90 per cent of the population, in each of the five surveys, said 'that they [were] against reductions in social spending, even in return for tax cuts'. On the other hand, only about 25 per cent of the sample felt that their current tax levels were acceptable, with almost two-thirds feeling that they were too high. Moreover, over three-quarters of people in all income groupings felt that the less well-off paid too much tax. When it came to people's public spending priorities the proportion naming health care as their first preference has always been higher than that for any other item. This rose from 37 per cent in 1983 to 52 per cent in 1987. 'Indeed, almost four in every five respondents (79 per cent) now give health first or second priority from among the ten items offered.'[22]

The data on people's satisfaction with particular aspects of the National Health Service indicate, almost without exception, relatively high levels of satisfaction. On the other hand, more respondents over the years are expressing a general sense of dissatisfaction with the way the service is being run. In 1987 the ratio of satisfied to dissatisfied respondents was 1:1, compared with 2:1 in

1983. Younger women and those aged between thirty-five and fifty-four were the most discontented groups. The factor underlying this discontent was 'a growing sense of public concern about the strains that NHS hospitals in particular [were] seen to be under, leading to too-long queues for treatment of one sort or another'. Even so, people continue to express continuing content with 'standards of medical and nursing care in hospitals'.[23]

Table 22
Household division of labour in the UK, 1987   *(%)*

Household tasks (% allocation)	Mainly men	Mainly women	Shared equally
Washing and ironing	2	88	9
Looking after sick children[a]	2	67	30
Household cleaning	4	72	23
Preparing evening meal	6	77	17
Household shopping	7	50	43
Teaching children discipline[b]	13	19	67
Doing evening dishes	22	39	36
Organizing household bills	32	38	30
Repairing household equipment	82	6	8

Notes
a Sample size (weighted) 983 respondents, married or living as married.
b Asked of four hundred and twenty-two respondents, married or living as married and with children aged under sixteen living in the household.
Source: British social attitudes, London, SCPR, 1988.

Table 22 shows the household division of labour in Britain for 1987. It confirms that the majority of time-consuming household tasks were done by women amongst those who were married or living as married. Even in households where the woman worked full-time outside the home, the tasks were not shared equally. 'Women who have part-time paid jobs may have the worst of both worlds, extra responsibilities outside the home and only limited sharing of activities within it.' The authors of the fifth SCPR report do not attribute causes or motives to the data but it is clear that 'working men do not participate much in most household duties, including child care . . . when the woman does not herself work full-time outside the home'.[24]

There have, however, been enormous changes in attitudes about married women going out to work in the past twenty-five years. 'In 1965, nearly four in five women felt that mothers of under-fives should stay at home; by 1980 that proportion had fallen to around three in five; and by 1987 it had dropped further to well under a half.'[25] As indicated above, however, this has not been translated into a sense of egalitarianism in the allocation of household tasks and activities in the home.

The fifth report of SCPR also shows that the moral climate has become less liberal in recent years, which somewhat surprised the authors. Their results show that 'on attitudes to extra-marital sex, homosexuality, the availability of pornography, contraception for the under-sixteens and some methods of assisted reproduction, such movement as there is has been towards greater censoriousness'. Attitudes to abortion are the only exception. On these and related matters it is age and educational attainment which largely influence attitudes, with the young and the well educated tending to be more liberal. 'But it is equally true that the gap between graduates and others in their attitudes to moral issues has been diminishing since 1983, with graduates tending to become less permissive, rather than non-graduates more so.'[26]

In examining macro-social indicators in the UK, Halsey (1987) suggests that, out of a wide variety of choices in using the available data and empirical material, official statistics can be most usefully brought to bear on two widely accepted generalizations in contemporary social science. 'The first is that Britain has experienced a comprehensive renegotiation of the division of labour over the past 40 years.' The second is that the 'post-war period can be identified as having come to an end in the mid-1970s, followed by a decade exhibiting a new form of polarisation in British society'.[27] These developments have to be seen in the context of steadily rising living standards since the war, though they have risen less than in many European countries, and Britain's relatively minor position in the world political scene after 1945 compared with the heyday of its imperialist past.

According to Halsey, Britain emerged from the Second World War as 'a classical industrial economy, a centralized democratic polity, and a familistic social structure'. Within this established social order the division of labour was 'an essential triangle joining the family, the economy, and the state'. Traditionally, families raised children, men worked and women ran households. To quote Halsey: 'the economy produced, the family reproduced, and the state protected and redistributed'. But all this was to change in the post-war period with the extension of the Welfare State, government intervention in the economy and full employment. In the next generation a different pattern of relationships amongst these elements emerged and developed. The structure of the economy changed, with the State playing a more active role in it; the family consumed as well as produced; and the State became a redistributive agency of economic and social resources affecting the well-being of all ordinary women, men and children and the families in which they lived. 'All of these shifts, institutional and individual, together add up to a renegotiated division of labour in the Britain of the 1980s compared with that of the 1940s.'[28]

Halsey identifies a number of changes in the family, the economy and the State during these years. Changes in the family included:

1 More women, especially married women, in employment.
2 Less childbirth, but more illegimate childbirth.
3 More divorce and remarriage and more one-person households.
4 More men economically inactive, whether unemployed, retired or drawn into the domestic economy.
5 More men and women in adult education.
6 More children in extended schooling.
7 A population with higher formal qualifications.

The correlative changes in the economy were:

8 A higher gross domestic product [GDP] *per capita*.
9 A less manual work force.
10 Shorter hours of work.
11 Longer holidays.

Finally, the accompanying changes occurring in the State were:

12 Higher expenditure on education.
13 Increased numbers of parent surrogates in the employment of the State (police, teachers, doctors, social workers, etc.).
14 Increased nursery provision for the under-fives.
15 A higher proportion of the GDP spent by the State.

These changes in the relations amongst family, economy and government, claims Halsey, resulted in the renegotiation of the division of labour between the 1940s and the 1980s. At the same time 'the traditional meanings and loci of masculinity, femininity, adulthood, childhood, work, leisure and learning have all changed as the division of labour has shifted'.[29]

In analysing the country's economic transformation in the post-war years, and whether there has been a re-emergence of social polarization more recently, Halsey divides the period into two phases. The first begins at the end of the Second World War and ends with the oil crisis of 1973–74. This is the thirty years after 1945 which corresponded with economic boom, high rates of growth, full employment and an expanding public sector. The second phase was one of declining employment, shifting economic activity from manufacturing to high-technology and service industry, and struggling with inflation. This was accompanied with a determination by government 'to move decision-making out of Westminster and Whitehall into the market and the locality, and to implement policies designed to move activity from the public to the private sector'. Some indication of success in the latter is provided by the fact that whilst government spending as a proportion of GDP had been 49 per cent in 1975, having risen from 36 per cent in 1961, it had fallen to 45 per cent by 1985.[30]

Turning to the issue of social polarization, Halsey argues that this is demonstrated by a number of indicators. They show a widening social division emerging in the 1980s between a prosperous majority in secure, well paid employment and 'a depressed minority of the unemployed, the sick, the old, and the unsuccessful ethnic minorities'. First, he argues, there was an increasing inequality in the distribution of money incomes between the mid-1970s and mid-1980s, with the highest rewarded groups raising their share and the lowest groups becoming worse off. Second, whilst the expansion of the professional and technical middle class is a feature of late twentieth-century Britain, as it was in mid-century, the growth of unemployment in the 1980s 'emerged as a structure of negative opportunity which tends to polarize mobility chances, especially of those who begin in the working class'. Third, drawing on research by Hannett, and his study of trends in housing tenure, Halsey concurs that there has been 'an increasing degree of social polarisation' between owner occupation and local authority renting in recent years. Fourth, using research based on the inner-city areas, Halsey argues that there is evidence 'of deprived people being left in the urban priority areas as the successful move out to middle Britain'.[31] This reduces the life chances of the poor and works against the interests of the disadvantaged in the inner cities.

From the evidence provided, there is little doubt that the industrial, occupational and economic change of the 1980s has resulted in a more unequal society. It is epitomized by the existence of a prosperous majority who are increasingly segregated from an underprivileged minority, economically, socially and spatially. There is also a more prominent north-south divide. The minority live in marginal economic and social conditions and are trapped in the inner city areas with their decaying council estates. The majority population, meanwhile, has moved into the suburban areas of the newer economy and enjoys a quantity and quality of life much in advance of their deprived counterparts in the old cities. As a result Britain faces new challenges in the late twentieth century 'as it carries on its ancient struggle to combine freedom and equality in a United Kingdom'.[32]

The Implications for Management

Given the structure of social inequality, and the power and control that they have over rewards and positions in work organizations, managers need to understand the nature and existence of workplace and industrial conflict and manage it effectively. All modern organizations, whether bureaucratically or democratically controlled, are 'imperatively co-ordinated associations' and incorporate hierarchies of authority, power and influence. Some individuals and groups govern, others have executive authority, whilst others have relatively little discretion in their organizational roles and are required to follow instructions from those who manage. As Dahrendorf (1959) argues, managers have to make decisions as to who does what, when and how in enterprises, with subordinates being expected to accept managerial decisions if organizational objectives are to be achieved. Irrespective of the particular persons in positions of authority, 'industrial enterprises remain imperatively co-ordinated associations the structures of which generate quasi-groups and conflicting latent interests'.[33]

Other than the Marxist frame of reference, there are two main theories analysing the nature of conflict in organizations. One, the traditional view, argues that there are no basic conflicts but only frictional and limited ones which are purely temporary in nature. Any fundamental conflicts which emerge — between managers and subordinates, for example — are seen to be aberrant and deviant conditions. The second view is that differences of interest inevitably arise in organizations and need to be, first, recognized and, second, managed in order to maintain some degree of internal consensus and social stability. Indeed, Coser (1965) suggests that 'conflict may serve to remove dissociating elements in a relationship and to re-establish unity.'[34]

Fox (1966) describes the first view as a unitary frame of reference and the second as a pluralistic one. For Fox a unitary enterprise has a number of features. Management is its sole source of authority and its one focus of loyalty, with everyone striving towards a set of common corporate objectives. Management's right to manage goes unchallenged and there are no oppositionary groups or factions threatening or disturbing managerial rule. Conflict within the organization is viewed as disruptive of internal harmony and is believed to result from the anti-social behaviour of disloyal elements.

Those holding the pluralist perspective, in contrast, accept the existence of rival sources of leadership and authority within and outside organizations, including work groups, trade unions, professional bodies, and so on. They also accept that the degree of common purpose and internal consensus existing within enterprises is of a very limited nature. In the sense that organizational sub-groups are mutually dependent and interdependent on one another there is a narrow common interest in the long-term survival of the whole of which they are a part. But this has little impact on the day-to-day conduct of organizational participants and enterprise relationships. The implication for management, says Fox, is that 'there are other sources of leadership, other focuses of loyalty, within the social system it governs, and it is with these that management must share its decision-making'.[35] Conflict, in short, is seen to be endemic and has to be accepted and managed by those in authority who hold organizational power, if it is to be diverted into constructive channels of power containment and power-sharing.

Since the class composition of society is reflected in the occupational structure, subordinate workers rarely, if ever, view work and work organizations in the same way as their managers. Whilst managers generally have higher salaries, recognized social standing, reasonable job security and professional careers at work, their non-managerial subordinates are often wage-earners, with less job security, lower status and low discretion in their jobs. Also, working people bring their own social values and personal attitudes to the workplace, and these are normally beyond the ability of managerial leaders to influence, even if they wanted to. At the same time, with the growth of middle-class white-collar occupations in recent years, at the expense of blue-collar manual employment, the new professional workers who have taken their place need more sensitive and skilled handling in their work roles, compared with the manual working class of the past. Yet at the same time middle managers are themselves often in an ambiguous position in the organization, neither fully integrated with senior management nor completely separate from those they manage.

Given the changing nature of gender and race relations, as well as the statutory duties placed on employers and their managerial agents not to discriminate against individuals on the grounds of sex, race, ethnic origin or nationality, increasing numbers of organizations are describing themselves as equal opportunity employers. Some employers go beyond the basic minimum required by the law, operating equal opportunities policies for very practical reasons. These include:

- Making full use of the talents of all the members of the work force, thus ensuring the best return on what is often a costly investment in recruitment and training.
- Improving employee motivation and performance.
- Broadening the talent base of the organization.
- Improving communications.
- Raising the external view of the organization, thus encouraging talented outside people to join it.

According to the EOC, employers have found that 'by focusing attention on the treatment of all staff at work, the implementation of equal opportunities policies stimulates a healthy and more productive atmosphere and creates a better quality of working life'.[36]

Equal opportunity employment policies place considerable responsibilities on managers in creating them, applying them and monitoring them. The act of becoming an equal opportunity employer requires a statement from senior management setting out its intention, with directness and clarity. Management then has to develop and apply internal procedures and practices which, whilst not discriminating against individuals, provide equality of opportunity to all job applicants and existing employees. In providing a written policy statement on equal opportunity management has to cover a number of areas. These include:

● Defining discriminatory practices.

● Stating the organization's commitment to equal opportunities.

● Naming the managers responsible for policy.

● Creating structures for implementing policy.

● Obliging employees to act in accordance with policy.

● Devising procedures for dealing with complaints.

● Providing monitoring and review procedures.

Overall responsibility for an equal opportunity policy is often given to a senior member of management at the highest level, day-to-day responsibility being assigned to line and personnel managers. The EOC recommends that consideration should be given to establishing a joint management, union and employee working party chaired by a senior manager, with the responsibility for reviewing how an equal opportunity policy is working out in practice. The role of an equal opportunity committee of this sort is crucial. It includes:

● To analyse the information provided by the monitoring process.

● To assess this against the objectives of policy and how it is working in reality.

● To make suggestions for remedying any failures.

- To assess the validity of the proposed remedies over time.

The existence of an equal opportunity policy requires that all employees involved in personnel decisions, or who come into contact with job applicants, should be given training on the application of policy, relative to their own responsibilities. In particular, managerial, supervisory and personnel staff, especially those involved in employee selection, normally need additional training covering specific areas. These include:

- Explanations of the types of discrimination that take place.
- Information about stereotyping and personal prejudice.
- Guidance on the need to base employment decisions on objective rather than subjective criteria.
- The need to assess people on their individual merits and the ability to do the job.
- The avoidance of biased and uninformed assumptions which can distort objective judgements in employment matters.

Managerial monitoring of equal opportunity policies needs to be flexible and geared to the requirements of each enterprise. Much depends on the resources available and the personnel systems existing in each organization. In setting up a monitoring process, management sometimes develops it in three distinct stages. First, it gathers the information available on the number and position of women and ethnic minorities in or applying for employment. Second, it analyses the data collected to identify where there are blocks to equality and why they occur. Third, it then defines a positive programme of action necessary to overcome any inequalities at work. A systematic approach to equal opportunity monitoring leading to a positive action programme covers a wide range of employment issues. These include:

- recruitment
- selection
- training
- placement
- transfer

- promotion
- terms of employment
- fringe benefits, especially parental leave
- grievance and disciplinary procedures
- dismissals
- redundancies
- resignations.

Positive measures which managements use to remedy the effects of past discriminatory practices take a number of forms. These include encouraging applications from women and ethnic minority workers, training them, improving working arrangements and, for women returners to employment, setting up return-to-work schemes. Encouragement includes special recruitment measures and developing a positive approach to appraisal and career counselling. Training may take the form of special seminars and training courses for women and ethnic minority groups, including retraining and pre-training courses. Improved working arrangements can incorporate:

- Enhancing maternity leave provisions.
- Improving child care facilities.
- Taking positive measures to limit individuals resigning on account of maternity or similar reasons.
- Providing part-time, job-sharing or flexi-time working arrangements.

For certain categories of employees, some employers use 'return to work' schemes, incorporating a number of elements. Some managements encourage bridging interviews, inviting job leavers to participate in a career break/re-entry scheme. Others have regular updating sessions to ensure retention of skills or the acquisition of new ones where the work is affected by new technologies. Employees can also be notified of any opportunities for relief work to cover holiday and sickness absences or be kept informed of what is going on by regular mailing of the employer's newsletter. Retraining courses are sometimes organized prior to return, especially where the development of new skills is required. Employers can also enable employees involved in a career break to return to their previous post, or the nearest grade. Where this is the case they can be moved on to their previous grade at the earliest opportunity. It is through these and related approaches that recruitment, training, redeployment and promotion policies affecting all individuals in an organization can be based on the job requirements, and an individual's abilities, rather than on sex or racial stereotyping. Managers play a key role in facilitating this process.

References

1 LITTLEJOHN J. *Social stratification*. London, Allen & Unwin, 1972. p 9.
2 MARSHALL T H. *Citizenship and social class*. Cambridge, Cambridge University Press, 1950. p 30.
3 *ibid*. p 31.
4 FARNHAM D. *Personnel in context*. London, Institute of Personnel Management, 1986. p 215.
5 HALSEY A H. *Change in Britain*. Oxford, Oxford University Press, 1986. p 27f.
6 GIDDENS A. *Sociology*. Cambridge, Polity Press, 1989. p 209.
7 DAHRENDORF R. *On Britain*. London, BBC, 1982. pp 50 and 55.
8 GIDDENS. *op cit*. p 220.
9 HALSEY. *op cit*. p 62.
10 DEPARTMENT OF EMPLOYMENT. *Employment gazette*. March 1988. London, HMSO.
11 ROSE R. *Politics in England*. Basingstoke, Macmillan, 1989. p 179.
12 COMMISSION FOR RACIAL EQUALITY. *Ethnic minorities in Britain*. London, CRE, 1985. p 1.
13 GIDDENS. *op cit*. p 245.
14 LESTER A. 'Anti-discrimination legislation in Great Britain.' *New community* XIV, autumn, 1987. p 1.
15 *ibid*.
16 quoted in HUSBAND C. (ed). *'Race' in Britain*. London, Hutchinson, 1987. p 191.
17 HEPPLE B. 'The race relations acts and the process of chànge.' *New community* XIV, autumn, 1987. p 32.
18 BROWN C. *Black and white Britain*. London, PSI, 1984. p 31.
19 HEPPLE. *op cit*. p 38.
20 BROOK L, JOWELL R *and* WITHERSPOON S. 'Recent trends in social attitudes.' *Social trends 19*. London, HMSO, 1989. p 13.
21 *ibid*. p 14f.

22 *ibid.* p 18.
23 *ibid.* p 19.
24 *ibid.* p 20.
25 *ibid.* p 21.
26 *ibid.* p 16f.
27 HALSEY A H. 'Social trends since world war II.' *Social trends 17.* London, HMSO, 1987. p 11.
28 *ibid.* p 12f.
29 *ibid.* pp 13–15 and 19.
30 *ibid.* p 16.
31 *ibid.* pp 17–19.
32 *ibid.* p 19.
33 DAHRENDORF R. *Class and class conflict in industrial society*, London, Routledge, 1959. p 259.
34 COSER L A. *The functions of social conflict.* London, Routledge, 1965. p 80.
35 FOX A. *Royal Commission on trade unions and employers' associations research papers. Industrial sociology and industrial relations.* London, HMSO, 1966. p 8.
36 EQUAL OPPORTUNITIES COMMISSION. *Guidelines for equal opportunities employers.* London, EOC (no date). p 1.

5

Scarcity, Markets and Prices

The central economic problem continuously facing humankind is how to satisfy the infinite wants of the world's ever-growing population within the constraints of the finite resources available. Given that the economic demands of people, individually and collectively, are virtually unlimited, and that the supply of economic resources to satisfy those demands are relatively fixed, certainly in the short term, conscious economic choices have to be made in any society to determine economic priorities. Basically, four types of economy have evolved to deal with this central economic problem, historically and in the modern world. These are:

- Relatively closed local economies, operating at subsistence level.
- The open national economies of the developing countries or those nation States with a *per capita* income below one fifth of that of the United States.
- The open national economies of the advanced countries such as those of western Europe, north America and Japan.
- Until recently, the relatively closed economies of eastern Europe.

Economic goods are those human-made commodities whose production requires the use of scarce resources to create them, exchange them and distribute them. These commodities take different forms. They include finished goods and services, intermediate goods and services used in the production process, such as capital goods, and raw materials. Whilst there are a limited number of non-economic goods, such as fresh air and sunshine, which are freely available to those using them according to their needs without being rationed because of scarcity, they are increasingly the exception rather than the rule. More generally, economic goods are those commodities for which people's demand exceed the availability and output of the scarce resources needed to produce them. It is the task of any economic system to solve the range of economic problems associated with this universal feature of resource scarcity.

Economic Problems and Economic Systems

In all modern economic systems the fundamental economic units are households, firms and government agencies. It is households, firms and governments which act as units of consumption in using the goods and services produced and exchanged in an economic system. It is firms and government agencies, in turn, that act as agents of production in transforming and converting the scarce resources available into the goods and services that are demanded for consumption and investment purposes. In this sense the term investment is used to describe the flow of expenditure which is channelled into activities producing new resources that are not intended for immediate consumption within the economic system. It is through planned investment decisions that the future development of production capacity is made possible.

The scarce resources used by firms and government agencies in creating new economic resources for consumption and investment are referred to as the factors of production. They are usually defined as land, labour and capital. Land incorporates all those natural resources such as the oceans, forests, minerals and soil fertility used in the processes of production. Labour is the sum total of human resource skills, knowledge and competences which are available. And capital is those human-made aids to production, such as advanced technology, plant and communication systems, which raise economic productivity and real output over time. The total output of all the commodities that a country produces in terms of goods and services over a given period, normally a year, is its gross national product (GNP).

Given the scarcity of economic resources in all societies, and the inability of any economic system to satisfy all the economic wants of its individual, household and corporate consumers, those taking economic decisions have to make choices about how society's resources are to be used, allocated and distributed. This gives rise to one of the fundamental concepts of economics, that of opportunity cost. Lipsey (1983) writes that the concept of opportunity cost emphasizes the problem of choice 'by measuring the cost of obtaining a quantity of one commodity in terms of the quantity of other commodities that could have been obtained instead'.[1] Opportunity cost arises only where the resources available to meet human demands are limited, so that everyone's economic wants cannot be satisfied at any one time. Producing or consuming a commodity, in other words, can be achieved only at the cost of not producing or not consuming something else.

These twin issues of scarcity and choice mean that all economic systems have a number of common economic problems which they attempt to resolve. These are:

- What goods and services are to be produced and in what quantities? This consideration includes the balance to be achieved between producing consumption and capital goods and between providing manufacturing and service output.

- How are these goods and services to be produced, given the mix of current resources and the present state of technology and productive capacity?

- Who is to get the goods and services that have been produced? In other words, how is GNP to be divided among a country's economic and non-economic participants?

- How efficient are the methods being used in the production and distribution processes? Are the resources which are employed being used to their maximum potential and are the producers being rewarded according to sound economic principles?

- Are existing resources being fully utilized or are some of them underemployed?

- In monetary economies, are price levels stable or are they rising out of line with productivity? In other words, is inflation under control?

- Is the economy growing and increasing its capacity over time?

A variety of economic systems have emerged to provide an

institutional framework within which mechanisms for solving these economic problems have operated. These are:

- Market economies.
- Command, or planned, economies.
- Market socialist economies.
- Mixed market economies, with the latter comprising a combination of both market forces and indicative planning.

In essence a market economy is one in which economic decisions about the allocation of resources and the production of goods and services are made on the basis of money prices, generated by voluntary economic exchanges among producers, consumers, workers and the owners of the other factors of production in the market place. Decision-making in such an economy is decentralized, with mainly private ownership of the means of production, though there may be some limited forms of social ownership too. It is the market mechanism that allocates resources, adjusts production and consumption decisions, distributes incomes to those owning the factors of production and paves the way for economic growth. The market economy, according to Grossman (1967), is where:

1 The individual economic units by and large decide themselves what, how, where, and when they produce and consume.
2 They do so largely with reference to the terms on which alternatives are available to them, i.e. with reference to *prices* in the broadest sense of the word.
3 Prices respond, more or less, to the forces of demand and supply for the individual goods or factors. The end result tends to be the equilibration of demand and the co-ordination of the economic activities of innumerable individual units and agents.[2]

A command or planned economy is where society's economic processes are determined not by market forces but by a planning agency which implements the major economic goals of society. To quote Grossman again:

In this instance, the individual economic units (though

probably only the firms and not the households) are ordered what, when, where, how, and how much to produce and consume. If done rationally at all, these commands (directives, orders, targets, 'plans') derive from some sort of conscious attempt ('planning') to co-ordinate the activities of the individual units and to direct the economy as a whole toward certain definite goals.[3]

In such a system, the greater part of productive activity is determined by establishing obligatory input and output targets. These are generated by vertical signals from an administrative hierarchical agency. A centralized planning system can lead to inefficiencies in resource allocation, because of the need to co-ordinate large numbers of subsidiary plans at lower levels of the economy. On the other hand, a planned economy may be able to solve the perennial problems of unemployment and idle capacity experienced by market economies, as well as reduce environmental pollution and overdifferentiation of products.

A market socialist economy is one in which the day-to-day running of the economy is left to the market mechanism within a socially planned framework. It was Lange (1964 and 1967) who originated the notion that the means of production can be socially owned, and the basic direction of the economy may be centrally planned, whilst its operation may be left to market forces. With the recent rise to power of Mikhail Gorbachev in the Soviet Union and the emergence of *glasnost* and *peristroika* in eastern Europe, there are signs of a movement away from centrally planned economies to market socialist ones. The popular uprisings in Poland, East Germany and Czechoslovakia in 1989 are likely to hasten the process.

A mixed market economy combines competitive private enterprise with some degree of central control. Whilst resource allocation between alternative uses is determined largely by the actions of individual firms and private households, through the price mechanism, the central authorities play some role in determining either the level of aggregate output and demand and/or the efficient use of the factors of production in the economy. They do so by using appropriate monetary and fiscal policies. They also influence the distribution of income by their taxation and welfare policies. In some cases, governments control sectors of the economy by nationalizing key industries, the 'commanding heights' of the economy.

To what extent a convergence of market capitalist and planned socialist economies is taking place has been a matter of debate for many years. The convergence thesis suggests that both the market and the planned-economy systems are moving towards a common pattern of development, both evolving similar modes of behaviour and institutional frameworks. Some economic theorists put forward the hypothesis that the two types of economic system are converging, owing to the necessity of having common patterns of technological development. It is not only common technologies which are facilitating economic convergence in the late twentieth century. The opening up of the world economy, the growth of multinational business corporations and the diffusion of finance capital transnationally are having the same effect.

Markets and Prices

Put simply, a market is any context where the buying and selling of goods or services takes place. Thus people refer to the property or housing market, the labour market, the stock market, the second-hand car market, the market for fruit and vegetables, and so on. A market does not have to have a physical presence: the market in which shares are traded, for example, consists of a worldwide telecommunications network, transcending national boundaries. Markets may be local, regional, national or international and vary according to circumstances.

The essence of any market is that it consists of producers or consumers and sellers or buyers. Either of those two parties may be individuals, households, business corporations or government agencies. In modern advanced market economies it is business corporations and government agencies which dominate the supply side of markets and the household which is the normal unit buying consumer commodities. In any free market, a market in which the forces of supply and demand are allowed to operate without interference, it is the pressure produced by the interplay of market forces, or of market supply and demand, which induce adjustments in market prices and/or the quantities traded in the market-place. Prices are normally measured in monetary values, with equilibrium or market price being the price at which the quantity consumers are prepared to buy equals the quantity producers are prepared to sell. Price also denotes what has to be given up in order to obtain a particular type of goods or service. Prices thus act as automatic signals which co-ordinate the economic actions of individual decision-making units and provide a mechanism whereby changes in supply and demand affect the allocative efficiency of resources in the economy.

Although individual markets are kept separate from one another by commodity, space, government intervention and tariff barriers, they are also interlinked. All commodities compete for consumer income and there is some link between spatially separated markets, even where transport costs are high and market controls exist. Nevertheless, various ways of classifying markets have been proposed. For example, they can be defined according to the substitutes available, since the size of a market is determined by the range of commodities which are substitutes for it. A market is also determined by the extent to which suppliers react with other suppliers to any change in the price, quality or output of their product. Finally, a market can be classified by the extent to which new producers can enter it, even when there are barriers to doing so.

To understand how markets work, it is necessary to examine the basic concepts of supply and demand. The next two subsections consider the elements of supply and demand theory. These come together in the sub-section examining the nature of price determination. They are based on the unrealistic assumption of perfect competition, where there are a large number of producers, a homogeneous product and free entry to the market. This approach, however, enables the basic ideas of market theory to be explored and discussed.

Market supply

The quantity of a commodity supplied by a producer is the amount the producer is prepared to sell at a particular price at a particular time. It is influenced by four main factors:

- The price of the commodity.
- The prices of the factors of production.

- The goals of the producer.
- The current state of technology.

It can be hypothesized that in general the higher the price of a commodity the greater is the quantity the producer is willing to supply. This is because more profit is made in doing this. Conversely, the lower the price of a commodity, the smaller is the quantity the producer is willing to supply. Similarly, the lower the prices of the factors of production, the greater is the quantity of the commodity that the producer is willing to supply, whilst the higher the prices of the factors of production the smaller is the quantity that the producer is willing to supply. The quantity supplied also changes according to the producer's goals. It varies, for example, according to whether the producer is aiming to maximize profits, to maximize sales, to enter a new market or to maintain an existing market position. Finally, technological developments affect quantity supplied, because technological advances lower unit costs of production and ensure higher output at lower prices.

The market supply curve of a commodity is the aggregate quantity supplied by each producer at each price. It shows the relationship between a commodity's price and the quantities that all producers are prepared to sell of the commodity per period of time. Like individual producer supply, market supply varies with price: the higher the price the more producers are prepared to sell, and the lower the price the less producers are prepared to sell.

Market supply increases when there is a rise in the quantity supplied at each price. It decreases when there is a fall in the quantity supplied at each price. The factors causing an increase in market supply include: falls in the prices of other commodities; falls in the prices of the factors of production; changes in the goals of producers; and technological improvements. A decrease in market supply is caused by: rises in the prices of other commodities; rises in the prices of the factors of production; and changes in the goals of producers.

Market demand

The quantity of a commodity demanded by a consumer is the amount the consumer wishes to buy at a particular price at a particular time. It is influenced by a number of factors. These include: the price of the commodity; the prices of other commodities; the size of the consumer's income; consumer tastes; and various social factors. It can be hypothesized that in general the lower the price of the commodity the greater is the quantity the consumer is willing to buy. Conversely, the higher the price of the commodity the smaller is the quantity the consumer is willing to buy. Where commodities are substitutes for one another— butter and margarine, for example—a fall in the price of one causes a fall in the quantity demanded of the other. Conversely, a rise in the price of one causes a rise in the quantity demanded of the other. Where commodities are complementary to each other, such as pipes and tobacco, a fall in the price of one causes a rise in the quantity demanded of the other, whilst a rise in the price of one causes a fall in the quantity demanded of the other. Where commodities are unrelated, a change in the price of one does not normally affect the quantity demanded of the other.

Normally a rise in consumer income results in a rise in the quantity demanded of a commodity. Similarly, a fall in consumer income normally results in a fall in the quantity demanded. This is usually the case with consumer goods demanded by households. In other cases a rise in consumer demand results in a rise in the quantity demanded up to a certain level; it then falls away. Consumer demand for basic foods, for example, is not infinite. The quantity demanded may decline above a certain level of income as consumers transfer their income to more expensive foods. In other cases the quantity demanded rises up to a certain level of income and then remains unaffected. Social factors such as the sex, age, social class, educational attainment and occupation of a consumer affect the quantity demanded of commodities, whilst changes in consumer tastes have similar effects.

The market demand curve of a commodity is the aggregate quantity demanded by each consumer at each price. It shows the relationship between the commodity's price and the quantities of the commodity that all consumers are prepared to buy per period of time. Like individual consumer demand, market demand varies with price: the lower the price the more consumers are prepared to buy, and the higher the price the less they are prepared to buy.

Market demand increases when there is a rise in the quantity demanded at each price. It decreases when there is a fall in the quantity demanded at each price. The factors causing an increase in market demand include: rises in the prices of substitutes; falls in the prices of complements; rises in consumer income; and changes in taste in favour of particular commodities. A decrease in market demand is caused by: falls in the prices of substitutes; rises in the prices of complements; falls in consumer income; and changes in taste away from particular commodities.

Price determination

The best way to understand how price is determined in a free market is to refer to figure 3. It shows an imaginary market demand curve and an imaginary market supply curve for commodity X. Demand curve D is a graphical representation of the quantity demanded of commodity X at different prices, where price per unit is indicated on the vertical axis, with units sold per period of time on the horizontal axis. It is downward-sloping from left to right, since, other factors remaining constant, the higher the price of the commodity the less of it consumers demand and the lower the price the more of it is demanded. Similarly, supply curve S is a graphical representation of the quantity supplied of commodity X at different prices. It is upward-sloping from left to right, since, other factors remaining constant, the lower the price of the commodity the less producers supply of it and the higher the price the more is supplied of it.

As can be seen in figure 3, if a commodity is offered for sale on the market at £a, then x units of it are demanded per week and z units are supplied. This means that there is excess supply in the market, and there will be downward pressure on price to move from £a towards £b. This is because market producers, with unsold output, will ask a lower price for the commodity, whilst consumers will offer a lower price. In this case, £b is the equilibrium market price and y units per week is the equilibrium quantity bought and sold. Market equilibrium is reached where, in aggregate, consumers and producers are satisfied with the current combination of the price of the commodity and the quantity of the units bought and sold per period of time.

Similarly, if a commodity is offered for sale at £c, then z units of it are demanded per week and c units are supplied. This means that there is excess demand in the market and there will be upward pressure on price to move from £c towards £b, or the equilibrium

Figure 3   Market demand and supply curves for a commodity

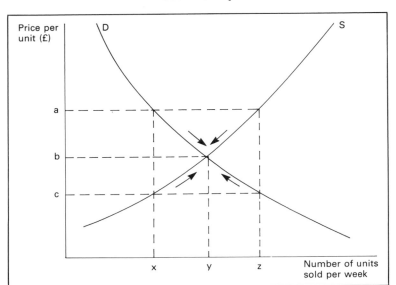

market price. This is because consumers, with unsatisfied demand, will offer a higher price for the commodity, whilst producers seeing the unsatisfied demand, will ask a higher price. Again equilibrium is achieved in the market at that price per unit, £b, where the total number of units which consumers are prepared to buy, y units, corresponds to the total amount which the producers are prepared to sell. In this case the market is cleared. This will continue until there is either a change in supply or a change in demand. Then the equilibrium price and the equilibrium quantity both change.

A diagramatic representation of the effect that an increase in market demand for a commodity has on equilibrium price and quantity bought and sold is shown in figure 4. In this case the initial market demand curve is represented as D1 and the corresponding supply curve is S. Here the equilibrium price is £b and the equilibrium quantity is y units per week. Other factors remaining constant, if market demand increases, owing (say) to an increase in consumer incomes, then more is demanded at each

Figure 4   An increase in market demand for a commodity

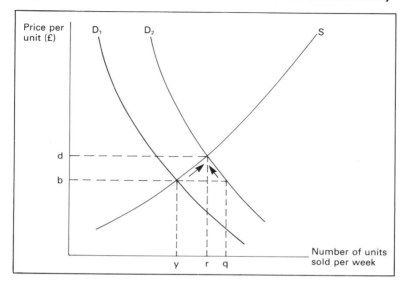

market price. This is shown by a shift of the demand curve to the right, from the position D1 to D2. Thus at the original market price £b the quantity demanded will be *q* units per week but the quantity supplied will only be *y* units. With supply fixed in the short term, there will be excess demand in the market and price will rise to a new equilibrium, £d, and quantity will rise to a new equilibrium of *r* units per week.

Similar analyses can be undertaken to examine the effects of a decrease in demand, increase in supply or decrease in supply of a commodity, other factors remaining constant. Thus a decrease in demand results in a fall in equilibrium price and quantity, whilst an increase in supply results in a fall in equilibrium price and a rise in equilibrium quantity. Finally, a decrease in supply results in a rise in equilibrium price and quantity. These basic tools of supply and demand analysis are powerful instruments for understanding price determination in free markets.

Capital Markets and Financial Institutions

One of the most important markets in the UK, or more accurately set of markets, is the capital market, or the money market and the market for finance capital. In essence, the capital market is the market, or more realistically the group of interrelated markets, where money is bought and sold and finance capital is raised, lent and borrowed on varying terms for varying periods of time. It incorporates various sub-markets, such as the credit market, the stock market and the foreign exchange market. The latter, for example, is the international market in which currencies are transferred between countries. These transactions are between financial institutions which buy and sell foreign currencies, thus resulting in a profit where exchange rates and interest rates differ between countries. There are strong forces causing conditions in one set of financial markets to affect others, both nationally and internationally. This is notably the case where there is a propensity for some lenders or borrowers to switch between markets as opportunities for cheaper borrowing or higher returns open up.

A diagrammatic representation of the UK's most important money market institution, the London money market, is provided in figure 5. In outline, the London money market comprises three main sets of financial institutions: the banks, related institutions and the Bank of England; the discount houses; and the London Stock Exchange. Each of these is considered in turn.

The banks, related institutions and the Bank of England

Money is the lubricant of the modern economy. Whatever form it takes, money provides the main method of payment for goods and services in transactions between buyers and sellers in a variety of markets. It has four main functions, having to:

- Be acceptable as a means of exchange.
- Act as a unit of account.
- Act as a store of value.
- Act as a standard for deferred payment.

115

Figure 5 The London money market

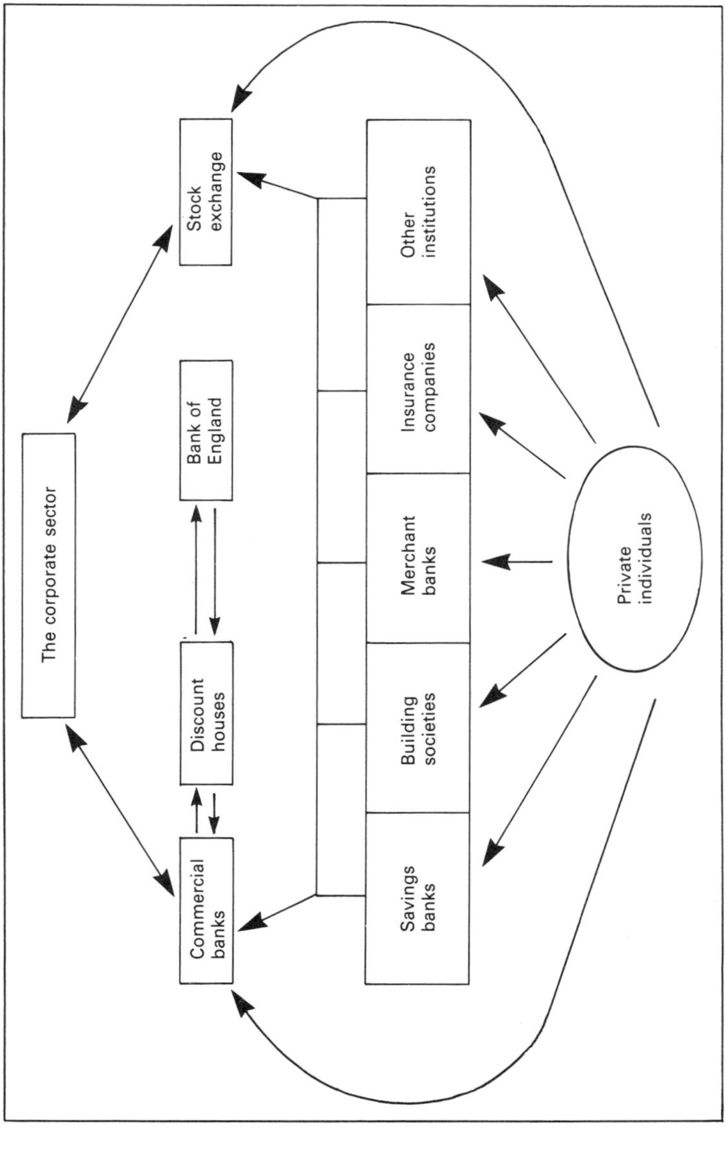

To perform these functions satisfactorily, money normally has the following qualities:

● Stability.
● Transferability.
● Durability.
● Divisibility.
● Portability.
● Recognizability.

There are three forms of money: coins, banknotes and bank deposits. In simple terms, bank deposits are funds deposited in bank accounts and are records of indebtedness of banks to their depositors. In the UK deposits are held in two main types of account, involving varying conditions of use or withdrawal: current accounts and deposit accounts. Current accounts are bank deposits which are withdrawable or transferable by cheque without notice, whilst deposit account balances are formally subject to seven days' notice of withdrawal.

In essence, banks are financial intermediaries. They take in funds, principally as deposits repayable on demand or at short notice, which they use to make advances by overdrafts and loans to their customers. They also discount bills and hold other financial stock, such as marketable securities, as assets. An important function of the banks is to maintain a money transaction mechanism by accepting deposits on current account and operating a system of transferring funds between banks by the use of cheques. Other important banking activities include providing foreign exchange services for customers, financing foreign trade, operating in wholesale money markets and providing a wide range of advisory services.

In a developed financial system, like that of the UK, only certain financial institutions cover all or most of these operations. The clearing banks satisfy all these criteria but the term 'bank' is sometimes applied to other related institutions such as savings banks, merchant banks and, increasingly, some building societies, all of which engage in some banking activities. The term 'clearing bank' denotes those commercial banks which traditionally operated and had access to a clearing house for the purpose of clearing cheques drawn against one another. With the admission of the Trustee Savings Bank and other banks to the London Clearing House from 1975, it was the Committee of London Clearing Bankers (CLCB) which subsequently became the trade association of the major domestic banks. In September 1985 the CLCB was replaced by the Committee of London and Scottish Bankers, which now acts in the interests of this wider group of banking organizations.

The clearing banks have a central position in the financial system and in the financial markets. This is by virtue of their control of the money payments mechanism and because their deposit liabilities form a major element of the money stock. These factors, coupled with their earlier dominance as short-term lenders to the corporate business sector, required them to be subject to special control under the government's monetary policy arrangements. In recent years, with the widespread diversification of many financial institutions and the growth of competition among them, the position is acknowledged to have changed. The quantity of bank deposits attracts special attention as part of the government's monetary control policy. Credit control arrangements, however, do not now normally concentrate on the clearing banks alone, as they did previously.

Financial institutions which are closely related to the clearing banks include finance corporations, savings banks, building societies, insurance companies and merchant banks. Finance corporations, for example, such as the Industrial and Commercial Finance Corporation and the Finance Corporation for Industry, were established after the Second World War to provide medium and long-term loans for firms experiencing difficulty raising finance capital from other sources. Savings banks provide somewhere for people of limited means to put their savings in deposit accounts attracting relatively low rates of interest but making it easy for them to withdraw money on demand. Building societies, in contrast, accept funds from the general public in the form of shares and deposits for relending, almost wholly to owner-occupiers for the purchase of houses and flats. Insurance companies enable individuals and corporate bodies to minimize risks to property, life and income with payment of premiums spreading the risks associated with any specified contingency over a large number of individual policy holders.

Merchant banks are a group of financial institutions carrying out a varied range of financial or finance-related activities. Amongst these activities the acceptance of commercial bills and the financing of overseas trade are prominent. As accepting houses, for example, merchant banks accept bills, drawn to finance trade or other commercial activity, from customers for a commission and from whom they eventually recover payment. Merchant banks also act as issuing houses which specialize in handling new issues of shares, debentures or bonds on behalf of companies, local authorities or the government. In recent decades the merchant banks have moved into corporate financial work, assisting in capital reconstructions and advising on company mergers and acquisitions. They are also involved in the expanding business of portfolio management, especially on behalf of pension funds. As bankers they take deposits, mainly in large sums and for defined periods, and they lend to corporate borrowers. Merchant bankers are also active as foreign exchange dealers, operating extensively in the Euro-currency market.

The Bank of England is the central bank of the UK. Established as a commercial bank in 1694, by the nineteenth century the Bank of England had become the manager of the country's external reserve. During the twentieth century its public role developed still further, so that at the time of its nationalization in 1946 the Bank had long conducted itself as a public rather than as a private institution. Today it is banker to the government, banker to the banking system and the financial institution which is responsible, in consultation with the Treasury, for implementing the government's financial and monetary policy. As the government's banker the Bank holds the accounts of central government departments, receiving government revenues and making expenditure payments. It also manages the national debt by issuing and retiring Treasury bills. These are a short-term borrowing medium and 'are similar to commercial bills in that they are issued at a discount and fall due for payment at specified dates'.[4] The Bank also makes advances to government by 'ways and means advances'. These are used to meet the short-term expenditure needs of government departments.

The Bank can implement monetary policy through open market operations on the money market, debt management in gilt-edged securities and other controls over the liquidity of the financial system. Open market operations involve the buying and selling of marketable securities, such as gilt-edged stock, equities and debentures, by the Bank. This can influence the quantity of reserve assets held by the banking system, as well as affecting the volume of lending by commercial banks and their holdings of other financial assets. Open market operations by the Bank may contract or expand the reserve base of the commercial banks and lead to a reduction or increase in bank loans and other assets. A further effect is to change the quantity of bank deposits and so the money supply. Open market operations may be conducted as an adjunct to interest rate policy, which may have a balance of payments objective. During the 1980s the Bank operated on interest rates by these indirect means, not directly through a minimum lending rate (MLR), which was abandoned in 1981. MLR was the financial rate at which the Bank would give assistance by loans or rediscounting bills to discount houses forced, by shortage of funds in the money market, to go to the Bank of England as the lender of last resort.

The discount houses

Discount houses are financial intermediaries in the London money market which acquire short-term assets with money repayable at very short notice, mostly on a daily or overnight basis, most of it coming from the commercial banks. Klein (1986) summarizes the principal functions of the discount houses as follows:

1   They provide a source of short-term funds for commerce and industry by discounting bills of exchange which have been accepted.
2   They accept funds from the banking system repayable at call or short notice, thus making it possible for the banks to maintain adequate but not excessive levels of liquid assets.
3   They cover the total tender at the weekly Treasury bill issue.
4   They provide a secondary market in dollar and sterling certificates of deposit.
5   They help the Bank of England by dealing in short-term bonds and gilts which are nearing maturity; this assists in funding the public sector debt.
6   They assist in the control of the money supply by buying

or selling Treasury bills and first-class commercial bills from or to the Bank.[5]

It will be appreciated, from this outline, that the discount houses occupy a key position in the banking and financial structure, including the right to borrow, on their own initiative, from the Bank of England as the lender of last resort.

A bill is a short-term debt instrument in the form of a document. It orders the debtor to pay the creditor a stated sum of money at a specified date. Once it is signed by the debtor and endorsed by the acceptor, a bill becomes negotiable and may be discounted, or sold at a discount off its face value, at a rate reflecting current short-term interest rates. A bill normally has a maturity date of up to six months. Historically bills were used to finance trade and industry, thus providing the working capital needed by agricultural and manufacturing businesses. An inland bill is one drawn to finance domestic trade, whilst a foreign bill, or bill of exchange, is drawn in the course of foreign trade transactions. Although inland bills were at one time largely superseded by bank advances or trade credit, they have now revived in the UK. The reason lay initially in their use to finance hire-purchase contracts and latterly as a means of raising general finance for major companies.

Another important type of bill is the Treasury bill, which is issued by government as a short-term borrowing instrument. Introduced at the end of the nineteenth century, the original purpose of the Treasury bill was to serve the purely seasonal needs for business finance. But since the First World War the Treasury bill has been a permanent feature in government debt. Treasury bills have a ninety-one-day term, though some sixty-three-day bills are issued at certain times of the year. They are sold by tender in weekly lots, with 'tap' issues of gilt-edged stock being continuously available for purchase from the government broker in the London Stock Exchange. The Treasury bill remains an important financial instrument, having a significant role in monetary management. By an arrangement dating from the 1930s the weekly Treasury bill tender is effectively underwritten by the London discount houses. Their total bids always cover the amount on offer. This arrangement, backed by understandings with the clearing banks, and by the discount houses' access to the Bank of England as the lender of last resort, provides a means by which the government can always find the funds it needs for expenditure purposes.

The London Stock Exchange

The London Stock Exchange is the principal stock market in the UK. In essence, it is the financial institution where stocks and shares are bought and sold. In this context, the stock of a company is its issued capital, or a particular issue of securities such as gilt-edged assets, equities or debentures. Stock is in a consolidated form so that it can be held or transferred in any amounts. Shares in a company, in contrast, are for fixed nominal amounts and are held or transferred in such units. Gilt-edged securities are all UK government debt, other than Treasury bills, in the form of marketable stocks. Equities are ordinary shares in the issued capital of quoted companies. They carry some risk but enable their holders to become members of the company, to vote at the company's annual general meeting and elect directors, and to participate, through dividends, in corporate profits. Debenture holders are provided with fixed rates of interest on their investments and are company creditors. Preference shares normally provide only limited voting rights, have more security than equities but have a higher return than debentures.

Although London is the main stock exchange, there are provincial exchanges in many towns. In the 1960s all but two of the provincial exchanges grouped themselves into three regional associations, with common membership and listings of securities, but with market business continuing to be conducted locally. During trading hours all exchanges are in constant contact with one another, especially with London, and in effect they form a single national market in securities. The existence of such a market is a vital condition for providing finance capital on the scale required in a modern mixed economy. It also provides a market in which claims created in the raising of finance capital can be easily transferred amongst stock holders. This facility encourages the holding of such claims and hence the provision of finance capital in the corporate sector.

Only members of the Stock Exchange may deal on it, and its membership and modes of trading are strictly regulated. Security-issuing bodies, in turn, are expected to meet specific requirements if their issues are to be listed or quoted on the exchange. Until recently there were two classes of Stock Exchange member: jobbers and stockbrokers. Now there are dual capacity firms which can act as both 'market makers' and 'broker dealers'. Jobbers were traders who dealt only with stockbrokers, and their role was to buy and sell quoted securities. Jobbers acted as principals and helped to make markets in particular securities, thus improving the functioning of the market. Their role was well described by Klein:

> Jobbers [were] guided in making prices by their experience and by any available information about their particular shares, but mostly they [relied] on the weight of buying and selling activity. Prices naturally vary according to supply and demand. If there [were] more brokers anxious to sell than there [were] to buy, the jobber [would] reduce his prices until buyers [were] attracted. If there [were] more buying brokers than there [were] sellers, he will put up his prices until more sellers [were] attracted.[6]

These principles of supply and demand still operate today. Broker dealers act on behalf of their clients charging a commission for doing so. Besides carrying out stock transactions, broker dealers act as advisers to their clients. They are also involved in new issues of securities, arranging for them to be listed or quoted on the stock exchange and to be underwritten. Some broker dealers handle new issues in their entirety.

Labour Markets

The labour market is where the activities of supplying and hiring human resource skills to perform certain jobs, and the process of determining how much is to be paid to whom in performing them, take place. The ways in which wages move and the mobility of labour amongst different occupations, geographical regions and employers fall within this definition. This is not to imply that labour as a resource is the same as inanimate commodities, such as capital or materials, but that the labour market is a place where labour supply and labour demand interact. The labour market is not homogenous. Workers provide a variety of skills, aptitudes and abilities to employers, who in turn, buy human resource inputs in a variety of labour markets. These include local labour markets, internal markets and external markets.

A local labour market, for example, is a limited geographical area and is a consequence of the monetary and psychological costs of extensive travel to work. These costs segment a labour force spatially that is already stratified occupationally, tending to restrict the labour market to that which is acceptable to given households and certain employers in a limited spatial area. This appears to be true of lower-level occupational skills at least. Changes in the structure of employment in a given market and the pattern and level of rewards offered, and changes in transport facilities, suggest in practice that a perfectly demarcated local labour market rarely exists. Such changes in the structure of costs and rewards affect the form and extent of worker job preferences. In reality, then, the definition of a local labour market assumes that its key feature is that the bulk of the area's population habitually seeks employment there, with employers recruiting most of their labour from that area.

An internal labour market is where labour is supplied by individuals and demanded by employers without direct access to the external labour market, which, in contrast, is more competitive and open to market forces. Different employment treatment is accorded to those recruited externally from those working internally. Most jobs within the firm are filled by the promotion or transfer of workers who have already gained entry to the employer. An internal labour market thus consists of a set of structured employment relationships which incorporate formal and informal rules governing each job and job interrelationships. This complex employment relationship develops, in part, because of the sort of tasks that are specific to certain jobs, such as requiring specific training which is acquired on the job. Sometimes internal labour markets develop because of union pressure for a seniority system. These are aimed at rewarding those having long service with an organization. This results in such jobs being unique to the enterprise and lacking an external source of labour supply.

The external labour market can operate locally, nationally or internationally. The labour market for senior managers, for example, is both national and, increasingly, international. This is one reason why business corporations use executive recruitment agencies, or headhunting consultancies, to assist in the filling of senior management posts. Other specialist and technical staff are also recruited nationally rather than locally, since their skills are in relatively short supply, given the demand for them. The coming of the European single market is likely to see the extension of a transnational labour market for certain types of skill as multinational companies extend their activities across frontiers in western Europe and possibly eastern Europe too.

From what has been outlined above, it is clear that the labour market, or more specifically its constituent components, is highly imperfect. Labour is notoriously immobile and there is considerable inertia getting individuals to move geographically, to develop new skills or to change their occupation. Bargaining power in the labour market is generally weighted towards employers, which is one reason why workers join trade unions to negotiate their terms and conditions for them. Some see trade unions as labour cartels artificially bidding wages up, and inflating unit labour costs, resulting in higher unemployment and job losses. Others see trade unions as defensive organizations, merely reacting to increases in commodity prices or to rises in company profits or labour productivity. Labour supply is relatively fixed in the short term, thus preventing firms expanding or resulting in higher wage settlements to retain existing workers.

Some economists support the 'dual labour market' hypothesis. This suggests that the labour market is segmented into two sectors, a primary and a secondary sector. The primary sector is characterized by 'good' jobs, whilst 'bad' jobs comprise the secondary sector. Good jobs provide high pay, promotion prospects, job security and attractive fringe benefits. Bad jobs are allocated to workers frozen out of the primary sector, with wages being established by competition in the labour market, where a sufficient number of jobs is normally available to those wanting them. However, they are low-paid, unstable and generally unattractive jobs. Workers in the secondary sector are precluded from entering the primary sector not only by their lack of human capital and trainability. They are also affected by discrimination, restrictive union practices and the dearth of good jobs. Workers in the secondary sector are thus underemployed.

Human capital theory suggests that investments are made in human resources to improve their productivity and monetary returns from working. Costs are incurred in the expectation of future benefits, hence the term 'investment in human resources'. Whether the investment is worth while depends on the benefits exceeding the costs by a sufficient margin. There is a direct analogy between investment in human capital and investment in physical capital, though there are differences. In particular, human capital is not collateral because it cannot normally be sold. Moreover, individuals cannot spread or diversify their risks in the manner that owners of physical capital can. But, like physical capital, human capital is subject to depreciation.

Human capital theory provides one of the main explanations of wage and salary relativities by age and occupation, the uneven incidence of unemployment by skill and the job regulatory practices of trade unions. The concept of investing in humans as economic resources has a wide application. It includes investment in formal schooling, post-school training and on-the-job training. It also covers domestic investments in the forms of family care in the pre-school years, improved health, labour market information and job search. Human capital theory also contributes to policy decisions on the allocation of resources to schooling and training in comparison with other claims on the limited resources of societies and individuals.

The public policy prescription of the dual labour market hypothesis is the creation by government of better jobs, or more primary-sector jobs, accompanied by legislation to remove discrimination. This conflicts with free market analysis, which interprets labour market disadvantage as reflecting deficiencies in human capital investments. Indeed, the lower level of human capital investment by secondary workers may be a rational response to a lower return on the investment experienced by such workers, as a result of labour market discrimination and segmentation.

The Limitations of Markets

The doctrine that the economic affairs of society are best guided by the decisions of individuals in the marketplace to the virtual exclusion of collective political authority is known as *laissez-faire* or economic liberalism. In 1776 Adam Smith (1976) provided one of the first analyses of economic liberalism. He argued that individuals acting out of pure self-interest are a progressive force for maximizing the total wealth of a nation. In this context wealth is anything which has a market value and can be exchanged for money or goods. It includes all those physical, financial and human assets which are capable of generating money income. Whereas wealth is a stock of valued resources, income is the flow of money earnings derived from the ownership of these resources. Within this framework the role of the State is to perform only those activities which the market cannot satisfy. It also has to maintain a legal apparatus in which the private enterprise economy and its markets can operate efficiently. Interference with the free working of the market, market liberals argue, results in misdirected resources, economic inefficiency and waste.

The main characteristic of a free market economy is that economic decisions are decentralized. The allocation of scarce resources between their possible uses is the combined result of millions of separate decisions. Consumers spend their incomes, firms make production decisions and workers find employment. The role of government is limited to maintaining internal law and order, enforcing contracts, defending the State against external threat and ensuring that markets are not distorted. Under such a system, it is believed, the market economy facilitates efficient resource allocation, thus maximizing the satisfaction of economic wants.

In practice, however, there are a number of ways in which the free market economy model can be criticized. The main ones are that in market-based economies there are: market imperfections, adjustment dislocations and social costs, and inequalities in income and wealth distribution. It is also necessary to make provision for the supply of public goods. Because of these and related factors, governments find it necessary to intervene in economic markets and economic affairs for economic, social and moral reasons.

Market imperfections

One problem with the free market model is that the market structure of an industry may not be sufficiently competitive amongst firms and producers to facilitate efficient resource allocation or real consumer choice. Most markets, in other words, are imperfect rather than perfect; firms are price makers rather than price takers. A perfect market has a number of features. These include: a homogenous product, a large number of buyers and sellers, freedom of entry and exit for buyers and sellers, perfect information about prices amongst buyers and sellers, no collusion between buyers and sellers, utility maximization by buyers, profit maximization by sellers, an insignificant impact is made by individual buyers and sellers on total market transactions.

In the real world, though some near-perfect markets exist, most markets exhibit varying degrees of imperfection, thus giving market advantage and higher than normal profits to the producers. This is where firms exceed that minimum amount of profit necessary to induce them to remain in business. Under monopolistic competition, for example, there are a large number of firms producing similar but not identical products. Although product differentiation gives each firm an element of monopoly power, other firms are free to enter the market and produce a different brand of product under equivalent cost conditions. With monopolistic competition, however, each firm produces its desired output at higher than minimum cost. It is argued, therefore, that the firm in monopolistic competition is less efficient than its counterpart in perfect competition, because it is producing with excess capacity.

An oligopolistic market is one where the number of sellers is few, with many potential buyers. The market structure is one in which firms are aware of the interdependence of their sales, production, investment and advertising plans. Where firms manipulate any of the variables under their control, it provokes retaliation from competing firms. Under oligopoly, each oligopolist acts either independently, basing its decisions upon assumptions regarding its rivals' reactions, or in collusion with its market rivals. The results are that market prices are usually artificially high, product supply may be restricted and the market is producer, not consumer-led.

In the strictest sense of the word, monopoly occurs where a firm is the sole supplier of a homogenous product for which there are no substitutes and many buyers. This enables the supplier to control either the market price or the output of the commodity it produces, resulting in profits well above the minimum necessary to keep the firm in business. Some degree of monopoly power exists where there are barriers to entering a market, patent rights giving exclusive use of a production technique or high costs of transport to producers.

Adjustment dislocations and social costs

However efficient the free market economy might be in allocating scarce resources to human wants in the long term, it requires time in which to adjust whenever changes in economic preferences occur. In advanced economies, human resource specialization, the high costs of capital investment and continuous technological change inevitably involve problems of adjustment and time lags between the production of one set of economic outputs and another. This has implications for producers, the suppliers of finance capital, workers and consumers. Some producers need to re-equip themselves, shareholders may find company dividends reduced, workers may become unemployed and need retraining and customer demand may be unsatisfied. Other economic participants benefit in the interim. But the fact remains that whilst part of the economy may be under-equipped and under-recruited for some purposes, other parts may be over-equipped and over-recruited.

A free market economy can also fail to make full use of the scarce resources available to it. Production generates output and incomes in the forms of wages, profits, interest and rents. These provide recipients with the means of buying the goods and services being produced. Where all available resources are fully used, and everyone who wants a job has one at the prevailing wage, full employment is achieved. But, to maintain full employment, the economic community must be prepared to spend the whole of its income on current output. If the community is not prepared to do this, total demand falls short of total output at full employment. Firms are then left with unsold output and are forced to cut back production. This results in people being laid off work, capital resources being unemployed and all resources being under-utilized. Conversely, with total spending in excess of full employment output, the economy overheats and prices rise. In practice, governments have to intervene in the economy to influence, either aggregate demand or impediments to the supply and efficient use of the factors of production.

Another difficulty arising in the marketplace is that the real costs of producing commodities are not measured by the money costs of doing so. Industrial pollution affects the environment, the eco-system and the quality of life of people and communities. Even where there are prohibitions on firms and companies harming the natural environment, it sometimes happens and damage is done to land, sea or the atmosphere. Yet the social costs, as measured by the total resources expended by society in this event, are far greater than the private costs of firms, or the resources for which firms have to pay, in producing environmentally damaging output. This is because corporate decisions about what and how much to produce depend on private, not social costs. Where these are less than social costs, from a social point of view a misallocation of resources occurs.

Inequalities in income and wealth distribution

In a market economy it may be possible to increase total satisfaction by redistributing and transferring income and wealth from some people to others. Extreme inequalities of income and wealth, in other words, must be regarded as incompatible with a satisfaction-maximizing use of total scarce resources, even where individuals are making the best use of their own resources from their human resource skills and accumulated wealth. Where two individuals have exactly the same capacity for enjoyment, for example, but one has an income of £10,000 per week and the other £50 per week, then transferring £10 per week from the first person to the second enables the poorer individual to satisfy wants which are far more urgent than those the richer person has foregone. The case for more equal income and wealth distribution, then, is based not only on moral grounds but also on economic ones.

As can be seen in table 23, the distribution of market income and of disposable income in the UK between 1976 and 1984 shifted in favour of those in the two highest quintiles and away from those in the two lowest quintiles. In 1976, for example, those households with the top 20 per cent of market incomes received 71 per cent of the total, rising to 76 per cent in 1984. The market incomes of households in the bottom 20 per cent, in contrast, fell from 10 per cent of the total in 1976 to 9 per cent in 1984. Similarly, in 1976 those households with the top 20 per cent of disposable incomes received 62 per cent of the total, rising to

Table 23
UK distribution of original and disposable household income, 1976–84   *(%)*

	Quintile groups of households					
Year	Bottom fifth	Next fifth	Middle fifth	Next fifth	Top fifth	Total
Original income[a]						
1976	0·8	9·4	18·8	26·6	44·4	100·0
1981	0·6	8·1	18·0	26·9	46·4	100·0
1983	0·3	6·7	17·7	27·2	48·0	100·0
1984	0·3	6·1	17·5	27·5	48·6	100·0
Disposable income[b]						
1976	7·0	12·6	18·2	24·1	38·1	100·0
1981	6·7	12·1	17·7	24·1	39·4	100·0
1983	6·9	11·9	17·6	24·0	39·6	100·0
1984	7·1	12·1	17·5	24·3	39·0	100·0

Notes
a Households ranked by original income.
b Households ranked by disposable income.
Source: Central Statistical Office, *Family expenditure survey*, London, HMSO, various years.

64 per cent in 1984. The disposable incomes of households in the bottom 20 per cent, by contrast, fell from 20 per cent of the total in 1976 to 19 per cent in 1984.

From table 24 it can be observed that whilst wealth distribution in the UK was less unequal in 1984, compared with 1971, the wealthiest one per cent of the population still retained over a fifth

Table 24
UK distribution of marketable wealth, 1971–84   *(%)*

Marketable wealth	1971	1976	1981	1984
Percentage of wealth owned by:				
Most wealthy 1%[a]	31	24	21	21
Most wealthy 5%[a]	52	45	40	39
Most wealthy 10%[a]	65	60	54	52
Most wealthy 25%[a]	86	84	77	75
Most wealthy 50%[a]	97	95	94	93
Total marketable wealth (£ billion)	140	263	546	762

Note
a Of population aged eighteen or over.
Source: Inland Revenue. Various years.

of total marketable wealth, the wealthiest 5 per cent almost two-fifths and the wealthiest 10 per cent over half. Given the importance of the ownership of wealth as a source of income in the forms of interest, dividends and rents, it is still the situation in the UK that the least wealthy 50 per cent of the population probably owns only some 7 per cent of total marketable wealth. This is compounded by the unequal distribution of household income already referred to. The evidence raises the question as to whether 'a new version of the two nations' has emerged in the last decade. What appears to have happened is that there is now 'a widening division between a prosperous majority in secure and increasingly well remunerated employment by contrast with a depressed minority of the unemployed, the sick and the unsuccessful ethnic minorities'.[7]

On the grounds of seeking to increase total economic satisfaction and social justice, therefore, governments in practice intervene in the markets for income and wealth distribution. They do so to varying degrees by their fiscal and taxation policies and their concomitant public spending programmes. The problem is getting a balance between maintaining economic incentives, to facilitate risk-taking and economic initiatives by the skilled and able, on the one side, and removing economic deprivation and social disadvantage amongst the poor and unskilled on the other.

Public goods

There is one group of economic commodities which cannot be provided through the market mechanism; these are what are known as public goods. Public goods are commodities or services having two main characteristics. The first is that they have no rival in consumption. The second is their non-excludability, so that where they are provided to any one person, it makes them automatically available to others. One person's consumption of public goods, therefore, does not reduce their availability to anyone else. This is not the case with private goods, where one person's consumption precludes the consumption of the same unit by another person. The characteristic of non-excludability prevents private markets operating, because a producer is unable to ensure that only those individuals paying for the goods can obtain them, since if the goods can be obtained without paying no one will be willing to buy them.

When there is no rival in consumption for certain goods, charging a price for them is inefficient. This is because adding extra units of consumption provides benefits to the consumers without imposing any costs. Charging a price, however, prevents some consumption taking place, thus causing a net loss of satisfaction or utility. Even where it is possible, providing public goods through a private market does not enable an optimal level of output to be produced. As outlined above, with non-excludability, a market cannot operate at all.

The provision of public goods is a matter of collective or social choice. The study of market economies is largely concerned with individual choice. Yet many decisions on resource allocation are made by governments, so public goods are generally provided by governments and paid for indirectly through taxation rather than directly through the market. Typically, public goods, such as national defence and environmental protection, are provided by the public corporate sector, though the size of the public sector varies according to the political ideology of the government in power. Although public goods could be provided by voluntary agreement amongst the community, individuals could conceal their true valuation of the goods to escape paying for them, thus becoming free riders. In practice, then, public goods are provided by the public authorities and are financed out of public taxation.

Merit goods are sometimes included in the definition of public goods. These are goods the consumption of which is deemed to be intrinsically desirable. In such cases, it is argued, consumer sovereignty does not hold. If consumers are not willing to buy sufficient quantities of such goods, they should be compelled or encouraged to do so. The argument is sometimes deployed in defence of compulsory education or tax-financed health services. Some economists would reject this reasoning, whilst others would claim that there is great difficulty in determining which goods are in fact merit goods.

The Implications for Management

Managing scarcity is a major task facing managements in all organizations. In practice, as for individuals, there are never enough resources available for business corporations to satisfy all their economic wants. Indeed, organizations compete for scarce resources with one another. In order to fulfil their economic and other goals, private and public-sector enterprises require skilled human resources and finance capital and access to intermediate goods and services and raw materials in the production process. Since these are in limited supply, organizations compete in factor of production and commodity markets for such resources. Within these markets it is prices which act as signals and indicators to firms, businesses and public enterprises in their continuous search for resource sufficiency and economic success.

Managements also have to decide what resources to use, in what quantities, how to use them and how to maximize efficiency in the production process. In carrying out these organizational activities, managements are continually faced with the problem of opportunity cost. In other words, utilizing one set of resources in a particular combination implies not using an equivalent set of resources for the same purpose, or the same resources for other purposes. Similarly, producing one set of outputs from a given resource base can be done only at the expense of not using alternative combinations. Making choices amongst resources, work methods and products or services are tasks continually facing management in every organization, with financial costs and opportunity costs in taking these decisions.

This raises the question: to what extent are managements reactors to market forces as opposed to controllers of market forces? In organizational product markets, it seems likely, given the relative imperfections of most market structures in the modern world, that business corporations are generally price makers rather than price takers. Certainly, anecdotal and research evidence suggests that big business organizations are able, in varying degrees, to influence market prices and hence returns on their finance capital and corporate profitability. With such vast amounts of finance capital at stake, management's ability to work market forces in its favour and to facilitate product success and corporate viability is not without its benefits to the business corporation. Whether it benefits the corporation's business clients or individual customers is more open to debate. As Galbraith (1967) writes, 'the control or management of demand [by big business] is . . . a vast rapidly growing industry itself'. In everyday language, 'this great machine, and the demanding and varied talents that it employs, are said to be engaged in selling goods. In less ambiguous language, it means that it is engaged in the management of those who buy goods.'[8]

When we turn to money and finance capital markets, management influence on these seems to be less apparent. Indeed, some commentators argue that there is increasing divergence between so-called City interests and those of the manufacturing and service sectors. The money markets are internationalized and demonstrate more propinquity to free markets than do many other markets. With the advent of high-speed computer technology, and an interdependent money market system, there appears to be greater volatility in the money markets of the world, compared with the past. It is also apparent that the major actors in international equity and security markers are themselves corporate bodies rather than individual investors. Increasingly, it is business corporations which own other business corporations, with corporate ownership traversing national and continental boundaries. Those supporting this interpretation of corporate capitalism argue that real economic power has passed out of the hands of the managerial elite running companies to the relatively small group of entrepreneurial capitalists who work the money markets and concentrate financial ownership in their own hands.

Others such as Marris (1964) argue that managerial capitalism better describes the power structure of the modern mixed economy. This is a situation where the economy is dominated by large business corporations, with power over resources being located in a definable managerial class, distinctly separate from the property-owning class and independent of its control. It is posited that the managerial class pursues goals and aims which are independent of workers, shareholders and the State. Theories of managerial capitalism are closely linked with managerial theories of the firm. They have developed out of the belief that contemporary capitalism is characterized by the dominance of large enterprises in the private corporate sector where ownership and control are divided between shareholders and managers respectively. Given the nature of imperfect capital markets and uncompetitive product markets, it is argued, managers have the scope to pursue business goals other than profit maximization, such as corporate growth or sales maximization.

With the emergence and growth of environmentalism in recent years, and the greening of politics, managements are having to pay far greater attention to their wider social responsibilities in taking economic decisions, certainly in comparison with the past. Consumers, local communities, environmental pressure groups and employees are all demanding that, in taking investment, marketing, production and employment decisions, managements must take their views into account. One way of doing so rationally is through the use of sophisticated cost-benefit analyses by organizations in both the private and public sectors.

Cost-benefit analyses differ from simple financial appraisals by considering all potential gains and losses in making a decision, irrespective of whom they accrue to. In essence, benefits are any gains in utility and costs are losses in utility, measured as opportunity costs. In practice, many costs are not capable of quantification in money terms, such as the destruction of natural beauty, loss of wildlife or threats to the environment, whilst benefits are measured in money terms. For this reason, shadow prices are often used in cost-benefit analyses. These impute valuation of an economic good or economic bad which has no market price. Shadow prices thus represent the opportunity cost of consuming or producing a commodity which is not normally traded in the economy. Done strictly, cost-benefit analyses should value all inputs and outputs at their shadow price.

Understanding the nature of economic scarcity and the principles underlying markets and price determination, then, is important for managerial decision-makers. Managers need to know the types of product, capital and labour markets in which their organizations operate. They also need to be sensitive to the sorts of market changes likely to affect their organization's product, capital and labour markets. In this way they are better able to anticipate the opportunities and threats facing their organization in conditions of change and market instability. It is also expected that managements can anticipate the actions of their product competitors, thus maintaining or even improving their organization's market position wherever possible. Managers also need to understand the ways in which governments intervene in markets in order to protect consumers, provide workers' rights, maintain the environment or prevent price-fixing. Finally, it has to be recognized that the introduction of competitive tendering and internal markets into the public sector is bringing important changes in organizational culture and managerial practices in public enterprises.

References

1 LIPSEY R. *Positive economics.* London, Weidenfeld & Nicolson, 1983, p 53.
2 GROSSMAN G. *Economic systems.* Englewood Cliffs, Prentice Hall, 1967, p 14.
3 *ibid.* p 15.
4 KLEIN G. *The elements of banking.* London, Methuen, 1986, p 77.
5 *ibid.* p 80.
6 *ibid.* p 93.
7 HALSEY A H. 'Social trends since world war II.' *Social trends* 17. London, HMSO, 1987, p 17.
8 GALBRAITH J. *The new industrial state.* Harmondsworth, Penguin, 1967, p 204f.

6
The Macro-economic Framework

The last chapter focused on some of the basic micro-economic elements of economic analysis. Micro-economics is concerned with the behaviour of individual economic units such as households and firms and their interaction in determining prices in market-based economies. More advanced micro-economic analysis concentrates on theories of consumer demand, the production decisions of firms, and price theory. Much intermediate and advanced micro-analysis is related to the types of markets in which producers and firms operate, especially with the degree of competition amongst them. Macro-economics, in contrast, studies the behaviour of the economy as a whole. Essentially, macro-economics dates from the 1930s, when significant contributions were made to the development of macro-economic theory by John Maynard Keynes. Under macro-analysis the economy is disaggregated into what are believed to be broadly homogeneous components. The determinants of the behaviour of each of these components, such as consumption, investment, government spending and overseas trade, are examined. They are then integrated to provide a model of the whole economy. Macro-economics is especially concerned with the income-generating effect of total expenditure and the role of the investment spending component in determining the level of economic activity, particularly employment.

National Income

A country's national income, normally described as its gross national product (GNP), measures the money value of the goods and services available to that country from economic activity over a given period, usually a year. As can be seen from figure 6, GNP can be measured in three ways, by adding up the sum of the outputs of the various industries of a country, the sum of expenditures or the sum of the incomes. Figure 6 indicates that in a simple two-sector economy, comprising just businesses and households, it is the business sector which produces the total goods and services making up national output, demanding factor inputs from the household sector to do so. It is the household sector, in turn, which is paid total factor incomes by the business sector and then spends them on the output generated.

The output approach to measuring GNP aggregates the sum of the values added at each stage of production by all the industries and productive enterprises in the country. The sum of these added values gives gross domestic product at factor cost, which, after an adjustment to include net property income from abroad, gives GNP. The expenditure approach aggregates consumption and investment expenditures to obtain total domestic expenditure at market prices. It aggregates only the value of final purchases and excludes all expenditure on intermediate goods, i.e. goods used in the production of other goods. Since final expenditures at

Figure 6   Output, income and expenditure in a two-sector economy

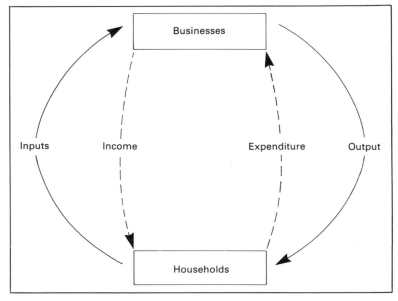

market price include the effects both of taxes and subsidies and of expenditures on imports, whilst excluding the value of exports, they have to be taken into account in measuring GNP by this method. Net national income or net national product is GNP adjusted to take account of capital consumption, the annual reduction in the value of a country's national assets.

Figure 7, page 142, shows in more detail the flows of income resulting from the buying and selling of goods and services in the economy. Gross revenue received by firms, for example, comes from a number of sources. These are consumption expenditure by households; investment or capital expenditure by the corporate sector via the financial institutions, firms or households; government or public expenditure; expenditure received from overseas sales; and expenditure from other firms buying intermediate goods and services for production purposes. Payments made by firms to households, government, overseas companies and other firms take the forms of: wages for employment services; interest on loans; rent on property; dividends to shareholders; corporate savings through profits retained to finance corporate investment, either directly or through the financial institutions; taxes to government; revenues to overseas companies for imported goods and services; and incomes to other firms selling intermediate goods and services used in the production process. Household income, in turn, goes on consumption spending, personal savings, taxes, and payment for imported goods and services such as consumer products, holidays abroad or overseas investments. The national expenditure and income accounts for the period 1978–88 are shown in table 25.

National income not only indicates general living standards but is the primary determinant of the level of employment. It is the determination of national income which is at the centre of macro-economic analysis. To understand how the level of national income is determined, it is necessary to outline the determinants of each of the main aggregate components of national expenditure, namely consumption, investment, the government sector and the overseas sector. Consumption expenditure, for example, is aggregate expenditures on goods and services that satisfy current wants in the economy. Its major determinants appear to be: the level of national income itself; changes in national income, expectations based on this; and taxes on incomes. Other determinants

Table 25

UK gross domestic product by income and expenditure at factor cost, 1978–88   (£ million)

GDP	1978	1979	1980	1981	1982	1983	1984	1985	1986	1987	1988
Factor incomes											
Income from employment	98,843	115,866	137,614	149,573	158,622	169,586	180,145	194,865	209,830	225,945	249,775
Income from self-employment	13,539	15,811	17,928	19,937	22,076	24,314	27,382	29,466	33,600	38,044	42,617
Gross trading profits of companies	22,382	29,240	27,918	27,295	31,460	39,837	44,967	52,572	48,327	61,281	70,242
Gross trading surplus of public corporations	5,393	5,594	6,162	7,821	9,347	9,847	8,204	7,025	7,953	6,713	7,286
Gross trading surplus of general government enterprises	216	180	180	236	216	50	−117	243	145	−58	−70
Rent	10,036	11,951	14,243	16,365	17,699	18,763	19,807	21,646	23,406	25,258	27,464
Imputed charge for consumption of non-trading capital	1,445	1,707	2,103	2,334	2,403	2,465	2,578	2,776	3,005	3,214	3,408
Total domestic income	151,854	180,349	206,148	223,561	241,823	264,862	282,966	308,593	326,266	360,397	400,722
less Stock appreciation	−4,228	−8,837	−6,391	−5,974	−4,276	−4,204	−4,509	−2,739	−1,766	−4,746	−6,116
Gross domestic product (income-based)	147,626	171,512	199,757	217,587	237,547	260,658	278,457	305,854	324,500	355,651	394,606
Statistical discrepancy (income adjustment)	1,516	1,292	760	610	203	−259	926	5	−469	−96	181
Gross domestic product (average estimate) at factor cost	149,142	172,804	200,517	218,197	237,750	260,399	279,383	305,859	324,031	355,555	394,787
Expenditure at current factor cost											
Consumers' expenditure	87,187	102,055	117,414	128,956	140,400	154,253	165,425	180,013	196,709	215,276	241,873
General government final consumption	31,535	36,201	45,426	51,275	55,811	61,296	65,392	69,418	74,560	80,161	86,061
Gross domestic capital information	31,243	36,572	36,334	35,686	40,449	46,694	52,693	56,797	60,212	69,010	86,125
Total domestic expenditure	149,965	174,828	199,174	215,917	236,660	262,243	283,510	306,228	331,481	364,447	414,059
Exports of goods and services	45,645	52,525	59,916	64,345	69,519	76,722	88,622	98,801	94,271	102,498	103,866
Total final expenditure	195,610	227,353	259,090	280,262	306,179	338,965	372,132	405,029	425,752	466,945	517,925
less Imports of goods and services	−45,555	−54,439	−57,814	−60,704	−68,064	−77,871	−93,020	−99,165	−101,565	−112,331	−125,194

Gross domestic product (expenditure-based)	150,055	172,914	201,276	219,558	238,115	261,094	279,112	305,864	324,187	354,614	392,731
Statistical discrepancy (expenditure adjustment)	−913	−110	−759	−1,361	−365	−695	271	−5	−156	941	2,056
Gross domestic product (average estimate)	149,142	172,804	200,517	218,197	237,750	260,399	279,383	305,859	324,031	355,555	394,787
Net property income from abroad	806	1,205	−204	1,210	1,449	2,857	4,449	2,763	5,364	4,987	5,619
Gross national product (average estimate)	149,948	174,009	200,313	219,407	239,199	263,256	283,832	308,622	329,395	360,542	400,406
less Capital consumption	−19,378	−22,827	−27,952	−31,641	−33,653	−36,150	−38,725	−41,886	−45,178	−48,366	−54,769
Net national product at factor cost (average estimate) 'national income'	130,570	151,182	172,361	187,766	205,546	227,106	245,107	266,736	284,217	312,176	345,637

Source: *UK national accounts*, London, HMSO, 1989.

142

Figure 7 The circular flow of income in the UK economy

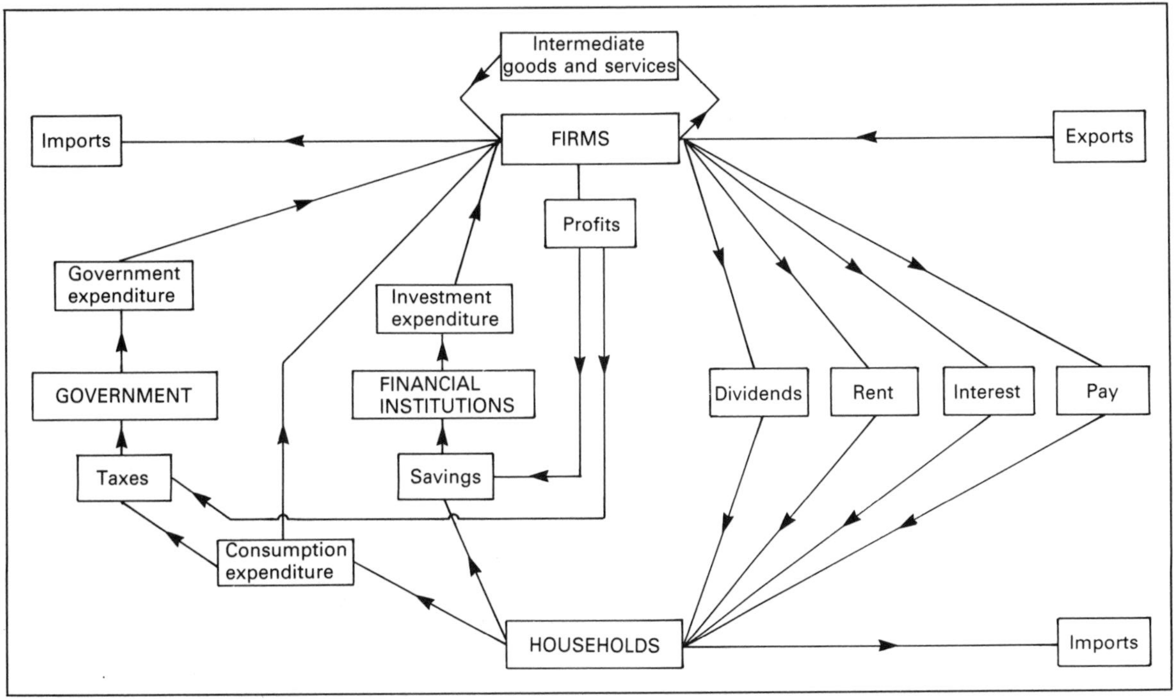

Source. D. Farnham, *Personnel in context*, London, IPM, 1986

of aggregate consumption include national wealth, interest rates, the availability and cost of credit, and social expectations. Other things being equal, aggregate demand increases when there is a rise in consumption expenditure and falls with a decrease in consumption expenditure.

Investment is defined as the flow of expenditures devoted to economic activities producing goods which are not intended for immediate consumption in the economy. At aggregate level, it is expected that investment spending will depend on factors similar to those which determine investment at the level of the firm. These are: expected future demand in the economy; its degree of spare capacity; wage and material costs; and financial factors such as levels of interest rates and company profits. As at the level of the firm, there are likely to be two stages in determining fixed investment. The first is deciding what the optimum level of capital capacity is, given demand factors and financial considerations. The second is influenced partly by technological and operational considerations and partly by financial factors. Thus a rapid rate of investment is more likely to need high-cost external finance than a slower rate, even though the ultimate desired total addition to capacity is the same. As with consumption expenditure, other things being equal, rises in investment expenditure induce increases in aggregate demand, with falls in investment expenditure leading to falls in aggregate demand.

The government sector of expenditure comprises central and local government and the public corporations. This sector raises revenue through taxation and the sale of marketed products. Tax revenues consist of direct taxes on incomes, including profits, indirect taxes on expenditure, and taxes on capital. Expenditure by the public authorities is broadly of three kinds: current expenditure on goods and services, mainly wage and salary payments to public employees; capital expenditure on goods such as roads, hospitals and schools; and transfer payments such as State pensions, State benefits, and grants to specific groups of citizens. Tax revenue and public expenditure need not balance. A government deficit can be met by borrowing from the private sector, primarily through issuing gilt-edged government bonds and securities. Similarly, a government surplus can be used for repaying past public debt. Other things being equal, aggregate demand is increased by a rise in public expenditure, either directly through a rise in current and capital spending or indirectly through a rise in transfer payments to private individuals, thus raising their total consumption. Aggregate demand is also increased by cuts in taxation. Aggregate demand is decreased when public expenditure is cut or taxes are raised. The latter is done either by reducing private incomes through higher direct taxation or by reducing the real values of incomes through higher indirect taxation.

The overseas sector affects aggregate expenditure through exports, which are purchases abroad of goods and services produced domestically, and imports, which are supplies of goods and services produced abroad to meet domestic demand. Other things being equal, a rise in exports increases aggregate output, whilst a rise in imports decreases aggregate output. Demand for exports and imports is determined by the preferences of purchasers, relative prices and income. Demand for UK exports, for example, depends upon world demand and the prices of UK goods relative to those of the UK's competitors. Similarly, demand for imports into the UK depends on the level of domestic demand, the prices of imported goods relative to those produced domestically, consumer taste and product quality. In general, the level of exports is determined autonomously outside the UK economy, whilst imports depend essentially on the level of domestic demand.

In the elementary income-expenditure model, it is aggregate expenditure, or aggregate demand, which determines both volume of national output and the associated level of employment. This is where the supply of national output equals the quantity of output which people wish to buy with their incomes. Aggregate expenditure equals the total sum spent on consumption, investment, government goods and services, and exports, whilst national income equals the total value of consumption, savings, taxes and imports. Since aggregate expenditure equals national income at equilibrium, this means that investment plus government spending plus exports equals savings plus taxes plus imports. In this model, in other words, the equilibrium level of national income is established when total leakages from the economy—savings plus taxes plus imports—equal total injections—investment plus government spending plus imports.

This model concentrates exclusively on the demand side of the macro-economy. There is no reason to expect that the equilibrium which is eventually achieved will be associated with full employment. On the contrary, this simple representation of the Keynesian system indicates that an 'unemployment' equilibrium is possible. Even if wages and prices are fully flexible, the economy need not necessarily return to full employment when, after adjustments, total leakages equal total injections. Where aggregate expenditure falls short of that required to produce a level of national income which would ensure full employment, there is a deflationary gap. Where aggregate expenditure exceeds the maximum attainable level of output, beyond the full employment level, resulting in an upward pressure on prices, there is an inflationary gap.

International Trade

International trade amongst countries is an extension of the principle of economic specialization into the international sphere. Domestic economic specialization concentrates production capacity into those areas of activity in which individuals, organizations and geographical regions have some natural or acquired advantage. This promotes economic efficiency and, where it is accompanied by trade, raises standards of living beyond those which might be achieved had each individual, organization or region remained self-sufficient. Nation States, however, differ from geographical regions in a number of respects. First, factors of production are able to move more freely within countries than between them. Second, each country has its own national currency. Third, there are variations in taxation, economic policy and social policy amongst countries, resulting in economic and political barriers to international trading between them.

Nation States nevertheless find that they are better suited to participating in some types of economic activity than others. Hence international trade effects the exchange of one nation's products against those of others when it is economically advantageous to do so. Some of this exchange takes place because most countries are incapable of satisfying all their economic wants from their own natural resources. This is due to the uneven distribution of minerals, agricultural products and other resources throughout the world. These commodities can be obtained only by one country importing them from another in exchange for goods or services it produces domestically.

Another economic factor encouraging international trade is that though many nations can produce a wide range of commodities, they are better at producing some kinds of goods than others. These differences tend to be reflected in relative prices. It becomes profitable, therefore, for one country to concentrate on producing the goods and services for which it is best suited and exporting any surplus to other countries in exchange for commodities in which they have a comparative advantage. It is international differences in the skills and costs of labour forces, agricultural fertility and capital investment which are the principal factors making international specialization profitable.

The balance of payments

A country's balance of payments records all the economic transactions that its residents undertake with foreigners over a given period, normally a year. Table 26 provides a schematic breakdown of the main components of the balance of payments accounts. Vertically they comprise money receipts and payments abroad. Horizontally they comprise current account balances and capital account balances. In outline, money receipts are credit items in the balance of payments accounts and payments abroad debit items. Current account balances, in turn, record all transactions involving currently produced goods or currently rendered services, whilst capital account balances record all payments arising from transfers of finance capital and credit between the home nation and overseas countries.

Money receipts on current account cover income earned from the export of a country's visible goods and invisible services over-

Table 26
The main components of the balance of payments accounts

Account	Money receipts	Payments abroad
Current	Exports of goods and services	Imports of goods and services
	Property income from abroad	Property income abroad
Capital	Investment from abroad	Investment abroad
	Borrowing from abroad	Lending abroad
	Fall in reserves	Rise in reserves

seas. Visible exports are tangible manufactured commodities, whilst invisible exports are money receipts for services rendered to foreign individuals and organizations. Money receipts on current account are completed by adding in net property income from abroad in the form of interest, dividends and profits. Payments abroad on current account reflect the equivalent money payments made to overseas individuals and organizations for the goods and services imported into a country, including any property income paid abroad. The difference between money receipts and payments abroad is the current account balance. Where money receipts exceed payments abroad, the current account is in surplus. In contrast, a current account deficit indicates that income from abroad is less than expenditure abroad.

Money receipts on capital account cover all capital transactions resulting in credit flows of funds into a country from abroad. These may be for:

- The direct construction of new plant and machinery from abroad.

- The purchase of existing assets from domestic residents.

- Borrowing by individuals or organizations at home.

- Official borrowing by the government.

- Other short-term capital flows such as for speculative purposes.

Money receipts on capital account also contain any fall in government holdings of gold and foreign currency reserves in the central bank. The significance of these entries in the balance of payments accounts is that they represent decreases in the community's net wealth, including any physical assets which are bought by overseas interests or loans accepted from them. Payments abroad, in contrast, comprise all capital debts, including rises in reserves, and collectively are an increase in the community's net wealth. Where payments abroad exceed money receipts, the capital account is in surplus. In contrast, a capital account deficit implies that payments from abroad are less than money receipts.

As outlined above, a country's current account balance is split into visibles and invisibles. In the UK, visibles comprise net exports of foodstuffs, raw materials, machinery, textiles, fuel, transport equipment, chemicals, consumer goods and other commodities. Invisibles comprise net exports such as earnings from tourism, insurance, banking, shipping, aviation, other services, property income from abroad, transfers from abroad and payments for government services. The main components of the capital account balance are:

- Net capital inflows for governmental or private direct investment.
- Net portfolio investment in the form of purchases of real assets.
- Bonds, equities and official government net borrowing from overseas.
- Net inflows of short-term capital.
- Falls in the reserves.

If all transactions are recorded correctly, the overall balance of payments balances exactly. A summary of the UK balance of payments for the period 1978–88 is shown in table 27.

To see how successfully a country is performing in its foreign trade and trading payments, it is necessary to look at the balances between different subtotals in the overall figures. One is the visible balance of trade. This is the surplus of the value of visible exports over visible imports or the deficit of the value of visible imports over visible exports. Another is the current account balance, which is the surplus or deficit of the value of all visible and invisible trade items, including net property income from abroad. The third is the basic surplus or basic deficit on autonomous items. This is the positive or negative excess of credit or currency inflow items over debit or currency outflow items in the current account and long-term capital account. Since governments cannot easily influence these items, they are financed by accommodating monetary flows such as short-term borrowing and lending or changes in the country's reserves.

Determinants of the current account

Most international trade can be explained in terms of the costs of the factors of production, technology, taste and income. Countries

Table 27
UK balance of payments, 1978–88

(£ million)

	1978	1979	1980	1981	1982	1983	1984	1985	1986	1987	1988
Current account											
Visible balance	-1,593	-3,344	1,355	3,250	1,908	-1,509	-5,169	-3,132	-9,364	-10,929	-20,826
Invisibles											
Services balance	3,514	3,799	3,653	3,715	2,971	3,995	4,339	6,606	6,247	5,682	4,165
Interest, profits and dividends balance	806	1,205	-204	1,210	1,449	2,857	4,449	2,763	5,364	4,987	5,619
Transfers balance	-1,791	-2,210	-1,984	-1,547	-1,741	-1,585	-1,734	-3,034	-2,181	-3,411	-3,575
Invisibles balance	2,529	2,794	1,465	3,378	2,679	5,267	7,054	6,335	9,430	7,258	6,209
Current balance	936	-550	2,820	6,628	4,587	3,758	1,885	3,203	66	-3,671	-14,617
Capital transfers	–	–	–	–	–	–	–	–	–	–	–
Transactions in UK assets and liabilities											
UK external assets	-4,377	-40,189	-43,439	-50,769	-31,407	-30,173	-32,068	-53,279	-92,462	-83,922	-50,073
UK external liabilities	1,506	39,447	39,568	43,400	29,054	25,809	24,289	43,782	81,369	76,255	52,408
Net transactions	-2,871	-742	-3,873	-7,370	-2,353	-4,366	-7,780	-9,497	-11,091	-7,667	2,334
EEA loss on forward commitments	–	–	–	–	–	–	–	–	–	–	–
Allocation of special drawing rights	–	195	180	158	–	–	–	–	–	–	–
Gold subscription to IMF	–	–	–	–	–	–	–	–	–	–	–
Balancing item	1,935	1,097	873	584	-2,234	608	5,895	6,294	11,025	11,338	12,283

Source: UK national accounts, London, HMSO, 1989.

tend to import products which require a relatively high input of the factors of production which they lack. Another reason why countries import goods is the technological advantages enjoyed by other countries. Where exporting countries have a technological lead in the production of certain commodities, and there are no tariff barriers, this normally results in relatively lower commodity prices for importing countries, which, because of production inefficiencies, are unable to compete in the relevant product market. According to the theory of comparative advantage, goods are traded from areas where they are relatively cheap to produce to destinations where they are relatively expensive to produce. What is important is the ratios of the commodity prices between countries.

The terms of trade are the relationship between the prices of exports and the prices of imports. The net barter terms of trade are the quotient between an index of export prices and an index of import prices. This represents the import purchasing power of a given volume of a country's exports. Countries are concerned about movements in the terms of trade, since a rise in the net barter terms of trade means that a given quantity of exports commands a larger volume of imports to compensate for them. A rise in the terms of trade implies that fewer exports have to be sold to obtain the foreign currency necessary to buy a given volume of imports. A fall in the terms of trade implies that more exports have to be sold to obtain such currency.

In addition to price and cost influences on imports, there is the influence of consumer tastes and income. With incomes rising, for example, domestic demand for most commodities rises. Initially many domestic producers increase their sales and output to meet such demand. As stocks diminish, however, and bottlenecks in production occur, there is a sharp rise in imports. Further rises in demand then spill over almost entirely into imports. It is only when domestic demands ebb that the ratio of imports to national income first slows and then drops away.

If government wishes to influence the levels of imports, it attempts to do so by a number of measures. These include monetary and fiscal policy, tariffs and import quotas, and devaluing the currency. Deflation, for example, cuts back imports, whilst reflation expands them. Tariffs and quotas redirect expenditure away from imports to domestically produced goods. A devaluation results in holders of foreign currencies paying lower prices for domestically produced goods, with the prices of imports on the home market rising and the prices of exports falling. If there is no increase in domestic production of export goods, they earn less foreign currency, thus exacerbating the balance of payments problem.

From the previous discussion it can be appreciated that certain commodities are exported because endowments of resources, technology, or taste confer a comparative cost advantage on the home country's industries. Provided foreign demand is sufficiently responsive to price, the value of a particular category of exports is enhanced if there is a fall in the export price, especially a fall relative to the prices and costs of overseas producers. Besides price, or domestic supply, the other major factor influencing a country's exports is the size of demand in other countries, with overseas booms stimulating demand for exports and recessions diminishing them.

When government wishes to influence exports, it uses a variety of means to do so. Subsidies increase the volume of exports, with domestic deflation of aggregate demand having an effect similar to an export subsidy. This encourages producers to switch from selling at home to selling abroad. The exchange rate can be a powerful weapon, too, with devaluation raising the foreign exchange value of exports and a revaluation lowering it.

The capital account, interest rates and exchange rates

Determinants of the capital account are much more complex. The crucial influence on direct international investment, such as in overseas factories, manufacturing plant, and so on, is the expected relative rates of return on capital at home and abroad. The higher the rate of profit expected on investment domestically, the greater capital imports are likely to be. Conversely, a rise in expected returns overseas induces capital exports. Differing rates of expected returns from similar investment in two countries are generally explicable in terms of different labour costs, geography or government policies on taxation, industry subsidies or tariff protection. The motives behind international portfolio investment may or may not be financial. Some holders of wealth wish to maximize returns from it, whilst others are less concerned with yield than minimizing risk and so diversify their portfolios to avoid risky assets.

The characteristic of short-term capital movements is the high degree of liquidity of the assets bought and sold. The two major influences on them are relative interest rates and expected exchange rates. Even slight differentials in interest rates between financial centres tend to trigger short-term capital movements from centres with lower rates to those where the rates are higher. An exchange rate is the price of a currency in terms of another currency. Exchange rates are regularly quoted between all currencies but frequently one major currency is used as a standard for comparing all rates. Movements in exchange rates give opportunities for speculation in the foreign exchange markets for those with speculative money.

The exchange rate of all convertible currencies is determined by supply and demand in the market in which they are traded. An important factor is whether the country's basic balance of payments position is in surplus or deficit. Where there is no official intervention in the foreign exchange market the rate is free floating and it rises and falls to equate supply and demand for that currency. Since exchange rates ceased to be fixed in 1971 they have generally been subject to a system of managed flexibility. This enables central banks to intervene to smooth out what are considered to be inappropriate fluctuations in their own currency's exchange rate. In the case of some currencies, exchange rates are linked in order to limit the range of movements amongst them, such as in the European 'snake' or exchange rate mechanism. Under it, member governments maintain the value of their currency within limited bands. These make market conditions more predictable for companies planning foreign trade and capital investment.

The single European market

One of the provisions of the European Community's Single European Act, 1987, which brings about a major amendment to the Treaty of Rome, 1957, is the planned creation of a Europe without frontiers by 31 December 1992. This is aimed at facilitating the free movement of people, goods and services. It is expected that the completion of the internal market will help regenerate industry and services, create new jobs and facilitate economic growth.

A study by the European Commission identifies the heavy costs of partitioning the Community's economy into twelve separate markets. It also calculates the immense opportunities which the completion of the open market is likely to provide for member States, businesses and people. These include:

- job creation
- corporate growth
- economies of scale
- improved productivity
- greater profitability
- healthier competition
- mobility for firms and workers
- price stability
- wider consumer choice.

It is estimated that, with integration the Community's gross domestic product could increase substantially, especially 'if the right effort is made in economic policy'. The benefits include savings from removing barriers affecting intra-Community trade and production which currently hinder new market entrants and obstruct competition. The study also argues that integration of the Community market should avoid overheating the economy, since it is likely that consumer prices will be deflated by an average of 6 per cent. Economic integration is further likely to:

> Relax budgetary and external constraints, by improving the public accounts of the Member States by an average equivalent to 2·2% of GDP and by consolidating the external position of the European Community—its balance of trade and payments with the rest of the world—by approximately 1% of GDP.[1]

Moreover, the consequences for employment could mean that within a few years about 2 million or more jobs could be created.

The major micro-economic consequences of the completion of the internal market were estimated to be threefold. First, certain industries and services, currently subject to market entry restrictions, could have their costs and prices reduced substantially. Second, the economies of scale not yet exploited by European industry are considerable. It is calculated that 'the aggregate saving from economies of scale would be equivalent to approximately 2% of GDP'. Third, there should be further gains in efficiency as a result of increased pressure of competition on overheads, labour deployment and efficient stock management. The study concludes that, for all sectors and for all types of cost savings, there should 'be economic gains of the order of 4·25% to 6·5% of GDP for the Community as a whole', though it does not say how these gains will be geographically distributed.[2]

The macro impact of Community integration is expected to show itself initially in downward pressures on prices and costs, with increases in production, following a modest time lag. 'After approximately five to six years, a cumulative impact of +4·5% in terms of GDP and of −6% in terms of price levels could be expected'. Taking account of increased economic integration, higher productivity and economic restructuring, 'the impact on employment should be positive, with a net gain of about two million jobs'. With a more active macro-economic policy, however, the medium-term gains could be as high as 7 per cent of GDP, with the number of additional jobs reaching 5 million, 'which corresponds to close to one third of Europeans currently seeking work'.[3]

Keynesianism

The central ideas of Keynesian economics were first set out by John Maynard Keynes (1936). As outlined above, Keynes focused on macro-economic behaviour rather than on micro-economic behaviour. He argued that the signals produced by market forces were sufficient for micro-economic activity to proceed smoothly only where aggregate demand was properly sustained. And the responsibility for this rested with government economic policy, not market forces alone. According to Donaldson (1986), 'at the heart of the Keynesian analysis is the proposition that the volume of employment in an economy depends on the amount of spending that is taking place'. As Keynes argued, the level of aggregate demand needed to buy the goods and services produced with full employment is not an automatic outcome. 'It is most unlikely that the actual level of national income and spending and the amount required for full employment will be identical.'[4]

It was shown earlier how equilibrium national income is reached when total leakages from the macro-economy equal total injections into it. This is where savings plus taxes plus imports equal investment plus government spending plus exports. In practice, however, there is no reason to expect planned savings to equal planned investment, or demand for imports to equal demand for exports. Further, with a balanced government budget, either rises or falls in national income result, depending on movements in other budgetary components. It was Keynes's achievement to show that a stable level of national income and of employment requires positive government intervention. Full employment, in other words, is not a natural outcome of the workings of an unregulated market mechanism. It can be achieved only by deliberate management of the macro-economy on the part of government.

Keynesian economic policy dominated politics in the UK, and most Western democratic countries, from 1945 till the mid-1970s, as the dominant academic orthodoxy. Using Keynesian economic analysis, and Keynesian economic management techniques, successive governments were in agreement that the prime economic policy objective was the achievement of a high and stable level of employment. It was to be accompanied by three other policy goals: price stability; economic growth; and a sound balance of payments position. The Keynesian approach aimed at controlling the level of aggregate demand in the economy by using appropriate fiscal and/or monetary demand management techniques.

According to Keynes, the reason why an unregulated economy is unlikely to achieve full employment is that the components of aggregate demand—consumption, investment and export spending—are determined by the unco-ordinated decisions of millions of largely independent households and firms. The probability is that they will not produce a level of aggregate demand enabling resources to be used at the full employment level but one which is either greater or less than that. With a deflationary gap, there is demand-deficient unemployment and, without government intervention, a shortfall in private-sector spending. With an inflationary gap, there is full employment and human resource shortages, with an excess of aggregate demand. For Keynes the solution was to increase spending in the economy when there was a deflationary gap and to reduce it when there was an inflationary gap.

The process of demand management requires the government authorities to estimate the productive capability of the economy and to assess the probable level of aggregate demand within it, without any government intervention. Where there is a deflationary gap, for example, the authorities have to determine what level of additional spending is required to achieve full employment. They adopt one or more approaches. First, they take measures to stimulate demand in the private sector for consumption, investment and exports. Second, they raise government spending to compensate for any deficiency in aggregate demand. Third, they 'pump prime' the economy, using extra government spending to do so. This is done in the expectation that it will induce the private sector to expand also. Where there is an inflationary gap, the authorities take contrary measures. This means deflating the economy by reducing the level of total spending or aggregate demand, even though this is likely to have deleterious effects on employment opportunities.

One set of Keynesian tools of economic management is fiscal policy. This is the use of taxation and government expenditure to regulate the aggregate level of activity in the economy. Where there is a deflationary gap, for example, with unemployed human and other resources, government uses changes in taxation to increase aggregate demand. It does this by cutting taxes on households and firms, hoping to induce them to increase their spending. Government can also stimulate spending by providing higher welfare benefits to households or investment grants to firms. Another way of injecting more spending power into the economy is by increasing public or government expenditure. This can be done by investing in new public works such as motorway construction, education and training, hospitals and housing.

Economic measures of this sort are financed by deficit financing, where government expenditure deliberately exceeds revenue. Such deficits are funded largely by government borrowing. Although this approach has been challenged by the so-called monetarists and 'new classical macro-economists' in recent years,

Keynesians argue that deficit financing stands a good chance of being self-financing. More important, if it succeeds in getting the economy moving again, then output, income and employment begin to rise. On the other hand, where there is an inflationary gap, government increases taxation, cuts back public spending and is able to pay off its debts if it chooses to do so.

The other set of Keynesian tools of economic management is monetary policy. This attempts to control the monetary system by operating on the level and structure of interest rates and the availability of credit, particularly bank advances and hire-purchase arrangements. With a deflationary gap, for example, interest rates are lowered and credit arrangements eased. This is to encourage households and firms to increase the consumption and investment components of aggregate demand. Conversely, with an inflationary gap, interest rates are raised and credit is tightened to choke off excess demand and overheating in the economy. The aim is to lower consumption and investment spending and to slow the economy down.

In practice, however, governments have had little success with either element of monetary policy. Neither consumers nor investors seem to take much account of the price of money or of credit in making their spending decisions. Consumers want their consumer durables at almost any cost, whilst business corporations appear to be more interested in the future prospects of the economy than in the cost of borrowing money for investment purposes. Overall, the use of monetary policy in the post-war years has disappointed its devotees. As Donaldson concludes, 'it turned out to be blunt, harshly discriminative and difficult to administer effectively' and was 'relegated to a minor role, subordinate to the other major [Keynesian] weapon of fiscal policy'.[5]

Keynesian demand management strategies dominated macro-economic policy in the 1950s, 1960s and the early 1970s and were used to manage the so-called trade cycle. This had manifested itself in the pre-war years, with periods of economic boom, followed by economic recession. The cycle would start with buoyant economic activity, such as expanding consumer spending, substantial investment, high employment and general prosperity. This was succeeded by falling consumer demand, slower investment and rising unemployment, deteriorating into slump and depressed business expectations. This, in turn, gave way to gradual recovery, leading ultimately to another boom and economic expansion. The main successes of Keynesian demand management techniques, with their countercyclical effects, were:

- Evening out the trade cycle.
- Maintaining steady economic growth.
- Keeping unemployment to relatively low levels during these years.

In this period, unemployment was never above 3 per cent of the work force and was normally substantially lower.

Despite the apparent successes of demand management techniques, some weaknesses in the Keynesian approach are evident. According to Donaldson, these are, first, 'the crudities of the fiscal and monetary techniques themselves, and of the economic forecasting on the basis of which they are used'. Given the intrinsic difficulties of economic forecasting in a mixed economy, it is not easy to achieve realistic stabilization policies. Second, not all unemployment is cyclical and caused by deficient aggregate demand. Some is structural and regional, and cannot be resolved by demand management policies. 'The important factor is that regional and technological unemployment can only be dealt with by "supply-side" measures.' These aim 'at matching the necessary quantities of capital with appropriate labour skills'. Third, Keynes was largely concerned with finding an economic remedy for mass unemployment. Yet governments using Keynesian techniques seek to achieve a number of policy goals. What was shown 'during these years is that they cannot all be simultaneously and consistently achieved by exclusive reliance on the broad macroeconomic measures of the Keynesian package'.[6]

Monetarism and New Classical Macro-economics

If the immediate post-war decades were the heyday of Keynesianism and demand management policies, then the period since the mid-1970s has witnessed the emergence of a sea change in the nature and course of economic policy. This is associated with the re-emergence of monetarism and supply-side economics as the dominant orthodoxies guiding government economic policy. Whilst Keynesianism was linked predominantly with social democratic governments and the Welfare State, monetarism and supply-side economics in the UK and the United States have been particularly associated with the 'New Right' in politics and the 'enterprise culture' of the 1980s. In outline, monetarism is a school of economic thought which argues that changes in the money stock are the principal cause of instability in the macro-economy. Linked with monetarism is new classical macro-economics. Neoclassicism purports to show the futility of Keynesian demand management in achieving economic stability, focusing instead on supply-side economics.

The origins of the monetarist and supply-side counter-revolution in economic policy emerged in the early 1970s. They derived from the growing concern of some politicians, business leaders and of the electorate over the combination of rising inflation and rising unemployment apparent at that time. 'The nightmare of stagflation—simultaneous sharply rising prices and unemployment—had arrived.' As Smith (1987) writes:

> For monetarists, and in particular British monetarists, the early 1970s were what the Great Depression had been for Keynes and his followers. Existing ideas about economic policy had been dealt a savage blow by actual events. The Keynesians could neither predict accurately what was going to happen, nor offer a convincing way out of the morass into which Western economies were sinking.[7]

It needed a combination of conditions to advance the cause of the 'new economics': an intellectual reassessment of economic theory; economic recession; and political opportunity. The intellectual revisionism came from commentators such as Friedman (1963 and 1970), economic recession followed the oil price shock of 1973–74 and the Conservative Party, which now contained a strong monetarist element, won the 1979 general election. As Smith concludes, 'Milton Friedman must be credited with the intellectual revolution of monetarism, but Margaret Thatcher was, more than anyone else, responsible for turning it into a potent political idea.'[8]

Monetarism rests on pre-Keynesian principles. The term is most commonly employed to describe the school of thought which contends that inflation results from excessive growth of the money supply. This being the case, monetarists argue that, to be effective, government policy needs to adhere to the 'fixed monetary growth rule'. This allows the money supply to grow at a constant rate approximately equal to the growth in economic output. Monetarists also argue that expanding aggregate demand in Keynesian fashion results, in the long run, in higher prices. Both monetarists and Keynesians are concerned with the level of demand for the economy's output but they differ over how the government should seek to influence it. They also disagree about the consequences of their different approaches. Monetarists contend that changes in the quantity of money are the only important sources of change in the level of national income. Keynesians, in contrast, attribute a large role to fiscal policy in determining the level of aggregate demand in the economy.

In its earliest form, monetarism was based on an elaborated version of the simple quantity of money theory. This states that in the long run changes in the money stock have minimal effect on the quantity of output or employment. The central propositions of monetarism as it emerged in the late 1960s were, first, that the demand for money function is more stable, and better defined statistically, than many of the components of aggregate demand. Second, the unique properties of money are emphasized, such as its role as a commodity which is substitutable for a wide range of other commodities and financial assets. As a result, monetary policy is seen as likely to have a direct impact on aggregate demand. This contrasts with Keynesian analysis, which emphasizes that the initial impact of monetary policy falls on financial assets, with only a weak and uncertain impact on aggregate demand.

One of the more important aspects of modern monetarism is its concern with the role that expectations play in economic decision-making. Expectations are now recognized to be of great importance in determining the path of prices and output. Rational expectations in particular have become associated with extreme monetarist views and suggest that individuals do not make systematic forecasting errors. On the contrary, their guesses about the future are often correct. If this is the case, the outlook for the efficacy of any macro stabilization policy is bleak. This is because households and firms learn to interpret economic events, with the result that they anticipate government action and take measures in advance to offset or evade it. The implication is that only unanticipated policy is likely to have any effect on real output, even in the short run. This contrasts with Keynesian policies, which make no allowance for private-sector anticipation of government action.

The revival of interest in monetarism since the 1970s has done much to clarify the issues separating monetarists from their critics. The chief area of disagreement concerns the principal source of instability in the economy. Monetarists argue that the private sector of the economy is basically stable and that fixed policy rules are necessary to insulate the economy from ill conceived and badly timed government actions. It is the latter, monetarists argue, which are the principal source of economic instability. Non-monetarists, on the other hand, claim that the principal source of economic instability is to be found in the private sector. This group emphasizes the instability of private investment decisions and generally supports an active government countercyclical policy to achieve macro-economic stability.

It can be appreciated that two important policy implications follow from monetarism. First, stimulating aggregate demand is harmful, since it results in serious inflation. Second, money supply is crucial to economic stability, and governments are expected to pursue a fixed level of money supply increase, departing from it only with great caution. In contrast with Keynesianism, monetarism implies three things: 'a less active fiscal and monetary policy, a greater concern with inflation than unemployment and a focus on the long rather than the short term'.[9] Monetarists thus disapprove of fine-tuning the macro-economy through the use of Keynesian policy instruments, including the adjustment of government or public spending. For monetarists, increased government spending involves two unacceptable measures: increasing the money supply and public-sector borrowing.

If sound money is the first major precept upon which monetarist analysis is based, two related principles follow. They are the need to reduce government borrowing and the need to reduce the overall level of public spending. Whilst sound money is supposed to keep inflation down, the two other policy goals are intended to make the economy more efficient by replacing public spending with private spending. Government borrowing is known as the public-sector borrowing requirement (PSBR). The PSBR is the amount by which the revenue of public-sector organizations falls short of expenditure. Expenditure includes spending on goods, gross capital formation, grants and interest on debt. The public-sector financial deficit plus any net financial lending gives the PSBR. The deficit is financed by the sale of securities to the non-bank private sector, borrowing from overseas, bank lending to the public sector and increases in currency. According to monetarist analysis, the effects of public-sector borrowing are likely to be inflationary where the financing takes the form of new currency in circulation, but not where genuine borrowing takes place from the non-bank private sector.

Reducing government borrowing and overall public spending is also favoured by monetarists on the ground that the requirements of the public sector otherwise 'crowd out' the private sector. Public-sector borrowing, it is argued, raises interest rates through increased sales of government bonds and so makes borrowing by the corporate sector more expensive. And this may have adverse effects on private investment. The argument supporting cuts in public-sector spending for its own sake, whether or not there is a public-sector deficit, is that if the State takes more of a national 'cake' fixed in size, less is available for private spending. This follows the thesis of Bacon and Eltis (1976) that the rise of State spending in the post-war period, and of public-sector employment, was the main cause of de-industrialization in the UK. Seen in this context, public-sector expenditure, whatever its form, is an undesirable intrusion of the State into the marketplace, which must be kept to a minimum. Indeed, according to Gamble (1988), 'New Right economists have endeavoured to show that market solutions would in every case be superior to the established public provision, and that there are very few goods which cannot be supplied through markets.'[10]

New classical macro-economics, whilst developing out of monetarism, essentially restates, in a more rigorous form, orthodox classical economics. This restatement rests on the notion of rational expectations combined with a natural rate of unemployment which emerges as a result of efficient clearing of the market. According to the classical economists, the prices of products are derived from the 'natural' rates of reward of the factors of production. The reward to land is determined by its scarcity and differential fertility, to labour by the long-run cost of subsistence of labour, while profit is residual. The natural rate of unemployment is that determined by the structural and frictional forces in the economy and cannot be reduced by raising aggregate demand. Any attempt to hold unemployment below its natural rate, it is argued, results in accelerating inflation. The natural rate of unemployment, in other words, is that level remaining when the economy is in equilibrium.

New classical economists, in rejecting the idea that economic growth is achieved by manipulating aggregate demand, see the solution to the problem of growth lying in two directions. First, inflation has to be squeezed out of the economy by monetary discipline. Second, the economy has then to be freed from obstacles inhibiting the efficient working of the market mechanism, showing that 'the gap between monetarists and supply siders is not vast'.[11] Supply-siders emphasize that the principal determinant of the growth rate is the allocation and efficient use of labour and capital in an economy. Accordingly, they focus on the impediments to the supply of and efficient use of the factors of production. Chief amongst these impediments are believed to be disincentives to work and invest. These are claimed to result from the level and structure of taxes, institutional restrictions and customary barriers to the efficient allocation of resources. The policy prescriptions following from the analysis typically take the form of lowering taxes and facilitating competition in labour and product markets.

Like monetarism, 'supply-side economics is a conservative economic doctrine which views capitalism as a natural economic form, deriving from the individualist nature of society'. Individualism is seen to be the central feature of human society, with capitalist economic activity allowing it to be manifested in its purest form. In capitalist free markets, it is believed, the creative element of capitalism is provided by entrepreneurs pursuing profit opportunities, based on expanded knowledge and innovation. Supply-side economics focuses on the level of taxes and their consequences for economic activity. Its advocates believe that individuals respond to one key incentive – the money return on their labour and efforts. According to King (1987), 'all individuals are considered to be calculating utility-maximisers'. This implies that 'they will work harder for higher pay and lower taxes; and the lower taxes are, the fewer will work in the black economy'.[12]

UK Economic Performance

There is no doubt that UK economic policy in the 1980s was
guided by what in modern times were novel monetarist and associated supply-side precepts. There is debate, however, about the
efficacy of these policies and the extent to which they were effective in reforming and developing the economy, its underlying
infrastructure, its market efficiency and its capacity for sustained
growth. Opinions are sharply divided and fall into two schools of
thought. On the one side, there are the apologists for the 'free
market-enterprise culture' approach of monetarist-supply side
economists. On the other, there are those who question its
claimed successes and challenge whether its free market, anti-
statist rhetoric was fully translated into economic reality.

Brooke (1989) asserts, for example, that 'few would dispute
that the British economy has now been transformed: although
inflation is still too high, our economic performance as a whole is
the envy of Europe'. Supply-side reforms have enabled 'the proper
functioning of markets, above all the labour market, . . . which
in turn [has] helped new jobs emerge and unemployment fall'.[13]
He is supported in this by Nigel Lawson (1989), the former Chancellor of the Exchequer, who argues that 'this dramatic change
has been achieved because . . . Government came to office in
1979 determined to pursue sound financial policies and restore
market forces'. Lawson claims that demand management leads to
spiralling inflation, the breakdown of market forces and endless
controls on business enterprise. In his view:

> The Government's more limited, but essential role, is to
> maintain sound financial policies leading to low inflation
> while at the same time freeing markets from distortions and
> regulations that prevent them from working properly. That
> our approach is right is shown by the results.[14]

Minford (1989) sees the economic changes instituted by Conservative governments during the 1980s as 'no less than a
revolution . . . on three main fronts of economic policy: counter-
inflation, productive efficiency, and the market-based cure of
unemployment'. For Minford the success of the 'policy of monetarist gradualism' in the 1980s is demonstrated by the fall in
inflation, the shake-out of overmanned industry, the resurgence

of manufacturing growth, with 'the growth rate of the economy and of personal real incomes tell[ing] the same story in a more immediate way for the ordinary person'. Employers 'had their management power of hiring and firing essentially returned to them', whilst contracting out spread efficiency into the local authority sector too.[15]

Some leaders of the business community have also praised the economic policy initiatives of the 1980s. Lord Forte is on record as saying, for example, that 'the change achieved over the Government's decade in office has been dramatic'. In his view this is demonstrated by the fact that 'thanks to the strength of the public finances, the country is actually repaying debt', there 'is more employment, average wages are up, taxation is down, restrictions have been lifted' and the whole country has benefited from the prosperity of these years. Furthermore, investment since 1980 has 'grown more than six times faster than the Common Market average', whilst 'an impressive stock of investment overseas by UK companies has increased sevenfold during the eighties and now yields substantial earnings'.[16]

Critics of monetarism, on the other hand, such as Holmes (1985), 'conclude that the monetarist experiment failed to control the money supply and public spending', whilst inflation was brought down only 'by a monumental recession which occurred almost by accident through the exchange rate'.[17] Smith's (1987) diagnosis is that by the end of 1981 'Britain's monetarist experiment appeared to have been an unmitigated disaster. Inflation, at nearly 12 per cent, was higher than when [the government] took office . . . [and] unemployment rose by three-quarters of a million in 1981 alone'. It was the January 1985 sterling crisis which 'marked the changeover point from pragmatic monetarism to pragmatism'. Shortly afterwards, he claims, monetarism was to all intents and purpose dead. This was because the government's measure of money — 'sterling M3' — which was 'the symbol, . . . of the British monetarist experiment, had disgraced itself'. Further, whilst the government had aimed initially to achieve absolute cuts in real public spending, 'this gave way to the more modest ambition of holding spending constant in real terms'.[18]

King (1987) also argues that government did not reduce the aggregate size of the public sector in the 1980s. 'As a percentage of GNP, total public expenditure has grown every year since

1979.' What happened, according to King, is that there were significant shifts in the composition of public expenditure. Spending on housing fell, whilst expenditure on law and order increased. The government even failed to reduce the share of the public sector consumed by education, health, social security and social services. The outcome was that the rate of growth in public expenditure was not controlled. 'However, the priorities of public spending have altered—clearly challenging some of the major post-war consensus priorities . . . and placing a new emphasis upon law and order expenditure.'[19]

Similar critiques of monetarist-supply side economic policies are provided by MacInnes (1987) and Gamble (1988). MacInnes claims, for instance, that government economic policy in the 1980s 'gave a further powerful twist to the process of the decline of the British economy and society in the name of doing precisely the opposite'.[20] Gamble's litany of governmental policy errors and omissions include: monetary targeting proved impractical and was abandoned; economic management remained discretionary and interventionist; the overall size of the public sector had not been reduced by 1987; failure to cut public spending meant Treasury reliance on privatization revenue to finance public sector programmes; and no strategic priority was given to maintaining a strong manufacturing sector. Indeed, the opening up of the UK economy resulted in domestic manufacturing contracting, 'while the financial businesses of the City boomed as did many leading industrial companies whose operations were now international'.[21]

From the evidence outlined above, it is clear that the cases for and against monetarist-supply side economic policies are controversial and contentious. This is not the place to evaluate the debate, only to describe and identify the main elements in it. The most useful way to conclude the discussion here, though academic and policy debate will continue for years to come as more research evidence becomes available, is by reference to one of the leading independent economic surveys. A useful one for the purpose is that produced by Barclays Bank. It presents some of the principal macro-economic indicators of the 1980s and its summary contents are provided in table 28.

Barclays' economic reviews indicate that the UK growth rate in the early and mid-1980s increased by just under 3 per cent per year, rising to almost 5 per cent per year in 1987 and 1988, but fell

Table 28
Key UK economic statistics, 1982–90

Year average	1982–86 average	1987 out-turn	1988 out-turn	1989 forecast	1990 forecast
% change over previous year					
GDP (output measure)	2·9	4·8	4·5	2·5	2·5
Consumers' expenditure	3·3	5·3	6·4	2·7	1·1
Government consumption	1·1	1·1	0·5	0·5	1·1
Fixed investment	4·9	8·0	12·2	7·1	3·9
Export volumes (goods and services)	3·9	5·4	−1·1	5·8	6·3
Import volumes (goods and services)	6·0	7·4	12·0	6·7	2·2
Average earnings	8·1	7·8	8·8	9·3	8·3
Real personal disposable income	2·0	3·4	4·7	4·0	3·0
Retail prices	5·5	4·1	4·9	7·7	5·5
Levels					
Unemployment (million adults)	2·88	2·82	2·29	1·80	1·85
Current account (£ billion)	2·7	−2·9	−14·9	−16·3	−11·7
Sterling exchange rate index (1985=100)	102·2	90·1	95·5	94·0	94·0
Dollar/sterling	1·47	1·64	1·78	1·67	1·75
Deutschmark/sterling	3·77	2·94	3·12	3·14	3·10
PSBR (£ billion)	7·6	−3·5	−14·4	−16·0	−13·0
Interest rates (%)	11·1	9·7	10·3	14·0	N/A

Source: Barclays Bank, *Economic review*, August 1989.

back to 2·5 per cent per year in 1989 and 1990. Fixed investment averaged an increase of some 5 per cent per year in the period 1982–86, rising steadily to an increase of over 12 per cent for 1988. By 1990, however, the annual rate of change in investment spending was projected to fall to under 4 per cent. To put the early 1980s into context, it needs to be recalled that there was a fall in manufacturing output of 17 per cent between 1979 and 1981, whilst gross domestic product fell by 4·5 per cent over the same period.[22]

The annual rate of change in consumption spending rose steadily throughout the 1980s, only to fall away dramatically in 1989 and 1990, after peak years in 1987 and 1988. This steady rise in the annual rate of consumption spending for most of the 1980s is reflected in annual rates of change in average earnings and in real disposable incomes. The annual rate of change in average earnings was about 8 per cent for most of these years, rising to about 9 per cent in 1988–89. The annual rate of change in real disposable income was about 2 per cent in the early 1980s, then rose to some 4 per cent in the last years of the decade. Recorded unemployment, in contrast, did not fall below the 2 million mark until 1989, with a forecast increase for 1990.

The annual rate of change in government spending remained fairly constant throughout the period, varying between the limits of 0·5 to 1 per cent per year. The PSBR, in contrast, averaged some £7·6 billion in the years 1982–86 but was being repaid at a rate of some £14 billion per year in the late 1980s. The annual rate of change in imports rose from an average of 6 per cent in the period 1982–86 but had doubled to a 12 per cent annual increase in 1988, with a projected fall to a 2 per cent change for 1990. The annual rate of change in export sales over the decade was less dramatic at about 5 per cent per year, except in 1988, when exports of goods and services fell by some 1 per cent over the previous year. These developments were reflected in the steadily deteriorating balance of payments on current account, from a positive annual balance averaging about £3 billion in the early 1980s to a £16 billion deficit in 1989. At the same time, the sterling exchange rate index, which stood at 100 in 1985, had fallen to 94 by 1989–90.

Finally, the annual rate of increase in retail prices between 1982 and 1986 averaged 5·5 per cent, was 4·9 per cent in 1987 and was projected to rise to 7·7 per cent in 1989 and 5·5 per cent in 1990. Throughout the 1980s UK interest rates were on average continually in double digits, except in 1987, when they averaged 9·7 per cent. In 1988 they rose again, reaching a peak of 14 per cent in 1989.

The Implications for Management

The working of the macro-economy is complex and even today not fully explained by the most advanced economic theory. Nevertheless, changes and developments in the national and international economy have a significant impact on business corporations, public corporations and public service organizations. It is one of managements' tasks to plan for, and respond to, macro-economic changes and their likely effect on the organizations they manage.

Projected growth in GNP, for example, is the starting point of any business forecasting. The direction and projected rate of growth in aggregate demand and national output indicate likely demand for corporate products or services. They also have implications for employer and managerial demands for human resource skills and abilities. Too rapid a rate of growth in GNP can result in skill and labour shortages in the short term, with pressures on management to raise wages, since extra people tend to lag behind extra sales. On the other hand, where growth is sluggish, with national output falling, organizations find that they are using less of their capacity, thus finding it more difficult to maintain productivity and to keep labour costs down. This in turn affects corporate competitiveness and the ability to maintain market position.

The components of GNP growth are important when examining the possible effects on product and labour market demand. Strong consumer spending is good for producers of consumer commodities, retail outlets and service-related industries selling direct to final consumers, with weak consumer spending having the opposite effect. Investment spending trends are particularly important in those industries producing and selling capital goods in the domestic market. With interest rates falling, rises in capital expenditure can be expected, but with interest rates rising, falls in investment spending are likely to result. Changes in government spending affect not only the supply of public services but also demand for those human resources and intermediate goods used in servicing public-sector and welfare organizations. Any cutbacks in public-sector spending, then, can result in lower demand for private-sector goods, services and resources.

The balance between the domestic and overseas components of national income is important in considering the prospects for UK companies. Where there is falling domestic demand for UK products, they can offset it by going for higher exports. Rising domestic demand, however, can divert selling from hard overseas markets to soft domestic ones. On the other hand, where domestic demand is unsatisfied by home production it is likely to suck in imports, with implications for the balance of trade. The balance of trade is not important on its own account but because of its consequences for interest rates, exchange rates and inflation. All these variables are interconnected and each one has differential importance for individual firms and different parts of the economy.

Capital-intensive industries tend to borrow more heavily than other sectors and so are considerably influenced by interest rates and their movements. But the relative proportion of debt capital to equity capital in a company is no indication of the impact of high interest rates on it, since one company may have raised its debt at a low rate of interest, whilst another may have to cope with a much higher rate of interest. High interest rates help to attract foreign money into the economy, which is needed to finance any current account deficit, but they also push up the exchange rate. This, in turn, worsens the balance of trade by making exports dearer and imports cheaper. Again this is not in the interest of companies with overseas subsidiaries, whose earnings are devalued by a rising pound.

On the other hand, if the pound begins to fall, as it does when interest rates come down, or overseas investors become worried about the state of the UK economy, this threatens to add to inflation by pushing import prices up. This is not the only influence on inflation, since as UK demand falls firms use less of their total capacity, unless lower home sales can be offset entirely by exports. As domestic economic activity winds down it becomes more difficult for domestic producers to increase productivity. Also, as output falls it is more difficult to keep unit labour costs down.

This, combined with greater pressure for higher domestic wages, leads to cost-push inflation.

Inflation does not affect all companies equally. Some can pass on their cost increases to their customers in higher prices, thus enabling corporate profit margins to be maintained, even if it is not beneficial for the economy at large. In these circumstances, firms with heavy working capital, such as stocks of material and finished products, have to use some of their profit to keep going at their current level of activity. Others with low working capital do much better.

This chapter has outlined the complex theories seeking to explain the working of the macro-economy. To some managers these theories may seem remote and unrelated to the everyday problems facing them as corporate decision-takers and business executives. At the minimum, however, managers need to be aware of changes in the macro-economy, and in the components of national income, and how these are likely to affect their organization's business plans and operational activities in the short and medium term. They also need to appreciate how different government fiscal and monetary policies can affect business in terms of tax liabilities, profitability, product markets and the raising of finance capital. Where business enterprises are operating in overseas markets, or are substantial importers of raw materials or other foreign-made commodities, their managements must have regard to the likely effects of changes in the terms of trade and in exchange rates on business prospects and corporate activities. Finally, with the moves towards European economic integration and a single European market, some larger companies in the private sector are setting up their own research departments, and task forces, to examine further transnational investments and international marketing strategies.

References

1 COMMISSION OF THE EUROPEAN COMMUNITIES. *European file: the big European market – trump card for the economy and employment.* London, August, 1988. p 4.
2 *ibid*. p 7.
3 *ibid*. p 8.

4 DONALDSON P. *Economics of the real world*. Harmondsworth, Penguin, 1986. p 35.
5 *ibid*. p 51.
6 *ibid*. pp 56–62.
7 SMITH D. *The rise and fall of monetarism*. Harmondsworth, Penguin, 1987. p 45.
8 *ibid*. p 72.
9 KING D S. *The new right*. Basingstoke, Macmillan, 1987. p 67.
10 GAMBLE A. *The free economy and the strong state*. Basingstoke, Macmillan, 1988. p 49.
11 *ibid*. p 46.
12 KING. *op cit*. p 142.
13 BROOKE P. 'The conservative revolution' in CONSERVATIVE PARTY. *The first ten years*. London, CPC, 1989. p 38.
14 LAWSON N. 'We're growing to win the league' in *ibid*. p 42.
15 MINFORD P. 'Keeping faith with the future' in *ibid*. pp 56–61.
16 FORTE Lord. 'The lady at No. 10 means business' in *ibid*. p 64f.
17 HOLMES P. 'The Thatcher government's overall economic performance' in BELL D (ed). *The Conservative government 1979–84*. London, Croom Helm, 1985. p 32.
18 SMITH. *op cit*. pp 104, 123 and 128.
19 KING. *op cit*. pp 120–23.
20 MACINNES J. *Thatcherism at work*. Milton Keynes, Open University Press, 1987. p 168.
21 GAMBLE. *op cit*. pp 121–26.
22 MACINNES. *op cit*. p 65.

7

Politics and Power

For many people, the term 'politics' denotes activity about which they 'feel a combination of cynicism, scepticism and mistrust. It is experienced as something distant and remote from everyday life.'[1] This is somewhat surprising, because politics is about power—power being the ability of individuals, groups or organized interests to influence or ultimately enforce changes of behaviour in others. All activity involving humans collectively is potentially political, since politics starts whenever there are disagreements or conflicts of interest amongst people over resourses, decisions or ideas. The purpose of any political solution is to resolve or accommodate the conflict between competing parties, wherever it arises, in order to achieve political stability and social peace. Contrary to much popular opinion, politics is not the cause of human conflicts, it merely reflects differences of interest between individuals, organized groups and nation States. If political disputes are not settled peaceably between those involved, social disorder or even physical violence can result. It is through the machinery and process of politics that such conflicts are identified and channelled in order to contain them and settle them peacefully, if only temporarily.

If politics is about power, it is also about the forces influencing and reflecting the distribution of power, as well as the effect of power on the use of society's resources and their allocation. Indeed, politics is ultimately about 'the "transformative" capacity of social agents, agencies and institutions: it is not about Government or government alone'.[2] Crick (1964) calls this macro-politics, and he defines it as the activity by which differing interests within a 'unit of rule are conciliated by giving them a share in power'. It is 'a way of ruling divided societies without undue violence— and most societies are divided, though some think that this is the very trouble'.[3] But politics also takes place at other levels—for example, in families, social clubs, trade unions, management,

173

work organizations and between nations. These are called micro-politics and international relations respectively.

Liberal Democracy

There are various ways of classifying political systems. They include autocratic, totalitarian, socialist and democratic ones. According to Ball (1983), in autocratic political systems important limitations are placed on open political competition, coercion is used to enforce obedience, there is weak support for civil liberties and little judicial independence. The basis of rule is either traditional or military elites. Totalitarian political systems are characterized by:

- Official ideologies.
- A single party, often with a dominant leader.
- The use of terror to enforce political obedience.
- Governmental monopoly of communications.
- Central direction of the economy.

In socialist political systems there is also an official ideology, usually a single political party and central economic planning of the economy.[4] But terror is not now used as a normal instrument of State policy. Some socialist political systems are also moving towards multi-party politics and some market-based economic decision-making. This means that the political authorities in such States are no longer seeking blind political obedience from their citizens but genuine legitimacy and popular support.

The political systems of Western capitalist countries are typically liberal democracies. The term is difficult to define with precision, since variants of liberal democracy exist. In essence, 'liberal democracy is a system of representative government by majority rule in which some individual rights are none the less protected from interference by the state and cannot be restricted even by an electoral majority'.[5] A central problem in any liberal democratic society, like that of the UK, is how to reconcile the economic liberties associated with freedom of contract and free market exchange, clearly based on overt inequalities amongst people, with individual political and social rights, embodied in the law, which are based on some degree of equal citizenship amongst them.

The ideas underpinning modern liberal democracy derive partly from those of 'classical liberalism' and partly from the concepts of democracy and equality before the law stemming from the American and French revolutions at the end of the eighteenth century. Classical liberalism emerged from two main intellectual sources: political theories of civil society and of a social contract, and economic theories of market capitalism. This is why liberal democracy is rooted in capitalist social relations and why liberal democratic institutions have to date developed only in capitalist market economies.

The political theories of classical liberalism originate from the writings of Hobbes in 1651 (1946) and Locke in 1690 (1947), who were social contract theorists. Although their theories of human nature differ substantially, as do their analyses of political authority, both concur that the lawful State is instrumental to social peace, economic prosperity and greater human welfare. Hobbes's view of humankind is pessimistic and based on fear, whilst that of Locke is optimistic and rationalist. For Hobbes the state of nature is one in which people are selfish, aggressive and acquisitive, and life is nasty, brutish and short. In this war of each against the other, the strongest rule and might is right. To overcome this condition of social anarchy, people contract to surrender their right to govern themselves by giving power to the sovereign body within the State. For Hobbes it is absolute government which is the necessary condition for creating law and order in society, with political obligation by the citizenry being unconditional—except in defending one's own life. Hobbes, in short, is the apologist of the absolute State, but one based on a social contract.

Locke, in contrast, believed humankind to be rational, moral and social. In his view, individuals are born free, with certain fundamental human rights such as personal autonomy, freedom from tyranny and ownership of property. For him, the state of nature is one of relative peace and harmony, where everyone is responsible for enforcing the moral law themselves. In entering into a social contract with one another in society, and handing over the right to make and enforce civil law to the State, citizens consent to being ruled by a limited, neutral government. It is the role of government, under the Lockeian social contract, to uphold and extend individual and personal freedoms, including the right of 'life, liberty and estate'. Political obligation under this social contract depends upon government providing the political conditions for protecting property, defending individual freedoms and enforcing legal contracts.

The economic theories of market capitalism are associated with the writings of the classical economists, starting with Adam Smith (1776, pub. 1976), whose contributions to economic theory continued until the late nineteenth century. Classical economic theory is based on the assumption that individuals are the best judge of their own economic interests. It holds that individual pursuit of economic self-interest, in a freely competitive market economy, results in aggregate economic benefit to the community. For the classical economists it is market capitalism, where the 'invisible hand' of market forces co-ordinates the diverse activities of producers and consumers through the price mechanism, which ensures the most efficient use of scarce resources. And this takes place without the need for any governmental bureaucracy to intervene and manage the economy.

Neither Hobbes nor Locke was a democrat, whilst the market liberals like Smith and his successors were political economists, not political theorists. As political economists they emphasized the virtues of free economic markets and of possessive individualism. Like the economic liberals, the political liberals focused on individualism as the motivating force behind human action. If humankind is rational, moral, born free and equal, and endowed with certain natural rights, it was argued, then human beings were the best judge of their own political interests. However, only in an ordered society can individuals exercise their human rights and develop their full potential. Logically, people should govern themselves, but this is not possible in modern societies.

It fell to the political democrats such as Rousseau, (1776, pub. 1972) the American federalists, Paine (1791, pub. 1984) and John Stuart Mill (1851, pub. 1972) to provide the democratic and egalitarian ideas embodied in modern liberal democracy. Since direct personal involvement is not possible in the large modern State, citizens delegate the power to govern themselves democratically. In this way, political democracy becomes, as Abraham Lincoln once described it, 'government of the people, by the people, for the people'. Political sovereignty remains with the people, who participate in choosing the government. The government is then representative of and responsive to the wishes of the people, with political obligation conditional upon government meeting popular needs.

By the mid-nineteenth century the fundamental principles and tenets of liberal democracy had been established in both the political and the economic spheres, even though they were neither applied nor practised universally. They included such ideas as:

- Free market economics and the invisible hand of market forces.
- Popular sovereignty, with ultimate power resting with the people.
- Basic human freedoms such as freedom of speech, of association and of holding property.
- Political equality before the law.

Other underlying tenets of liberal democracy established by this time included:

- The principle of majority rule, with the need to protect minority interests from abuse of power.
- The principle of government as trustee of delegated power from the people it represents.

Additionally, if the ends of liberal democracy were to provide legitimate government for its citizens, then it was also to be the means of facilitating civic progress and of civilizing society.

Modern liberal democracy, then, has emerged in Western capitalist countries out of the ideas associated with social contract theory, market capitalism and representative democracy. In its modern form, liberal democracy in countries like the UK is characterized by a number of distinctive features:

- Liberal democracies are based on inter-party politics, where more than one political party competes for power.
- Competition for political power is open, with accepted and established procedures for political debate and the seeking of power.

- Recruitment to positions of political power is relatively open.
- They are representative democracies, with periodic elections of political representatives, based on universal suffrage.
- Pressure groups outside government can influence government policy.
- Individuals have certain political freedoms, such as freedom of speech and freedom from arbitrary arrest by the authorities. These individual freedoms are recognized and protected by an independent judiciary, which is able to protect citizens against the abuse of political power by government.
- To facilitate freedom of speech and ideas, the mass media are free to criticize government and its policies.

Above all, liberal democratic States have governments with limited rather than absolute powers. Governments are circumscribed constitutionally in what they can do and in the ways in which they exercise their political authority. Also, within the liberal democratic framework, there are private non-political areas of social and economic life in which the State does not intervene. Finally, the liberal democratic State seeks actively to protect minority rights and interests by law and legal convention.

The Machinery of Government

Figure 8 provides a basic model of the UK political system. It is a systems model, drawing on the work of David Easton, an American student of politics. It provides a useful framework for identifying and analyzing the 'inputs', 'processes' and 'outputs' of the political system. The inputs are the political system's demands and supports. Its demands are what individuals and groups want the political system to achieve, whilst its supports are the resources required to achieve them. The political process begins with individual activity. This is influenced by public opinion and the mass media and, to be effective, is channelled into collective activity through political parties, pressure groups and elections as political demands and supports. These demands and supports are fed into the process or machinery of government, where some are accepted, others are accepted in part and the rest are rejected.

179

Figure 8 A basic model of the UK political system

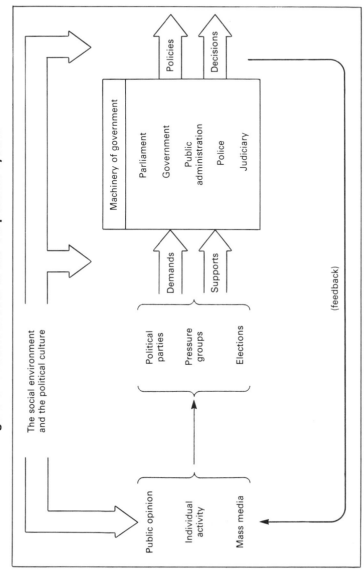

Source. D. Farnham and M. McVicar, *Public administration in the United Kingdom*, London, Cassell, 1982

The policies and decisions of the machinery of government are the outputs of the political system. They feedback into it, helping to generate further demands and supports by individuals and organized groups.

Since many of the demands of the political system are incompatible with one another, thus reflecting the inevitable social and political conflicts in society, liberal democracies have constitutional machinery aiming to manage these conflicts. The elements of the machinery of government are readily distinguishable, although their functions overlap. The elements are, first, a legislature, consisting of the monarch in Parliament, the House of Commons and the House of Lords. Second, there is a governmental executive which consists of the Cabinet and other Ministers of the Crown, led by the Prime Minister. Third, government departments, public corporations, non-departmental agencies and local authorities provide an administrative system. Fourth, there is a judiciary, largely independent of the legislature and executive, which interprets and applies parliamentary statute and common law.

Parliament

Parliament is the supreme legislative authority. In practice, however, it operates within a pluralist political system which incorporates external pressure groups and an organized opposition, both within and outside Parliament, seeking to influence policy decisions. Each element of Parliament—Commons, Lords and the monarch in Parliament—is outwardly separate and is based on different constitutional principles. Although both Houses meet at Westminster, they do so separately and come together only on ceremonial occasions such as the state opening of Parliament.

Parliament has four main functions. First, it establishes the laws of the State by enacting parliamentary statutes. These regulate those aspects of political, economic and social life regarded as being within the sphere of government. Second, it provides, through voting taxation and public funds, the means of carrying out government policy decisions. Third, it holds the government and public administration accountable for their actions by scrutinizing their activities through a number of parliamentary devices. These include asking parliamentary questions, arranging parliamentary debates and setting up select committees. Fourth, Parliament acts as a channel of representation through which the electorate's views and wishes can be communicated to the government through Members of Parliament, Ministers and political lobbying.

A Parliament sits for up to five years, though in practice it is normally dissolved before the five-year period elapses. Every Parliament has a number of sessions, each of which begins in October or November and continues, with adjournments, until the summer recess, beginning in July or August. The Commons sits for about 175 days per session, which is longer than any other legislative assembly, and the Lords for about 140 days. At the end of each session, Parliament is temporarily suspended, or prorogued. At the end of the life of a Parliament the monarch orders its dissolution by a royal proclamation, on the advice of the Prime Minister. The proclamation orders the issuing of writs for a general election and announces the date on which the new Parliament is to assemble.

Within Parliament the Commons is the dominant chamber. It is a representative assembly elected by universal adult suffrage. For electoral purposes the UK is divided into 650 electoral constituencies, each of which returns one MP to the House of Commons. At the 1987 general election there were 523 contestable parliamentary seats in England, thirty-eight in Wales, seventy-two in Scotland and seventeen in Northern Ireland. Election to the Commons is by secret ballot. All British subjects and citizens of the Irish Republic resident in the UK are entitled to vote, provided they are over eighteen, registered electors, not legally barred from voting and not 'Peers of the Realm'. Similarly, most British subjects are eligible to stand for election to the House of Commons, unless they are undischarged bankrupts or certain categories of clergy. Judges, civil servants, some local government officers, members of the armed forces and the police service, and members of the boards of public corporations may stand only if they resign their post.

The party system is central to the role of Parliament. At every general election, or by-election, the parties lay their policies before the electorate in their manifestoes and put up candidates for election. The candidate who polls the greatest number of votes in each constituency, not necessarily with an absolute majority of votes, is elected. It is the party with the majority of seats in the House of Commons after a general election which normally forms the government, even if it has not obtained a majority of the votes cast nationally. The distribution of seats by political party after the 1987 general election is shown in table 29.

Table 29

Distribution of seats in the House of Commons and percentage vote cast, by political party, 1987

Party	No. of seats	% of vote cast[a]
Conservative	376	42·3
Labour	229	30·8
Liberal and Social Democratic Alliance	22	22·6
Nationalists (Scotland and Wales)	6	1·7
Others (Northern Ireland)	17	2·6
Total	650	100·0

Note
a The electoral turnout was 75·3 per cent of the eligible electorate.
Source: D. Butler and D. Kavanagh, *The British general election of 1987*, Basingstoke, Macmillan, 1988.

By convention the leader of the majority party in the House of Commons is appointed Prime Minister by the monarch, with some 100 members from both Houses, but largely from the Commons, being appointed Ministers of the Crown on the advice of the Prime Minister. In both Houses, in government and opposition parties alike, control is maintained by the whips. Their task is to keep MPs and peers in touch with party business, to maintain party voting strength and to inform the party leadership of back-bench opinion.

The impact of the party system on the Commons makes the formal theoretical model of a supreme legislative assembly in the parliamentary system unrealistic. The Commons has all the potential powers implied in the formal model. It can use its legislative powers, hold government and administration accountable and act as the sovereign legislative body, but the exercise of these powers depends on the party composition of the House. This is because the Commons is divided on party lines, and the forces keeping the parliamentary parties apart are stronger than those drawing them together. The Commons therefore does not act as a central body able and willing to limit and control the power of the executive. When the government has a clear majority in the House, as in recent years, the opposition—especially when it is divided—is practically reduced to ineffectiveness.

The key relationship is between the Cabinet and the majority party in the Commons. Majority-party MPs are under great pressure to support the government, even where they disagree with some of its policy proposals. In most cases they support government policies anyway, since they have fought hard to secure the election of the government to office. Those having doubts are normally reluctant to criticize the government publicly, since it might harm the party's standing in the country generally. It might even cause them difficulties with local party activists. Few majority-party MPs press their differences with the government as far as voting against it on important issues. Also, party discipline in the Commons is very strict. Therefore, unless a substantial number of majority-party MPs are prepared to challenge their government, the legislature occupies a position subordinate to that of the executive. Whilst not necessarily ignoring its backbenchers' views, the government is the dominant force in the relationship between Ministers and majority-party MPs. Nevertheless, it is wrong to suggest that MPs have no influence in Parliament. Their work on specialist scrutiny committees in the House of Commons is important, when there is some cross-party agreement. MPs also play an important role in standing committees by improving and amending parliamentary Bills.

Under the Parliament Acts, 1911 and 1949, the formal powers of the House of Lords are strictly limited, especially regarding the passing of legislation. It has no power to veto or delay money Bills, though it can impose a temporary veto of one year on other Bills. It also has the right to amend Bills, subject to closure or shortened debate in the Commons. Although the majority of parliamentary Bills originate in the Commons, governments sometimes raise uncontroversial Bills in the House of Lords first, before proceeding with them to the Commons. The significance of the Lords is as a parliamentary long stop and as a revising chamber. This is important, given that most legislation is passed by the Commons without discussion of more than half the clauses in each Bill. The most striking feature of the Lords is that its members are unelected. They consist of 'lords spiritual', who are the leading archbishops and bishops of the Church of England, and over 1,000 temporal peers. The temporal peers consist mainly of hereditary peerages passed on within families from generation to generation. There are also a few hundred life peerages that are non-hereditary. Although the House of Lords has a large membership, relatively few peers attend its sittings; only about 250 of them take an active part and they tend to be the life peers.

Government

The government consists of approximately 100 Ministers appointed to executive positions in the Cabinet or in junior positions. It is the Prime Minister who provides the individual leadership of the government, and of the majority party in the House of Commons, whilst it is the Cabinet which provides the collective leadership. Most Cabinet Ministers are heads of major government departments with the title Secretary of State. Others hold office without departmental duties and are 'Ministers without portfolio'. The size of the Cabinet varies and is determined by practical and political considerations but normally it has around twenty members. Certain office holders such as the law officers of the Crown, including the Attorney General and the Scottish counterpart, are not members of the Cabinet. But they do attend Cabinet meetings for particular issues. Similarly, other Ministers without departmental duties serve on Cabinet committees, have access to Cabinet papers and attend Cabinet meetings when asked to do so.

The main function of the Cabinet is to take decisions on government policy and on matters to be submitted to Parliament, especially issues relating to public expenditure. It also traditionally oversees and co-ordinates government administration and arbitrates between Ministers or departments failing to agree between themselves. The Cabinet undertakes these duties through a system of Cabinet committees, assisted by the Cabinet Office. Full knowledge of the Cabinet committee system is confidential but the Cabinet would clearly not be able to fulfil its wide-ranging tasks without the complex committee structure. One purpose of Cabinet committees is to co-ordinate decisions between those different departments of state which are concerned with common policy issues.

As long as Ministers hold office they share the collective

responsibility of all Ministers. This requires them neither to criticize nor to dissociate themselves publicly from government policy decisions. Dissenting Ministers may, however, request that their views are recorded in the private minutes of Cabinet. They are also expected to support the government by voting for its policies in the Commons. Only when Ministers resign because of policy disagreements in the Cabinet are they permitted to explain openly their reasons. Collective responsibility reinforces the principle of the indivisibility of the executive and serves a number of political purposes:

- It reinforces party unity in Parliament and strengthens the party in power against opposition.
- It helps to maintain government control over legislation and public spending.
- It minimizes public disagreements amongst departments, such as between the Treasury and the spending departments.
- It helps maintain the authority of the Prime Minister.
- It reinforces the secrecy of government and cabinet decision making.

The role of the Prime Minister, like that of the Cabinet, has evolved by political practice and constitutional convention since the eighteenth century. Today the office of Prime Minister, which is customarily linked with that of First Lord of the Treasury, is of central importance in the system of government. Constitutionally, as leader of the majority party in the House of Commons, the Prime Minister is appointed by the monarch. Consequently the Prime Minister needs to have a firm hold over party loyalty inside and outside Parliament and command of the Commons. The real power of the office derives from the dominant influence the Prime Minister exercises over and in the Cabinet. As Benn (1980) writes, 'The premiership in Britain today is, in effect, an elected monarchy. No medieval monarch in the whole of British history ever had such power as every modern British Prime Minister has in his or her hands.'[6]

It is the Prime Minister who effectively makes all the appointments to ministerial office, since Crown Ministers are appointed by the monarch on the recommendation of the Prime Minister.

The Prime Minister may ask Ministers to resign, may recommend the monarch to dismiss them and may reallocate Cabinet posts. Orders of precedence are determined by the Prime Minister. By presiding over Cabinet meetings the Prime Minister is able to control Cabinet discussions and decision-taking within it. Although the Cabinet secretariat services the whole Cabinet, it has a special relationship and allegiance to the Prime Minister. It is the Prime Minister too who effectively controls the machinery of central government. This is facilitated by having the power to approve senior appointments and by deciding how the tasks and duties of government are to be allocated and distributed amongst different departments. In this way the Prime Minister can determine which departments are to be abolished, amalgamated or created. Above all, the Prime Minister has the constitutional right to recommend to the monarch that Parliament should be dissolved and a general election held.

Compared with other Ministers, the Prime Minister has far more opportunity to present and defend the government's policies to Parliament and the public, including control over what information and communications go to the press and other media about Cabinet business and government affairs generally. The Prime Minister may also take certain political decisions, or authorize them to be taken, without waiting for a full Cabinet meeting to take place. When a Cabinet committee is looking at a particular policy problem, the Prime Minister may take the chair personally and report back on the action taken to a later Cabinet meeting. Such developments as these led Crossman (1963) to conclude that:

> The post-war epoch has seen the final transformation of Cabinet Government into Prime Ministerial Government . . . [the Prime Minister's] powers have steadily increased, first, by the centralization of the party machine under his (*sic*) personal rule, and secondly by the growth of a centralized bureaucracy.[7]

Local government

In liberal democratic theory a strong case is made out for local government. John Stuart Mill, for example, argued that local democratic self-government is fundamental to any national democratic system. It is a means of political education, popular participation and training future national political leaders. In addition, it acts as a counterweight to central government, diffuses political power and accommodates local and minority interests, thus ensuring that government is responsive to popular demands. Local government is also justified on administrative grounds as the best means of providing public services at local level. Different communities have different needs, and a system of local elected bodies, it is argued, enables those needs to be identified and prioritized locally. Traditionally, therefore, local government has a dual role. First, it exercises a political function by managing conflicts arising out of the provision of public goods and services. Second, it has an administrative function of providing public services locally.

In the UK, local government consists of local authorities, with different systems in England and Wales, Scotland and Northern Ireland. Local authorities, which are elected bodies, are multipurpose organizations providing a range of local public services over defined geographical areas. They have the following characteristics:

- A distinct legal status.
- A degree of autonomy and decision-making power.
- Tax-raising powers.

Local authorities are subordinate governmental bodies and are entirely creatures of statute. Parliament enacts legislation determining the structure of local government, its powers and functions and its sources of finance. Unlike local government in other liberal democracies, there is no constitutional protection for local government in the UK. It has no rights embodied in a written constitution and no general powers to provide for the good government of the community. It has to operate within a legal framework determined by central government and is subject to a variety of administrative, financial and political controls.

The main types of local authorities are district councils and county councils, where councillors are elected to serve for a fixed period of four years. Many district council elections are held in three out of every four years, with one third of the council being elected each time. County council elections are held once every four years. Although 38 million people are eligible to vote, only 40 per cent do so. Electoral turn-out is low in the UK compared with most other west European countries, where it is often 80 or 90 per cent. Local councillors have to be local residents or work in the area and they usually stand for a political party. In the late 1980s some 85 per cent of local councillors represented the Conservative, Labour or Liberal Democrat Parties, with 5 per cent representing ratepayers or nationalist organizations. The remaining 10 per cent were political independents. Some 80 per cent were men, 20 per cent women, with about two-thirds drawn from the top socio-economic groups. The majority were over forty-five years of age.

Elected councillors collectively constitute the council of a local authority which is invested with political authority and legal powers. Traditionally, however, local government has operated through a system of committees, with delegated powers. The committees, some of them required by legislation, carry out the main work of councils, working closely with local government officers and their departments. Local government committees are administrative committees, and councillors get very involved in the running of services and the taking of administrative decisions. Councils tend to concern themselves with determining general outlines of policy, taking politically contentious decisions and acting as report-receiving bodies. Most decisions taken in committee are ratified by the full council. The only power which a council cannot devolve or delegate is the decision on the Community Charge, or 'poll tax', which must be made in a special meeting of the full council.

The committee structure of local authorities varies with the type of authority and its range of functions. Most follow the recommendations of the Bains report (1972) and have a policy and resources committee, with programme committees covering the major policy areas. Most committees, and their sub-committees, work closely with chief officers and their departments. The chief officers are led by a chief executive, who acts as the head of the permanent officials, and collectively they constitute a management team.

Political parties play an important part in local elections and in the running of local authorities. The Widdicombe report (1986) stated that 85 per cent of all councils were controlled by parties;

the remainder, where independents were dominant, were in rural areas. Although one view is that party politics has no place in local government, there is general consensus that political parties are indispensable in ensuring that local councils are responsible to their electorates. Political parties formulate policies which they present to the electorate, enable councillors to co-ordinate activities and to prioritize issues, and apply party principles to specific problems. In some councils, party dominates the internal organization, with committees faithfully reflecting the party structure. In others there is more flexibility and party is only one criterion in determining committee membership.

Party is also significant in central-local relations and is often a cause of friction when different parties are in power in central government and local government. Local political leaders may resist the attempts of central government to impose new policies or constrain local authority expenditure. Whether they are successful depends on the how determined central government is to get its way. Throughout the 1980s the relationship between central and local government was fraught with conflict. Successive governments, committed to fundamental changes in the role of the State and to restructuring society, demanded radical changes in local government. Unable to get the co-operation of many local authorities, central government used a range of strategies to compel or circumvent local government. These included legislation, financial reform, by-passing local government and adopting a directive policy style.

More than sixty major statutes affecting local government were passed between 1979 and 1989. They imposed new responsibilities on local authorities, removed some of their powers or compelled them to carry out national policies. Central government took more control of local authority expenditure, although it was initially unsuccessful because of the ability of local authorities to raise money from the rates. In 1988 the rating system was abolished and a new controversial Community Charge was instituted in Scotland in 1989 and in England and Wales in 1990.

In 1990 the local government structure bore a strong resemblance to that of 1979, except in the major metropolitan areas. The local authority sector is an important part of the machinery of government but it has less power and less autonomy than in 1979. For example, the policies of national government have changed local government's role in housing, education, social services, urban development and other fields. Local government has been partly privatized and has to compete in the provision of welfare services with the private sector. It is no longer the main provider of housing to let, sheltered accommodation for the elderly or homes for the infirm. The management of schools has been delegated to boards of governors, dominated by parents. Schools may opt out of local authority control, whilst council house tenants can choose their landlords. It no longer sets the business rate and only directly controls less than 25 per cent of its revenue income.

The politics of local government in the 1980s was about depoliticizing it and transferring a wide range of local authority functions to the marketplace, and bringing market criteria into local government decision-making. Local authorities are becoming enabling bodies providing, regulating or facilitating local services by both private and voluntary agencies, within a mixed public-private economy.

The European Community

The origins of the European Community (EC) lie in the Treaty of Paris, 1951. This created the European Coal and Steel Community a year later. In 1957 six countries signed the two Treaties of Rome, setting up the European Economic Community and the European Atomic Energy Community. These three European Communities were managed by common institutions, and on 1 July 1987 the Single European Act came into force throughout the member States of the EC. By this time the original 'common market' of the six had expanded to twelve member States, with over 300 million citizens. The six founding countries were Belgium, France, Italy, Luxembourg, the Netherlands and West Germany. They were joined by Denmark, Ireland and the UK in 1973, followed by Greece in 1981. The present EC was completed with the admission of Portugal and Spain in 1986.

The coming into force of the Single European Act, 1987, followed nearly four years of intense discussion and debate, both at Community level and in the national parliaments of the member States. The Single European Act brings about a major amendment to the Treaties of Rome and prepares the way for further developments over the next decade. The most important implications of the Act can be summarized as follows:

- The Act changes the way in which decisions are made at the level of the Council of Ministers, replacing the need for unanimity with voting by 'qualified' majority on all but the most important issues.

- The Act increases the powers of the European Parliament, replacing its consultative status with the power to amend or reject proposals by the council when they have been made by a 'qualified majority'.

- The Act calls for a comprehensive reform of the structural funds of the Community—the European Social Fund and the European Regional Development Fund—in order to aid regional economic and social development further.

- The Act creates an administrative framework for European co-operation in the sphere of foreign policy.

- The Act formally adopts 31 December 1992 as the deadline for the completion of the internal market, that is, the creation of a Europe without frontiers or barriers to the free movement of people, goods and services.

The implications of the Act are considerable. It undoubtedly marks a major step in the direction of economic union and the beginnings of a process that will lead to greater political union too.[8]

The European Parliament

The political institutions of the EC are shown in figure 9. These are the European Parliament, the European Commission and the Council of Ministers. There is also the Court of Justice. The Parliament is located at Strasbourg and has 518 members (MEPs): eighty-one from each of France, Italy, the UK and West Germany; sixty from Spain; twenty-five from the Netherlands; twenty-four from each of Belgium, Greece and Portugal; sixteen from Denmark; fifteen from Ireland; and six from Luxembourg. MEPs form political groupings rather than national ones. After the Euro-

192

Figure 9 The political institutions of the European Community

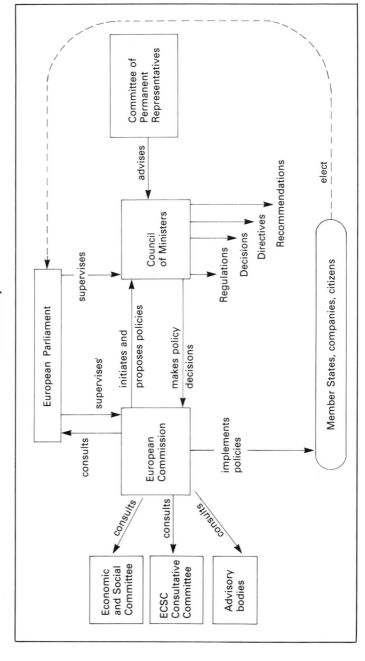

elections in June 1989 they were divided as follows: 182 socialists; 106 European People's Party; forty-eight European Democrats; forty-two Communists and allies; forty-four Liberal Democrats and Reformists; nineteen European Democratic Alliance; twenty-three Rainbow; sixteen European right; and thirty-eight others. The evolution of support for the main political groupings in the Parliament for the period 1979–89 is shown in table 30.

Table 30
Main political groupings in the European Parliament, 1979–89

Group	1979	1981	1984	1987	1989
Socialists	112	124	130	166	182
European People's Party	109	117	110	113	106
European Democrats	64	63	50	66	48
Communists and allies	44	48	41	48	42
Liberal Democrats and Reformists	40	38	31	46	44
European Democratic Alliance	22	22	29	29	19
Rainbow	11	12	20	20	23
European right	–	–	16	16	16
Non-attached	10	10	7	14	8
Other[a]	–	–	–	–	30

Note
a MEPs who have yet to associate themselves with a political group.
Source: Trade union information bulletin, (No. 3/87), Brussels Commission of the European Communities, 1987.

It is the Parliament's role to keep constant watch on the Commission's activities, ensuring that it faithfully represents the Community interest. It has to be ready to call it to order at any time if it gives the impression of yielding to the lobbying of member governments. The Parliament sits for one week a month, except in August, and for shorter periods in between to discuss special items such as the Community budget. It also has meetings set aside for its eighteen parliamentary committees. It is these bodies to which members of the Commission report to give account of the decisions taken by the Commission, the proposals presented to the Council of Ministers and the position adopted by the Commission towards the Council. According to Noël (1989), 'questions from Members of Parliament to the Commission, and to the Council and Conference of Foreign Ministers . . . , provide a much-used means of control . . .'[9] The European Parliament also holds urgent debates on current issues to bypass the lengthy alternative procedures available.

The European Parliament now has the last word on 'non-compulsory' expenditure, that is, expenditure which is not the consequence of Community legislation. Its budgetary powers cover the institution's administrative costs and certain operational expenditure such as the social and regional funds. The Parliament has the power not only to reallocate but also to increase this expenditure within certain limits. It can also propose modifications of the Community's 'compulsory' expenditure on the Common Agricultural Policy, provided it does not increase the total amount of such spending. It also has the right to reject the budget as a whole, as it did in 1979 and 1985. It is the president of the Parliament who is responsible for declaring that the budget has been finally adopted, once all the procedures have been completed. The Parliament thus holds a strong position in the budgetary process. 'The dialogue between Parliament and the Council has increasingly come into play and where it has not been possible to resolve differences, Parliament has on a number of occasions been able to impose its point of view.'[10]

The Parliament, however, is not a legislative body. Indeed, under the Treaties of Rome its involvement in the legislative process was restricted to giving its opinion on certain Commission proposals. In addition to this compulsory consultation, provision was later made for optional consultation at the Parliament's request, with the result that it now makes its voice heard in the legislative process whenever major legislation is involved. Further, whilst the Single European Act, 1987, does not give the Parliament all the legislative powers it wants, it does confer on it the power of assent—essentially a joint decision-making power—in relation to certain limited areas. It also introduces a co-operation procedure applicable to 'qualified majority decisions' bearing on the internal market, social policy, economic and social cohesion and research. Whilst the Commission remains the driving force behind the drafting of Community legislation, the co-operation procedure enables the Parliament to have a direct influence on decisions, even though the final word still rests with the Council of Ministers.

The European Commission

The Commission, which is based at Brussels and Luxembourg, consists of seventeen members, and is appointed by agreement between the member governments, for a four-year period. Currently there are two commissioners from each of France, Italy, Spain, the UK and West Germany, with one from each of the remaining seven countries. Members of the Commission must remain independent of governments and the Council of Ministers. The Council cannot remove any members but the Parliament can pass a motion of censure compelling the Commission to resign as a body. The European Community Treaties assign a wide range of tasks to the Commission. In outline, the Commission's role 'is to act as the guardian of the Treaties, to serve as the executive arm of the Communities, to initiate Community policy, and to defend the Community interest in the Council [of Ministers]'.[11]

The Commission has to ensure that the provisions of the Treaties and the decisions of the Community institutions are effectively implemented. The Commission investigates a presumed infringement of a Treaty either on its own initiative or on the strength of complaints from governments, companies or individuals. If, after investigation, the disputed practice continues, or the Commission's 'reasoned opinion' is rejected, the Commission may refer the matter to the European Court of Justice. The Court's judgement is binding on those concerned. Since most Community law is directly applicable, any individual or firm can invoke Community law in a national court. This complements the supervision carried out by the Commission.

The Commission is directly invested by the Treaties with wide executive powers. Additionally, extra powers have been conferred on it by the Council of Ministers to secure the implementation of secondary legislation. Under the Single European Act, 1987, the conferring of executive powers on the Commission is now the general rule. One set of powers is the issuing of decisions and regulations implementing certain Treaty provisions or Council acts. Decisions are binding in their entirety on those member States, companies or individuals to whom they are directly addressed. Regulations are of general application, binding in their entirety and applicable to all member States, applying directly as Community laws. A second set of powers enables the Commission to apply Treaty rules to specific cases involving governments and firms. These include the European Coal and Steel Community (ECSC) Treaty, common policy areas—such as agriculture and the environment—and completion of the internal market. Third, the Commission administers the safeguard clauses in the Community Treaties which allow Treaty requirements to be waived in certain circumstances.

Another responsibility of the Commission is to administer appropriations for the Communities' public expenditure and the three major Community funds. Most of the ECSC's operating budget, for example, is spent on grants for research, interest subsidies on investment and conversion loans, grants for the retraining and redeployment of workers, and other measures linked to the restructuring of the steel industry. The three major funds administered by the Commission have relatively substantial resources. They are:

● The European Social Fund.
● The European Agricultural Guidance and Guarantee Fund.
● The European Regional Development Fund.

The Single European Act, 1987, provides for these funds to be reorganized to improve their co-ordination and effectiveness as a contribution to greater European integration. There is also a European Development Fund which is the EC's main overseas aid fund.

The Commission also initiates Community policy, defends the Community interest and sees that Community policy forms a consistent whole. The European Economic Community Treaty, for example, confines itself to outlining the policies to be pursued in the main areas of economic activity. It leaves it to the EC's institutions, such as the Commission, in conjunction with the Council of Ministers and the Parliament, to work out the actual arrangements to be applied within this framework.

The Council of Ministers and the Court of Justice

The Council meets in Brussels and is made up of representatives of the governments of the member States. Each government normally sends one of its Ministers. The composition of the Council thus varies with the subjects down for discussion. The Foreign Minister is probably regarded as a country's main representative but Ministers of agriculture, transport, economic and financial affairs, social affairs, industry and the environment also meet frequently for specialized Council meetings and sometimes sit alongside the Foreign Ministers. The presidency of the Council rotates between the member governments at six-monthly intervals. When decisions are taken by majority vote, France, Italy, the UK and West Germany have ten votes each, Spain eight, Belgium, Greece, the Netherlands and Portugal five each, Denmark and Ireland three each, and Luxembourg two. Where there is a 'qualified majority' it means fifty-four votes out of a total of seventy-six.

Effective working arrangements between the Council and the Commission are essential for formulating and implementing Community policy. The most commonly used procedure, in dealings between the two institutions, is that laid down in the Treaty of Rome. Once a proposal is lodged, dialogue begins amongst Ministers in the Council, who put their national points of view, and the Commission. It is the Commission which draws up the proposal which the Council is to discuss, and only on that basis can the Council deliberate at all. The Council can either adopt the Commission's proposal as it stands by a majority; or it can depart from the proposal if there is unanimity; or it may fail to come to a decision at all. The increasing tendency to use majority voting in the Council has been reinforced by the Single European Act, 1987. This 'has substantially extended the Council's scope for taking majority decisions, particularly as regards the internal market'.[12]

Since the mid-1970s the heads of state and government, often accompanied by their Foreign Ministers, meet regularly, with the president of the Commission, as the 'European Council'. It meets both as the Council of the Communities and as a forum for political co-operation. After 1986 these meetings were restricted to two per year. This was done largely to limit intervention by the European Council in the general running of the Community. The Court of Justice of the European Communities, whose centre is at Luxembourg, consists of thirteen judges appointed for six years by agreement amongst member governments. They are assisted by six advocates-general and are charged with ensuring that implementation of the Community's Treaties is in accordance with the rule of law. The Court also gives preliminary rulings on questions referred to it by national courts. Community law, made up of the Treaties and the secondary legislation based on them, is becoming more interwoven with the national law of individual member countries. Its implementation is attracting more of the national courts' attention.

The Distribution of Power

It is one thing to outline the theory and concepts of liberal democracy and to describe the formal structures of its central, local government and trans-European institutions. It is a different matter altogether to explain where ultimate power lies in a liberal democratic State, like the UK. There is no consensus on this issue. Three main models are used to illustrate the range of ideas and perceptions about the distribution and location of power in liberal democratic societies. They derive from pluralism, ruling class or Marxist theory, and elite theory respectively.

Pluralist theory

In essence 'political pluralism recognizes the existence of diversity in social, institutional and ideological practices, and values that diversity'.[13] More specifically, pluralists argue, political power in liberal democracies is fragmented and dispersed amongst many different organized groups. All these groups are able to influence policy on different issues, with no one group or interest dominant. A central thrust of pluralist theory is that it is through organized groups—such as political parties, for example—that individuals have access to political power, enabling them to influence political decisions in a liberal society. Such groups are secondary and intermediate associations between individuals and society and may be either manifest or latent ones. Manifest groups are organized and active, whilst latent groups only emerge when events provoke them to do so.

Pluralists argue that all associational groupings have access to the political system, if they wish to influence political activity. Moreover, they see no impediment to groups organizing in response to changing circumstances. Thus if one group becomes too dominant another emerges, organizes itself and begins acting politically on behalf of its members. The purpose of such groups is to represent and be responsive to the needs of the rank-and-file membership on whose behalf they operate. These organized groups act upon government and other groups to achieve their objectives. No single group is involved in all areas of decision-making, since each is limited to particular issues. The essence of associational groupings is organization, representation, influence and feedback.

For pluralists the role of government is to arbitrate between competing groups and competing interests. The State is seen as neutral, with its institutions acting independently of any particular interest. Since power is perceived as being widely dispersed amongst society's diffused groups, it is assumed that every group is able to influence political decisions when its interests are affected. Pluralists accept that elites exist but see them as accessible, accountable and responsive groupings, not as exclusive bodies. For pluralists, too, elites are not coherent but competitive groupings. Moreover, every latent interest is a potential power group. Since relative power positions change, today's most powerful organized group may be tomorrow's least powerful one. And today's least powerful group may be tomorrow's strongest one.

The main evidence given to support pluralist theory is the very existence of the many different groups attempting to influence government policy. Their membership is drawn from a cross-section of society and they act with varying degrees of success. It is also contended that pluralism is aptly demonstrated by the fact that no single organized group is dominant. Further, groups tend to be issue-specific and to cover one area of government policy such as education, defence, health or agriculture. As some groups wax others wane, and power shifts occur. Nor does any particular group appear to be completely successful in getting its own way. It gains on some issues and loses on others.

The weaknesses of pluralist theory are, first, that it fails to take account of the structural bias in liberal democratic States. It is 'insider' groups such as employers, business groups and trade unions, for example, that can organize themselves effectively. 'Outsider' groups such as those representing pensioners, 'gay rights' or radical feminists may have inadequate access to social resources, as well as failing to attract the leadership and commitment necessary to sustain them. Second, access to associational groupings is limited in other ways. Not all interests are able to organize themselves, and the difficulties of organizing new legitimate interests can be severely underestimated. Third, whilst pluralism assumes the existence of basic freedoms in society, such as freedom of speech, association and belief, not all interests are seen as legitimate. This means that their demands never appear on the political agenda and are excluded from organization, representation and influence.

Last, pluralism assumes that government and the State have no direct interest themselves in accommodating associational groups to their own political purposes. This is mistaken, since these institutions are power groupings themselves and want to perpetuate their own power position in society.

Ruling class theory

Ruling class theory holds that politics reflects the class structure of society, with the capitalist class on the one side and propertyless wage-earners on the other. The basis of class domination is the relationship to the means of production. Those who own and control the means of production are the ruling class, whilst those who own only their labour are the subordinate class. It is the purpose of the State to protect the capitalist or ruling class, which dominates political institutions, at the expense of workers and their families. It is the ruled, in turn, who are subjugated and exploited. The relationship between these two classes is therefore one of conflict. The conflict is inevitable and endemic because the relationship between rulers and ruled is exploitative.

One means by which the ruling class sustains its position, it is claimed, is through the inheritance and ownership of private property. Another is by using its economic power to maintain its social and economic position. It does this by colonizing the power centres of society and by using the State to protect its power bases within it. In these ways the ruling class upholds capitalism, maintains its own position and manages class conflict to its own advantage. The class structure incorporates government, industry, commerce, the established Churches, the law, the media and the arts. These institutions, it is contended, reflect the interests of the ruling class and provide means of controlling the major decisions taken in society. Out of the objective existence of classes comes the consciousness of the ruling class's common interest: the ruling class is a class in and of itself.

The working class, on the other hand, is not always conscious of its common interest or of being exploited. It is indoctrinated, it is argued, into believing that the capitalist social system does not exploit working people. It accepts existing class relationships as the natural order of things. Subjective consciousness is not important, since it is objective conflict which is the engine of social change. It is only when the basis of class power is removed that capitalist class domination will no longer be necessary. Then no person will exploit another, economic and political equality will coexist and the State will wither away. This will create a socialist society, which is the highest order of social organization.

The evidence supporting this theory is, first, that no elected government in the UK has seriously sought to abolish the capitalist economy which is based on market allocation and private property. Even the Labour Party, it is claimed, seeks only to reform industrial capitalism, not to transform it. Second, whilst business interests are only one amongst many, they are seen to be the most significant and best organized economic power group. Third, City interests, such as the commercial banks, insurance companies, the Stock Exchange and merchant banks, are claimed to be the best protected of UK economic institutions. Unless this continues, whatever government is in power, it is argued, the economy could be seriously harmed and international confidence in the country's economic performance would be drastically eroded.

Critics of ruling class theory suggest that it is too much a uni-dimensional model of politics which focuses largely on economic power. It appears to be both a complex and a simplistic theory of power distribution in liberal democracies and fails to take account of the social diversity inherent in industrial capitalist societies. It seems to ignore the empirical evidence of the widespread involvement of political parties, interest groups, pressure groups and occupational associations in political and economic decision-making in advanced market economies. Above all, perhaps, ruling class theory sidesteps the conflicts within the capitalist and working classes themselves. In other words, there is neither a homogeneous capitalist class nor a homogenous working class. Manufacturing and financial interests clash in the Confederation of British Industry, just as unions of skilled workers clash with unions of less skilled workers in the Trades Union Congress.

Elite theory

Elite theorists argue that political power tends to be concentrated in the hands of the few. It is the social and political elite which provides the leadership of organized groups and those at the apex of society's key institutions. Such elites control society's political processes, with political decisions tending to favour their interests. Society consists, in short, of an elite and a mass. The elite is the minority which rules; the mass is the majority which is ruled.

Since it is the elite which by definition dominates the decision-making processes, the elite's power is cumulative. The elite may be drawn from a single sub-group but, more usually, from several overlapping sub-groups. The elite is not simply a collection of top persons but is a united, coherent, self-conscious social group. Its control stems from its ability to organize and its possession of scarce attributes and resources. These may include land, power, wealth, capital and knowledge. These attributes are valued in society and are legitimated and aspired to by the mass who are largely excluded from access to them.

Elites, who are not answerable to the mass, may either exploit or act benevolently towards their social inferiors. But, whatever their behaviour to others, it is elites which facilitate social change. As Wright Mills (1956) noted, in the context of the United States, the power elite traditionally consists of those in a position to make decisions having major consequences for the masses. It is the power elite which commands 'the major hierarchies and organizations of modern society'.[14]

Supporters of elite theory argue that a number of social institutions in the UK are run and dominated by elites. They include Parliament, the civil service, the judiciary, the armed services, business corporations, the media and communications. Each has its own elite and each is recruited in similar ways. It is also contended that these elites dominate and control the political process as well as decisions favouring their own interests. There is little evidence, moreover, of any substantial change in the distribution of wealth, income or power in liberal democracies. Whilst national income and social wealth can increase with time, and some of the new resources trickle down to the masses, power is a fixed resource or a positional good to which the elite clings with determination.

The problem with assessing the validity of elite theory is defining what is meant by an elite. If elite groups are equivalent to those within a pluralist polyarchy, then elite theory becomes merely a variant of pluralism. It is also difficult in practice to test elite theory empirically. For example, if elites possess negative power, then it is very difficult to identify and eradicate this. Further, it cannot be assumed that membership of an elite group, of necessity, determines its members' behaviour. It may be that behaviour results from role and institutional factors rather than from membership of elite groups *per se*.

The Implications for Management

The UK is a liberal democracy and incorporates a political culture dominated by the ideas of individual freedom, political pluralism and representative government which originated in the seventeenth and eighteenth centuries. In a liberal democratic society, like the UK, there is a reciprocal relationship between the political system and the corporate sector. Decisions and laws made in the political system, such as parliamentary statutes, the directives and regulations of the EC, local authority by-laws and economic policy, affect business corporations in their role as producers and employers of resources. But the corporate sector, in turn, can influence the political system. It can, for example, lobby those in political authority, and their civil servants or equivalents, at local government, central government and EC level if business leaders consider it to be in the interests of the organizations for which they are responsible. Pressure-group politics is as relevant for the business sector as it is for trade unions, professional associations, consumer groups and the environmentalist lobby.

Managements need to establish effective relations with the political authorities, therefore, if they wish to influence political decision-making. This can be done either by corporations acting individually on an *ad hoc* basis or collectively through membership of the relevant employers' or trade association, including organizations such as the Confederation of British Industry, the Institute of Personnel Management and the British Institute of Management. Managements also need to know how central government, local government and, increasingly, EC institutions operate. The idea that the business sector is non-political does not stand up to scrutiny. Whilst it is only a minority of companies which make financial donations to the Conservative Party, and are therefore overtly party-political, most companies need to be sensitive to the political environment as it affects their own interests. There is plenty of anecdotal and case study evidence to demonstrate that companies and their senior managements do not remain politically inert when their organizational interests are threatened by intervention by the political authorities.

In the public sector, of course, management operates in a political environment by definition. In central government and the public corporations, changes of government sometimes have a significant impact on the ways in which the civil service, the National Health Service or other public authorities operate and are organized. In the 1980s it could be observed how organizational and operational changes were imposed on the public services and public corporations, whilst substantial parts of the nationalized industries were privatized and returned to private ownership. Policies like contracting out and competitive tendering for services such as catering, cleaning and building maintenance had a number of effects on management. These affected personnel and industrial relations activities, financial control and the role of managers in the public sector. In essence, the role moved away from administering services to managing resources and a preoccupation with cost, efficiency and quality control.

In local government, managers have been even more dramatically affected by government decisions since 1979. In addition to competitive tendering and contracting out, the local authority sector has had to change its role as a provider of services to one of enabling a variety of public, private and voluntary organizations to meet the needs of the community. The impact on management has been to facilitate these changes and to implement a vast amount of legislation concerning all areas of local government activity. All the management systems have changed and the pressures on management have been enormous. Managing local government is becoming more like managing private business, with some mobility of managers between the two sectors.

The policies and decisions taken by locally elected councils also affect managers and business corporations. They include planning decisions, building control, public health and business enterprise initiatives. These and other local authority functions regulate business activities, and can provide a supportive infrastructure for local firms and stimulate business opportunities, all of which have implications for management. On the other hand, where the priorities of the local authorities are less business-centred, or where welfare needs consume most local authority resources, support for the interests of local firms may be relegated in importance. This puts quite different pressures on managers.

The impact of EC decisions on management policies, planning and practices is increasing too. European Community directives and regulations, for example, affect the way in which managerial policies are made and implemented and have to be taken into account in corporate decision-making. Proposals for a draft Community Charter of Fundamental Social Rights include a range of intended measures likely to affect management handling of employment issues. These include workers' rights to:

- Employment with fair remuneration.
- Improvement of living and working conditions.
- Social security protection.
- Freedom of association and collective bargaining.
- Vocational training.
- Equal treatment between men and women.
- Information, consultation and participation in companies.
- Health protection and safety at the workplace.

When finally agreed, the charter will form an important part of

206   *The Corporate Environment*

the overall social dimension of the internal single European market which management will have to implement in their respective organizations across the EC.

As closer European integration and a unified European economy move nearer it is likely that the task will need the active support and participation not only of governments and national administrations but also of the business community and its leaders. Governments will respond more constructively, if they know what it is the business sector wants. In this sense the corporate sector has a vital role to play in making the single market an economic reality, and in ensuring that governments respond constructively to its interests and needs, within a new Euro-political consensus.

References

1 LEFTWICH A. *What is politics?* Oxford, Blackwell, 1984. p 138.
2 *ibid*. p 144.
3 CRICK B. *In defence of politics*. Harmondsworth, Penguin, 1964. pp 22 and 33.
4 BALL A. *Modern politics and government*. London, Macmillan, 1983. pp 44–46.
5 *ibid*. p 6.
6 BENN T. *Arguments for socialism*. Harmondsworth, Penguin, 1980. p 126.
7 CROSSMAN R H S. Introduction to *The English constitution* by W. BAGEHOT. London, Fontana, 1963.
8 EUROPEAN COMMUNITIES. *Trade union information bulletin: No. 3/87*. Brussels, Commission of the European Communities, 1987. p 3.
9 NOËL E. *Working together: the institutions of the European Community*. Luxembourg, Office of the European Communities, 1989. p 33.
10 *ibid*. p 34.
11 *ibid*. p 13.
12 *ibid*. p 27.
13 DUNLEAVY P. *and* O'LEARY B. *Theories of the state*. Basingstoke, Macmillan, 1987. p 13.
14 WRIGHT MILLS C. *The power elite*. New York, Oxford University Press, 1956. p 19.

8

Political Parties, Pressure Groups and Voting Behaviour

The UK's macro-political culture is rooted in its history, geography and wider social and political structures. There is broad agreement amongst the population not only on how the political system should operate but also on its central political values. Foremost amongst these is a firm attachment by most people to the principles of parliamentary democracy, involving as it does political party organization, pressure group politics and interest group lobbying. Overall there is a fundamental consensus on the acceptability of the political system. Few would argue against the principles of government by consent, parliamentary supremacy or the rule of law. There is general acceptance of the legitimacy of government and its political authority, coupled with a trust by the majority of the electorate in elite political leadership.

Another feature of the political culture is the acceptance by the vast majority of citizens of the legitimacy of peaceful, non-violent political protest. At one level this manifests itself in party political organizations. Individuals are free to form or join political parties and to seek political power and political office through the ballot box. At another level, trade unions, employers' organizations, pressure groups, professional associations and other bodies aim to represent their constituents' viewpoints in political and economic affairs, as special interests. Individuals are also free to organize and participate in peaceful demonstrations, and political rallies, which in some other States would be banned or otherwise suppressed.

Linked with this is a belief in gradualism, or incrementalism, in politics. There is a preference for political change being effected through the relatively slow and piecemeal process of the parliamentary system. It is underwritten by a dislike of political extremism, sectarianism in Northern Ireland being an anomaly in this respect. There is also a strong libertarian tradition in the political culture. This means that political priority is accorded to individual rights and personal liberty. Where possible, the government is not expected to limit individual liberty in pursuit of its own political goals. What individuals do in private is not normally considered to be of public concern and what they say in public is not normally a matter of government regulation. However, the boundary between the public and private spheres of social life is constantly changing.

Another basic element in the political culture is political tolerance. This is reflected in public acceptance not only of legitimate protest by individuals and organized groups but also of the right of political dissenters to disseminate new ideas. Some people argue that tolerance of this sort is the hallmark of a truly free society. By this view, conflicts of ideas and of political goals are the lifeblood of democracy and of personal and collective freedoms.

There is general consensus about the political process and its institutions. But there is less consensus about the goals of politics. Whilst both the Conservative and Labour Parties support the concept of liberal democracy, each differs from the other about how it chooses to use political power when it has a parliamentary majority.

Political Parties

The political system, like that of all liberal democracies, is based on inter-party competitive politics. Organized political parties seek the support of the electorate in voting for their candidates in local, national and European elections. Although some observers argue that the UK is moving towards a period of multi-party politics, Ball (1987) concludes that by the mid-1980s the 'party system could still be characterised as a two-party system in that the majority of seats were won by the two largest parties, one of them having won an absolute majority of seats . . . and willing to govern alone'.[1]

Table 31 summarizes the results of general elections since 1945. It shows that it is the two major parties, the Conservative Party and the Labour Party, which have dominated the elections. Nevertheless, a number of minor parties have won an increasing proportion of parliamentary seats since the mid-1960s. In the context

Table 31

Number of UK parliamentary seats, by political party, at general elections, 1945–87

Party	Election year												
	1945	1950	1951	1955	1959	1964	1966	1970	Feb 1974	Oct 1974	1979	1983	1987
Conservative	213	298	321	344	365	304	253	330	297	277	339	397	376
Labour	393	315	295	277	258	317	363	287	301	319	269	209	229
Liberal	12	9	6	6	6	9	12	6	14	13	11	17	19
Social Democrat	*	*	*	*	*	*	*	*	*	*	*	6	3
Communist	2	–	–	–	–	–	–	–	–	–	–	–	–
Plaid Cymru	*	*	*	*	–	–	–	–	2	3	2	2	3
Scottish Nationalist	*	*	*	*	–	–	–	1	7	11	2	2	3
National Front	*	*	*	*	*	*	*	*	–	–	–	–	–
Others (G.B.)	20	3	3	3	1	–	2	6	2	–	–	–	–
Others (N.I.)	*	*	*	*	*	*	*	*	12	12	12	17	17
Total	640	625	625	630	630	630	630	630	635	635	635	650	650

* No seats contested by these parties in these elections.
Sources: D. Butler and A. Sloman, British political facts, Basingstoke, Macmillan, 1980. Kessing's contemporary archives, Harlow, Longman, 1983, 1987.

of liberal democracy, a political party has a number of characteristics.

- [It is] an organisation that has a recognized degree of permanence.
- This organisation contests elections and seeks to place its members in positions of influence in the legislature.
- It either attempts to occupy executive positions in the political system, such as those in the Cabinet, or to exercise influence on those occupying such offices by virtue of its position in the legislature.
- It has a distinctive label which distinguishes it from other political groupings.[2]

As organizations, political parties have six main functions. The first is a representative one: providing a choice of representatives to the electorate and representing the electorate in the legislature. Second, political parties 'present labels to the electorate and seek electoral support' for their programmes and policies. Third, political parties perform a political recruitment and governing function, since in the UK, for example, government office is limited to nominees of the majority party in the House of Commons. Fourth, political parties are 'one of the agencies engaged in the formulation of government policy'.[3] Fifth, parties mobilize people, raise their levels of political awareness and persuade them to go out and vote. Finally, they provide a communication function and an institutional link between government and the people.

The Conservative Party

Like most political parties, the Conservatives are a coalition of diverse political and social interests. King (1987) claims that there are three traditions in the party. The first is 'a pragmatic tradition' rooted in the belief that the Conservative Party is not bound rigidly to any particular ideology. The second tradition explains the durability of the Conservatives' political success 'by their consistent support for certain key values'. The third strand is 'the mixture of the "Tory" tradition of belief in a strong state and state authority as the basis for a durable social order with a "liberal" tradition based on free market principles'.[4] It is arguable that the second tradition overlaps the other two, with the first tradition being strongly associated with pragmatic 'Modern Conservatism' and the third tradition with the ideological 'New Right'.

The ideas associated with one-nation Modern Conservatism, and the role of the party in defending it, emerged out of the premierships of Stanley Baldwin in the inter-war years and reached their apotheosis during the Macmillan era of the 1950s and 1960s. Modern Conservatism developed out of the belief that it is the role of a Conservative government to defend existing institutions and traditions. In this way the community is protected against the turmoil likely to arise from unregulated social change and possible social revolution. The fundamental goal of Modern Conservatism is to support existing political and social institutions, and the distribution of power in society, in order to sustain social stability and national unity. Social reform must be controlled, considered and acted upon only in response to specific social problems. What has stood the test of time is assumed to be virtuous, in the natural order of things and not to be lightly cast aside.

Modern Conservatism also claims to be largely pragmatic and not to be identified with any ideological political philosophy. Modern Conservatism is seen by the Party and its supporters to be the means of forming practical responses to given political situations. Its thinking is based on the assumption that society is a unity, greater than the sum of the individuals comprising it. Society is believed to be founded upon consensus social values, reflecting its citizens' common purpose, national unity and respect for tradition. Hierarchy and a stable social structure are seen by Modern Conservatives as natural, orderly and desirable. There is therefore strong commitment to the monarchy, the House of Lords, the armed services, the established Church and law and order.

Modern Conservatism is strongly identified with belief in elite political leadership, patriotism and deference to recognized social and political authority. Conservatives of this tradition defend family thrift, personal initiative and self-help. Individual liberty of this sort, it is argued, can be maintained only where the State upholds certain fundamental human freedoms. They include the right to own property, to spend one's income as one chooses, and to go about one's business without undue interference from the

State or its administrative bureaucracy. In upholding these values the Conservative Party accepts inequality as normal and inevitable, with private property and free enterprise being the necessary conditions for personal liberty and political freedom.

On economic matters, the Modern Conservative tradition normally favours decision-making based on market forces rather than on government intervention, with private enterprise having the major role in 'wealth creation'. By the 1940s and until the late 1970s, however, it needs to be recognized that the Modern Conservative Party accepted, like all other UK political parties, an interventionist role for the State in managing the economy. The aim was to ensure high levels of employment and economic activity, consistent with steady growth and rising living standards. Thus Modern Conservatism came to be associated with the mixed economy. Yet the Modern Conservative tradition has always been ambivalent about the role of the unions in the economy. Although some third of trade unionists regularly vote Conservative at general elections, the Conservative Party normally wants to weaken the unions' power because of their impact on wage determination and their political links with the Labour Party.

It is out of such ideas that Modern Conservatism, and the policies associated with it, emerged. More recently, however, another set of ideas and policies has emerged within the Party, largely from its right wing. These emphasize two main themes: the primacy of markets in wealth creation and resource allocation; and the necessity of reducing the role of the State in economic and social affairs, enabling individuals to take greater responsibility for their own welfare and that of their dependants. Bell (1985) claims that this 'new Conservatism—Thatcherism, the New Right, or whatever it is called—is more akin to Powellism than to old-style Butler-Macmillan Conservatism' and 'it flatly repudiates the Keynesian interventionist policies of the post-war years'.[5] Although the ideas and policies of the New Right have been in the ascendant in the Conservative Party and Conservative governments during the 1980s, it cannot be assumed that the Modern Conservative tradition is redundant. Nor can it be assumed that it will not be revived in the party at some time in the future, since its roots lie deep in the party and amongst many of its supporters.

The ideas of the New Right developed amongst the Conservatives when the party was in opposition after 1974. The Party undertook a thorough review of its economic and social policies. Out of this review, and in response to the country's apparent economic weaknesses and social malaise, a distinctive set of radical economic and social policies emerged. They reflected a new dominant right-wing orthodoxy in the party. Its underlying aims were to make the economy competitive, to facilitate growth and to combat the welfare dependence culture of post-war Britain. This orthodoxy claims that the major economic policy objective of government must be to squeeze inflation out of the economy, irrespective of the impact on employment or other economic indicators, and change the balance of the mixed economy by reducing the role of the public sector in it. Central to this policy have been attempts to control the money supply, to reduce and eventually eliminate the public-sector borrowing requirement and to use interest rates as the main tool of economic management. People are also encouraged to assume personal responsibility for their own welfare provision and to relinquish dependence on the 'nanny' State.

This approach has been described as supporting a 'free economy' and a 'strong state'. Gamble (1988) sees ambiguities in this position which derive in part 'from the fact that the New Right has two major strands: a liberal tendency which argues the case for a freer, more open, and competitive economy, and a conservative tendency which is more interested in restoring social and political authority throughout society'.[6] The liberal tendency in the New Right embraces the ideas of monetarists, supply-side economists and supporters of privatization. The economic causes espoused by supporters of the New Right include:

- Restricting money supply targets to reduce inflation.
- Floating exchange rates.
- Limiting government spending, leading to balanced budgets or even budget surpluses.
- Reducing income tax to increase economic incentives.
- Abolishing trade union immunities to weaken the unions and free the labour market.
- Privatizing public-sector industries.

'It is taken as axiomatic that markets are inherently superior to any other way of organizing human societies.' Thus there have been campaigns for 'sound money, a major reduction in taxation and public expenditure, and a programme of deregulation and privatisation'.[7]

The conservative tendency in the New Right argues that the State must be strong. This is necessary 'firstly to unwind the coils of social democracy and welfarism which have fastened around the free economy; secondly to police the market order; thirdly to make the economy more productive; and fourthly to uphold social and political authority'. By this view, public spending must be cut, taxes lowered and public assets privatized in order to restore a free economy. Policing the market order 'means maintaining a central authority strong enough to maintain formal exchange equality between all economic agents'. Other arguments favouring a strong State are to facilitate economic efficiency, industrial modernization and reform of the remaining public services, including the education system. Lastly, 'a free economy is seen as a prop for a strong state instead of the other way round'.[8]

Another strand in the New Right is social authoritarianism which is basically anti-libertarian. It holds that personal discipline, duty and responsibility, and social stability, are higher-order social values than is unrestrained individual freedom. It is the role of the State—a strong State—to impose that order and prevent civic anarchy. As Scruton (1980) indicates, the social authoritarian strand of Conservatism is collectivist rather than individualist and emphasizes patriotism, nationalism, political allegiance and the concept of family. 'Society exists through authority, and the recognition of this authority requires the allegiance to a bond that is not contractual but transcendent, in the manner of the family tie.'[9]

From this analysis, it can be appreciated that whilst the New Right has been dominant in the Party since the late 1970s, the national Conservative Party is none the less a coalition of political interests and ideological positions. Moreover, compared with other political parties, it is successful at recruiting party members. According to its Central Office, there is no central membership roll 'but unofficial estimates put the membership at over a million. [There is] no accurate figure. It's very much up to the local constituency associations.' The party structure consists of the parliamentary party and the National Union of Conservative and Unionist Associations. The centre of power, however, is the parliamentary party, one of whose roles is to elect the party leader, who, provided the role holder has the confidence and support of MPs, is virtually unchallengeable. The role of the local constituency associations, in contrast, is limited to raising party funds, choosing parliamentary candidates and fighting elections.

There are financial links between the Conservative Party and some business leaders and business corporations, though it is possible that the party is less reliant on company donations than is commonly supposed. Indeed, it is estimated that corporate contributions 'supply just over half the party's central income, but only about a quarter of the local and national income combined'.[10] Nevertheless, the Party continues to receive large donations from some private businesses, especially from certain well known public companies. It was revealed, for example, that in the election year 1987 '333 companies gave a record total of £4,528,553 to the Conservative Party'. This compared with 235 companies giving a total of £2,094,619 the previous year. Of these 333 companies, seven gave at least £100,000 each in party donations, with eighty-four doubling the donations they made in previous years.[11]

The Labour Party

The Labour Party, which was born out of a trade union-working class alliance, underwent significant changes in terms of its ideas and policies during the 1980s. After three general election defeats, in 1979, 1983 and 1987, the Party and its leadership were forced to review what it stood for, its policies and its electoral strategy. Unlike the Conservative Party, however, the Labour Party never claims to be non-ideological. Webster (1981) claims that there are three main sets of ideas in the Labour Party which have had varying degrees of influence throughout the party's history: 'ultra-democracy', 'modern British Trotskyism' and 'social democracy'. He sees the guiding spirit of ultra-democracy being the right of people to make decisions for themselves, 'not only in the area of collective decision-making but also in that of private behaviour, so that the decriminalization of homosexuality and abortion are part of the same trend'. Several political developments were organized around the theme of ultra-democracy in the late 1970s. They included Welsh and Scottish devolution, demands for industrial democracy, participation in local planning, and the revival of the co-operative ideal.[12]

The essence of modern British Trotskyism, which revived among sections of the Party in the late 1970s and early 1980s, 'is a doctrine of conflict: struggle and violence are wholeheartedly accepted'. This pursuit of conflict, it is claimed, leads to a conscious disregard for the truth, with Trotskyist supporters of a British workers' revolution pressing 'for reforms which they do not believe to be attainable, as part of a "politics of exposure" of capitalism – and also of "reformist" labour leaders'. The revival of Trotskyism in Britain, and the growth of Trotskyist entryism into the Labour Party at that time, is traceable to the growth, since the 1960s, of varieties of western Marxism hostile to the orthodox communism of the Soviet bloc. Webster concludes that permanent control over the Labour Party 'of the degrading and inhuman ideas of political Marxism', with its totalitarianism and intolerance, the acceptance of violence and the glorification of conflict, 'could set back for a very long time what generations of Labour supporters have really meant by socialism'.[13]

Subsequent events, however, saw the third strand of Labour Party ideology, that of social democracy, once again come to the fore by the late 1980s. This was buttressed by the surprising break-up of orthodox Marxism in eastern European States at that time. The central idea of social democracy, which is sometimes referred to as democratic socialism, is that of equality. The aim is to create equality 'of wealth, income and opportunity; equality of esteem, in the sense of the repudiation of class, caste or status; and, crucially, equality of political rights and political power'. Social democracy insists on the exclusive use of political persuasion within a parliamentary system and on the repudiation of violence. Social democrats are also committed to the mixed economy and representative democracy. The latter stems from the belief that elected representatives are responsible to the wider electorate which they represent, not exclusively to the Party and party members.[14]

Contemporary definitions of democratic socialism are provided in the Labour Party's 1988 statement on democratic socialist aims and values. As democratic socialists Labour want 'a state where the collective contribution of the community is used for the advance of individual freedom . . . real freedom and real

chances'. The overall aim of the Party is 'the creation of a genu-
inely free society, in which the fundamental objective of government is the protection and extension of individual liberty irrespective of class, sex, age, race, colour or creed'. As the party claiming
to represent democratic socialist aspirations, the principal aim of
Labourite socialism is creating 'for all the people, material ability
to make the choices that a free society provides'. It is also necessary to create a 'more equal distribution of power as well as of
wealth'. This means that all men and women should have the
right to determine the decisions influencing their daily lives 'by a
major extension of democratic control'. Further, if they are to be
free and equal, 'men and women must have the fullest possible
access to education, training, information, technology and satisfactory modern employment'.[15]

In setting out its contemporary political philosophy, the Labour
Party discusses seven themes: socialism and equality; freedom to
choose; government and freedom; socialism, the community and
democracy; socialism and redistribution; socialism and the productive economy; and power for freedom, equality and justice. In
seeking to achieve equality between the sexes and the races, for
example, the Party remains 'committed to the redistribution of
wealth and power [in Britain]', arguing that a 'more equal distribution of wealth increases the sum of freedom'. Real freedom, in
turn, the Party argues, can be extended only by co-operative
action, by participation in democratic institutions 'and by collective provision to gain and sustain individual liberty'. Moreover,
for socialists, 'the state is an instrument for sustaining and enhancing the liberties of the whole community'. In the Party's view,
democratic government should be the main guarantor of fundamental citizenship freedoms. These include freedom of
expression, of the press and of worship, as well as freedom to
dissent, to be equal under the law and freedom from fear.[16]

For the modernized Labour Party, democratic socialism is based
on the rationale that to survive and prosper individually people
need to co-operate collectively. It believes that it is the duty of
the politically strong to help the economically weak, both nationally and internationally, and 'that everyone should have the
chance to participate in the decisions which affect our lives'. For
this, power must be decentralized and diversity of ownership and
equality of access ensured. Also 'there is nothing natural about

inequality. It is simply the characteristic . . . impressed upon society by those who benefit from great disparities in power and wealth.' For democratic socialists the social divisions of contemporary Britain 'are not only wrong in principle, they are damaging in practice'. But this does not mean that socialists want conformity. They 'rejoice in human diversity. Human differences are the work of nature. Inequalities are the result of human institutions.'[17]

Turning to the economy, Labour insists that in the modern world, with its fierce competition for resources, trade and wealth and the demands it makes on the environment, 'these demands can and must be balanced by a collective approach to common economic problems'. To promote economic success and efficiency, large-scale investment in research, development, schooling, further and higher education, and in training, depend on a positive lead from government. Support of the mixed economy is endorsed, since there are many areas where market allocation and market competition are 'essential to serving the consumer by meeting changing needs, responding to demand and promoting efficiency'. But the objectives sought by Labour 'clearly require a greater sector of the economy to be socially owned'. Common social ownership is to be encouraged for the purposes not only of greater efficiency and better economic performance: its 'fundamental justification is greater social justice and individual fulfilment and satisfaction'. Whilst democratic socialists believe in the market allocation of goods and services, it must be 'market allocation guided by agreement that the competitive system should pursue the objective of greater freedom, greater equality and greater choice'.[18]

It is in the context of the dominance of democratic socialist values in the Labour Party in the late 1980s that its policy reviews must be judged. By 1989 the Party had received reports from the seven policy review groups established by the annual conference in October 1987. These were directed at reassessing the Party's position on key aspects of economic and social policy for the 1990s. They started from the assumption of Labour's 'commitment to individual freedom, to a more just and more democratic society, to an efficient economy providing a better quality of life in a clean and safe environment, and to peace, security and fairness across the world'. Throughout the policy reviews Labour develops the case for a democratic and decentralized form of government, 'involving people as directly as possible in decisions which affect them' and 'using the power of the state to help create a society in which citizens have the means and the self-assurance to take responsibility for their own lives and to fulfil their obligations to others'.[19]

The policy review report on a productive and competitive economy sets out Labour's strategy for 'supply-side socialism' and argues that the economic role of modern government is to help make the market system work more efficiently. This means establishing a new partnership with business and enabling companies to produce quality commodities, with government investing in education, training and science and creating incentives to success. In its report on people at work, Labour wants a strategy to create a 'skills culture' offering new opportunities not only to children but also to everyone at work, so that Britain can succeed as a talent-based economy in the 1990s. The report on economic equality tackles the country's growing social and economic divisions. It sets out policies dealing with poverty, taxation and social insurance. In its report on consumers and the community the Party wants more protection for consumers. It offers a new framework for public and private services, aimed at putting people first, including a commitment to excellence in schools and the Health Service.[20]

The remaining policy review reports cover democracy for the individual and the community, the physical and social environment, and Britain in the world. The first of these argues the case for a directly elected legislative and administrative assembly in Scotland, with equivalent bodies in England and Wales. The report on the physical and social environment urges that protecting the environment is one of the greatest challenges facing humankind. In Labour's view, concern for the environment has to be integrated into economic, industrial, energy, transport and social policy, so that individuals, industry and government can work together in the interests of a balanced eco-system. Finally, in considering Britain's role in the world, the Labour Party argues that Britain is in a unique position to contribute, with other powers, in fighting environmental damage, deprivation, debt in the Third World and abuses of human rights.[21]

Organizationally, the Labour Party has two elements: the Parliamentary Labour Party (PLP) and the extra-parliamentary party.

The PLP consists of the party leader, the deputy leader and Labour MPs. The extra-parliamentary party has a number of elements, including the constituency Labour parties, trade union affiliates and the socialist societies, each of which sends delegates to the party's annual conference. The annual conference is the Party's supreme policy-making body which, among other tasks, elects the national executive annually. At the beginning of 1988 there were some 290,000 individual party members and about 5 million union-affiliated members, drawn from twenty-two Labour Party-affiliated trade unions. They sponsored 164 candidates at the 1987 general election, 129 of whom became MPs.[22] Although the institutional and financial connection between Labour and some of the main trade unions has its political critics, links between the two wings of the Labour movement remain firm. As the fraternal delegate from the Labour Party declared at the TUC's 119th annual conference at Blackpool in 1987, 'The message I bring to all trade unionists is: affiliate, delegate and participate within the Labour Party and help us to be rid of the most reactionary government of our time.'[23]

The Liberal Democrats

Although the British parliamentary system is essentially a two-party one, for many years there has been a distinct but volatile third party element within it. This role has traditionally been focused on the Liberal Party. At the time of writing, this 'third force' appears to be declining in popular support. But it needs to be recognized as an unstable feature of British political life which could re-emerge at a later date. It also represents a distinctive humanist tradition in British politics, associated with the radical centre of the political spectrum. The current heirs to this tradition are the Liberal Democrats which were known for a short time as the Social and Liberal Democrats.

The Social and Liberal Democrats were created in 1988, after a merger between the former Liberal Party and a majority of the Social Democratic Party (SDP). For a short period the new party was known simply as the Democrats but in 1989, after a ballot of members, it was renamed the Liberal Democrats. At the beginning of 1989 the [Liberal] Democrats claimed 'a national membership of 90,000, of which 78,000 [were] in England'. Before the

1988 merger the two separate parties jointly claimed some '150,000 members, of which 52,000 were SDP'.[24] Compared with the two major political parties, the Conservatives and Labour, the Liberal Democrats are a relatively small party at the centre of the political spectrum.

The roots of the former Liberal Party, like those of the Conservatives, can be traced back to the early nineteenth century but it was the formation of the Birmingham Liberal Alliance in 1865 which was 'to lead to imitations throughout the country and to the establishment of the National Liberal Federation in 1877'. The Liberal Party reached the peak of its power in the early twentieth century but was a spent force after 1922. This was due to the emergence of the Labour Party 'as the second largest party and as the alternative to the Conservative Party', thus drawing to an end the political significance of the once great Liberals.[25]

The SDP, in contrast, had been formed only in 1981, with the initial support of fourteen former members of the PLP, 'together with the active backing of several members of past Labour governments and approving noises from the leadership of the Liberal Party'.[26] Although a formal electoral alliance was forged between the Liberals and SDP at the general election of 1987, it subsequently broke down, largely over the issue of the proposed merger between them. After the bitterness of the merger debate, the [Liberal] Democrats emerged as a new party consisting of the bulk of the old Liberals and some of the SDP membership, with what remained of the SDP claiming some 25,000 members at the beginning of 1989.[27]

As a party new to the political scene the Liberal Democrats promptly set out to elaborate what they saw as their distinctive political philosophy and values in a Green Paper published in 1989. The paper develops, in essence, out of the party's constitution, which emphasizes 'a fair, free and open society, in which we seek to balance the fundamental values of liberty, equality and community, and in which no one shall be enslaved by poverty, ignorance or conformity'. The Green Paper claims to draw its inspiration from the traditions of both the Liberals and the Social Democrats, with their different though parallel philosophical and political paths. The intellectual and political roots of the Liberal Democrats go back, it is argued, 'through the great reforming Governments of 1945–1951 and 1905–1914, to the popular radicals of the nineteenth century who fought for the rights of the common people and against privilege and oppression'. On the basis of this common ancestry, the Liberal Democrats claim, 'we stand for three basic values – liberty, equality and community'.[28]

In setting out the Liberal Democrat alternative, the Green Paper analyses the changing nature of British society and some of the political implications. It focuses on changes in the patterns of production, social and demographic change, cultural and political change and the changing nature of international economics and politics. The central message of the Paper is that 'only a new politics, embracing new institutions, new habits of mind and, above all, a new flexibility and openness, can realise the full potential of the new order which is beginning to take shape around us'. The Green Paper savagely attacks the Conservative government's political and economic policies after 1979, and their consequences for people and society generally. In the Liberal Democrats' view, 'no recent government has evoked such bitter opposition from its enemies or such hysterical adulation from its friends'. It describes the Conservatives' position as 'the retreat to the past', where government uses 'the rhetoric of modernity, but its underlying message is hopelessly antiquated'.[29]

The Liberal Democrats argue that Britain needs a different political vision, based on different social values. For Liberal Democrats the good society is one in which all have the freedom to 'develop their own potential, to learn from their own mistakes, to realise their capabilities for growth and in which all recognize their responsibilities to the communities to which they belong'. The Liberal Democrats draw two crucial implications from their view of human nature. One is that there is no simple litmus test of policy. The other is that Liberal Democrats are 'not Utopians, trying to create a perfect society . . . the balancing has to be done here and now'. Liberal Democrat values imply four commitments. First, Liberal Democrats stand for 'an open, tolerant, diverse and pluralistic society', with protection for minorities and where power is dispersed. Second, they stand for community power as well as individual power. Third, they stand for equal citizenship, since 'a society without citizenship is not a true political community'. Fourth, they hold 'that each generation is the steward of the Earth's resources, with an obligation to hand them on, unspoiled, to future generations'.[30]

The Liberal Democrats identify six central themes around which the party's policies should take shape: citizenship in an open society; community power; 'taking a long view'; quality of life; life chances for all; and only one world. In outline, the Liberal Democrats argue that 'the extremes of Left and Right both concentrate power, in order to remodel society from top down, in accordance with a predetermined ideal'. In the Democrats' view, the foundations of British liberties have always been fragile, whilst 'the basic principles of pluralist democracy have never been adequately protected in this country'. Accordingly there is a need to secure a new constitutional settlement, embracing explicit protections of basic human rights. These include devolution of power, reform of Parliament, and electoral reform. Linked with this, Liberal Democratic 'policies must re-emphasize the importance of community as a buffer between the individual and the state'. By community government the Liberal Democrats mean government where individuals in the community exercise control over their own lives. The notion is wider than that of locality. 'It implies a society of self-governing associations . . . in every sphere where men and women can pursue common purposes, hammered out through free discussion and debate.'[31]

The Liberal Democrats condemn the short-termism of economic decision-making in the UK, fortified in recent years by the 'free market dogma which has become the reigning orthodoxy'. The country's past economic failures have not occurred by accident, they claim: 'they are the product of the short-sighted individualism of managers, investors, workers, politicians and civil servants over many generations'. Free-market theory fails to recognize that the market is effective only when information flows between producers and consumers; 'where the market fails, public power . . . must intervene'. Three critical areas demanding public intervention are: environmental protection, long-term investment, and urban regeneration. The Liberal Democrats would seek, therefore, to facilitate a sustainable economy developing recycling, conservation and pollution control technologies and smaller and more energy-efficient products. They would seek to invest in the development of human capital, by being 'the party of skills and knowledge in a world in which skill- and knowledge-intensive activities hold the key to quality of life, to self-fulfilment, and to competitive success'. And they would seek to regenerate inner-city blight.[32]

The Liberal Democrats also believe that the quality of life matters. 'It crosses the spectrum of environmental enhancement, consumer rights, the quality of public services, and the quality of our democracy itself.' Here there are three essential tasks for government. First, government must identify those public goods which the common interest demands must be secured, such as education, effective policing and crime prevention. Second, government should ensure that public services are provided in an efficient and sensitive way. Third, the common interest requires that government should set high standards for the private and voluntary sectors and for specific goods and services.

Central to Liberal Democrat beliefs is the positive view of freedom, with the State's responsibility being 'to ensure that *all* have access to what life offers'. To make this a reality, two things are required. First, it rests with the State to ensure that all have a decent level of income enabling everyone to participate in society and not to feel excluded from it. Second, the State must also make opportunities widely available for personal develop- ment, enabling people to break free of the limiting conditions of their present circumstances. In the Democrats' vision it is in a society 'where individuals are not only free to develop their tal- ents, but are afforded the opportunities to do so, that cultural, as well as material, poverty will diminish'.

Finally, the Liberal Democrats are committed to working closely with other countries, with this co-operation finding its closest expression in Europe. 'Just as the single market is becom- ing an extended domestic market for the businessmen [*sic*] and consumers of Europe so, we believe, the Community should achieve closer political union with democratic institutions account- able to its citizens'. This implies that it is Europe which should be the principal channel through which the UK makes its contri- bution to world peace and prosperity.[33]

Other parties

The other political parties are a heterogeneous group of political interests and ideologies, including the nationalist parties, the Northern Ireland parties, and the Green Party. Scotland and

Wales both have nationalist parties, the Scottish Nationalist Party (SNP) and Plaid Cymru respectively. Although the SNP took about 30 per cent of the popular vote in Scotland in the mid-1970s, its influence and support have declined since then. Compared with the SNP, Plaid Cymru has always been a more radical party and has laid some stress on Welsh cultural and linguistic roots as a basis for Welsh independence. Like the SNP, Plaid Cymru has been unsuccessful in raising its share of the vote in Wales. It remains a reservoir of protest votes, drawing on sentiments of Welsh nationalism and local frustration with English domination of the political agenda.

Party differentiation in Northern Ireland is based not on class and economic interests as in the rest of the UK but on religious and sectarian differences. Even the religious parties are themselves sectarian. Amongst the protestant groupings, for example, there are the Official Unionist Party and the Democratic Unionist Party. The Catholic groupings include: the Social and Democratic Labour Party, the Catholic Workers' Party and Sinn Fein. Sinn Fein is the political wing of the revolutionary Provisional Irish Republican Army, which maintains close links with radical Irish nationalists in the Republic of Ireland. The nationalists' basic aim is political union with the republic.

The smaller parties in the UK include the SDP, the Greens and a number of left-wing sectarian groups. Of these parties, only the SDP has had elected MPs, whilst the Greens managed to attract a rising number of protest votes in parts of Britain in the late 1980s.

Pressure Groups

In modern society, formal participation in the political system, beyond voting in elections, is normally channelled through pressure groups. Where individuals or organizations, for example, become involved politically, they join and participate in those organized groups which reflect their political interests and opinions. Organized political groups are of two kinds, political parties and pressure groups. Whilst it is possible to draw an analytical distinction between political parties and pressure groups, in practice it is not always easy to distinguish between them.

Both sorts of group pursue political demands through the political system and both are concerned with power and the ways in which power is used. Sometimes their memberships overlap. This happens, for example, with some Labour Party and trade union members or those individuals who are members of both the Conservative Party and an employers' organization such as the National Farmers Union or the Confederation of British Industry.

Nature and scope

As discussed earlier, political parties seek to influence policy decisions directly by getting their leading members into formal positions of political authority in the European Parliament, the House of Commons or local government. Political parties attempt to win political control to use political power. What largely distinguishes pressure groups from political parties is that pressure groups seek to influence policy decisions, not to get their representatives into positions of formal political authority. Whilst some pressure groups, such as Shelter or Age Concern, are politically independent, others have close links with political parties, or even one political party, and may help them fight elections. But they do not normally put up candidates for political office. British United Industrialists, for example, is an influential pressure group with strong links with the Conservative Party but it does not sponsor BUI candidates in elections. Similarly, trade unions with political objects and political levies are free to sponsor Labour Party candidates and provide them with financial help at elections. Those candidates are Labour Party candidates, however, they are not candidates of the Transport and General Workers Union, Manufacturing, Science or Finance or the Amalgamated Engineering Union, for instance.

Whilst it is relatively easy to distinguish between the Conservative Party and the National Union of Teachers (NUT), for example, it is less easy to distinguish between the roles of minor political parties and pressure groups. In the first example, the Conservatives are a broad-based national political party which fights elections and the NUT is a narrowly based teachers' union which, amongst its other roles, acts as a pressure group for schoolteachers. The political roles of Plaid Cymru or the Green Party, on the other hand, are more akin to those of pressure groups than to those of political parties. Neither is likely to win enough parliamentary seats in the House of Commons to form a government, thus making them in effect interest-centred pressure groups rather than full-blown political parties. More realistically, they seek to influence policy rather than to determine it.

Both political parties and pressure groups, then, are concerned with power and may themselves be powerful. The power of political parties depends on electoral success and support in the ballot box, whilst the power of pressure groups depends on a number of factors. These include their membership base, the resources at their disposal, their political appeal and organizational effectiveness. Since political parties need to have relatively wide appeal to win votes for their candidates, their political programmes tend to be broadly based. Pressure groups, in contrast, have much narrower political objectives and are sometimes based on a single issue, such as the Society for the Protection of the Unborn Child or the Abortion Law Reform Society. These factors lead to differences in organization between parties and pressure groups. Because political parties contest elections, they are organized nationally and locally. Most pressure groups, in contrast, may have branches locally but tend to be more active nationally, except where they are dealing with specifically local campaigns including planning, building and development issues.

Pressure groups may be defined in general as 'social aggregates with some level of cohesion and shared aims which attempt to influence the political decision-making process'.[34] Various typologies have been proposed but there is no clear agreement on the labels to be used in categorizing pressure groups. Those which are used include: 'cause' and 'economic' groups; 'promotional' and 'protectional' groups; and 'interest' and 'attitude' groups. Where the 'interest' and 'attitude' group dichotomy is used, the term 'interest group' is normally applied to those organizations which are created because of their members' common socio-economic goals. Members of the Engineering Employers Federation, for example, combine to protect the common interests of federated engineering firms, which may be large or small, multi-plant or single-plant, and geographically concentrated or geographically separated. The managers representing these firms may be young or middle-aged, professionally well qualified or less well qualified, and practising Christians or otherwise. What brings these enterprises and corporate representatives together is their common commercial interest as manufacturing organizations, not their organizational characteristics or the personal aspirations of their managers. It is really quite surprising how common economic interests can bring quite disparate individuals or organizations together, for limited economic purposes at least.

Attitude groups, in contrast, are based on the commonly held beliefs and values of their members. The motivating force behind joining the Royal Society for the Protection of Birds, for example, is not economic self-interest but concern for the protection and well being of such creatures. Similarly, members of Age Concern share a compassion for and commitment to the elderly. Such groups contain men and women, professional people and non-professional people, agnostics and religious people, and so on. What draws them together is the attitudes they share as individuals and their wish to organize collectively to defend or extend the rights of the political interests they represent. Other examples of attitude groups are the Campaign for Nuclear Disarmament, Amnesty International and the Society for the Protection of Rural England.

Activities and power

In attempting to influence government decisions in their favour, pressure groups try to gain access to those who take decisions and, to do so, they lobby key individuals at different levels of power. Their activities range from trying to influence the Prime Minister, the Cabinet and government at one level to local government councillors and officers at another. They also seek to influence public opinion. Thus the methods and levels which each pressure group uses to communicate its opinions and demands vary widely and according to its specific power and the circumstances of the time. Although the most powerful pressure groups have almost instant access to the important parts of the political system, the weakest groups have to improvise to make their views heard at all.

Some powerful pressure groups have well established relations with government, on a permanent or semi-permanent basis. These relations are sometimes channelled through advisory or standing committees, staffed jointly by civil servants and pressure-group representatives. The National Farmers Union, for example, has close links with the Ministry of Agriculture and government Ministers. Whilst relatively few pressure groups have the necessary power to gain access to policy-making machinery at these levels, they use their representatives skilfully to pursue their objectives. If pressure groups cannot influence the main decision-makers directly, that is, government and its senior civil servants, they are forced to lobby MPs or members in the House of Lords. In lobbying Parliament they want MPs to put pressure on government to change or maintain its policies. They may even lobby MPs to introduce legislation from the backbenches, where this is possible, although it is very difficult to achieve in practice. But they can get MPs to put forward amendments and speak for or against legislation in either House.

If pressure groups cannot influence Parliament, or if their parliamentary supporters do not carry enough political weight, they are forced to operate outside Parliament. They may try to influence political parties, for example, and thus slowly build up support for their policies within them. The Campaign for Nuclear Disarmament (CND) is an example of an organization using this approach. For many years its main policy objective has been unilateral nuclear disarmament. This has never been accepted by any UK government and there is little support for it amongst senior civil servants. Although CND has some supporters in Parliament, they are too few in number to have any impact. To circumvent this, CND supporters tried to induce both the former Liberal Party and the Labour Party to accept non-nuclear defence policies. Whilst they were unsuccessful with the Liberals, they were eventually successful with the Labour Party. Since then Labour has moved away from a policy of unilateral nuclear disarmament to a more complex multilateral position, thus requiring CND to adapt its political strategy in response.

Where it is not possible for pressure groups to influence national political parties even outside Parliament, or if they are unsuccessful in doing so, they are forced to try influencing the mass media and public opinion. The objective of campaigning at grass-roots level is to try and create shifts in public opinion in the hope that those in political power, and those with political influence, will feel the need to respond positively. The tactics used to achieve this include rallies, marches, petitions and media campaigns to get the message across to the general public. These activities, in turn, can lead to extensive media coverage, television documentaries and other in-depth analyses, thus putting pressure on Ministers and government to modify their policy. An example in recent years has been concern for the environment. Various attitudinal environmental pressure groups, such as Friends of the Earth and Greenpeace, have mounted strong grass-roots campaigns to influence public opinion and governmental policies on such issues as lead-free petrol, the use of chlorofluorocarbons, and organic farming. In some areas they have been fairly successful, in others less so.

It is clear, then, that pressure groups vary widely in their power bases and influence, and this affects the ways in which they operate. Sometimes the more visible a pressure group is the less is its influence, and the more likely it is to operate at media and grassroots levels. The most powerful groups rarely need to use such tactics. The most important determinant of pressure-group power is its position in the economic system and the sanctions it has to back its demands. Sanctions may be positive, such as co-operating with the authorities, or negative, including the withdrawal of financial resources or taking punitive actions against those in power. Large employer pressure groups, such as those representing the banks, financial interests and insurance companies, are crucial to the economy and most governments listen to their views with some degree of deference. Some trade unions had a great deal of power in the 1970s but they were rarely consulted or listened to during the 1980s, since the government purposely excluded them from the policy-making process.

It follows that interests groups are generally more powerful than attitude groups, since the latter normally lack effective economic sanctions. Pressure groups which are powerful and influential have close relations with the machinery of government. These normally include the Police Federation, the Law Society, the Bar Council and the British Medical Association. All these bodies have professional expertise which governments usually need to draw upon. Thus, in general, these and similar pressure groups have developed good working relations with government rather than antagonistic ones.

The financial resources and leadership of pressure groups are also important determinants of group power and influence, since they affect the types of campaigns and activities they pursue. Even the size of the membership of a pressure group is secondary. What is important is the group's representativeness and the proportion of potential members actually in the group. The National Farmers Union (NFU), for example, represents the great majority of farmers. Hence government channels all its agricultural communications through that body. If there were several farmers' unions, each individually would be much weaker than the NFU is collectively. Public support is particularly important for attitude groups, since they have few sanctions to use against the authorities. Also, those powerful pressure groups whose aims are generally acceptable to members of the political system, such as the business community and the Churches, find it much easier to influence policy decisions than do those whose views clash with dominant opinion. The latter include the National Association for the Care and Resettlement of Offenders, the National Council for Civil Liberties and the Child Poverty Action Group.

Many sections of society, however, are represented by weak pressure groups or by no pressure groups at all. Generally, consumer groups are less powerful than producer groups, whilst the economically weak, such as one-parent families, the unemployed and pensioners, are far less influential than the economically strong. This reflects one of the major problems of liberal democratic societies, the unequal distribution of power. Nevertheless, pressure groups are an important part of the political system. Critics argue that certain pressure groups are so powerful that they can force governments to change their policies. They claim that this is undemocratic, since government is based on an electoral majority in the House of Commons, and represents the whole electorate, whereas pressure groups represent only their members' sectional interests.

Supporters of pressure groups, on the other hand, maintain that they are important channels of political communication between government and the public. They inform government and the administrative machinery of specific problems and opinions. Elections, they suggest, are too general and infrequent to be of value as genuine channels of communication. Pressure groups are especially vital between election times, when they become important vehicles of communication between the political authorities and the electorate. In this way they are seen to extend political democracy and reinforce liberal democratic political culture and values.

Elections and Voting Behaviour

Party politics begins with individual behaviour. Some individuals join political parties, some participate in them actively and a few seek public political office in elections. Most adults over the age of eighteen have the right to vote in local, national and European elections, though the participation rate varies. About three-quarters of the electorate turn out at general elections but only about a third in local and European elections.

There is no simple explanation why people vote as they do. Nevertheless, there has always been a relationship between voters' social characteristics and their party choice. These characteristics include class, age, gender and occupation as well as religion and ethnic group. Traditionally, there has been a tendency for the middle-class, professional and higher-income groups to vote for the Conservative Party and for working-class voters to support Labour. At least a third of the working class, however, always votes Conservative. Most women vote Conservative, whilst ethnic minorities generally favour Labour. Votes for the Liberal Democrat, centre and nationalist parties tend to come from across the class, occupational and ethnic divisions.

Table 32 outlines how Britain voted in the general election of 1987. It indicates that whilst the correlation between voting behaviour and social class has diminished in recent years, 'divisions between the manual and middle classes remain important'. According to MORI, 54 per cent of the middle class (groups A, B and C1) voted Conservative, compared with 18 per cent voting Labour. Similarly, 48 per cent of unskilled manual workers (groups D and E) voted Labour, compared with 30 per cent voting Conservative. The most significant feature of the Conservative Party's support in this election, and in recent ones, was its strength amongst the working class (groups C2, D and E). Here 'it gained 36% of the vote (compared to Labour's 48%), its largest post-war share'. As in 1979 and 1983, Conservative support was built on what Crewe calls the 'new working class': manual workers living in the south, who are home-owners, employed in the private

233

Table 32
How Britain voted in 1987

| Allegiance | Class | | | Union members | Sex | | Age | | | | All |
	ABC1	C2	DE		Men	Women	18–24	25–34	35–54	55+	
All	43	27	30	23	48	52	14	19	33	34	100
Conservative	54	40	30	30	43	43	37	39	45	46	43
Labour	18	36	48	42	32	32	40	33	29	31	32
Alliance	26	22	22	26	23	23	21	25	24	21	23
Other	2	2	2	2	2	2	2	2	2	2	2

Source: MORI, British public opinion: General election, 1987, London, MORI, 1987.

234 *The Corporate Environment*

sector, and not union members. The MORI poll also shows how housing tenure divides the working class. 'The Conservatives had a 12% lead over Labour among working-class homeowners, but ran 32% behind working-class council tenants'.[35]

Other features of table 32 include the Liberal-Social Democratic Alliance's consistent share of the vote amongst all social classes, all trade unionists, all age groups and between the sexes. It ranged between 20 and 25 per cent in all cases. Among trade union members, 42 per cent voted Labour and 30 per cent voted Conservative. Compared with the 1983 election, this was an improvement for Labour, when only 39 per cent of trade union members voted Labour, 31 per cent Conservative and 29 per cent Alliance. Support for the Conservatives tended to increase with age, whilst support for Labour tended to decrease with age. Conservative support was strongest among those aged fifty-five and over and accounted for 46 per cent of those voting in this age cohort. Labour support was strongest amongst those aged between eighteen and twenty-four, where 40 per cent of this cohort voted Labour.[36]

Table 33
Main regional changes in voting behaviour, 1983–87

Region	Conservative	Labour	Alliance	(No. of seats)
North/West Britain	−2·7	+6·5	−4·2	(344)
South/East Britain	+1·2	+1·6	−2·5	(273)
Devon and Cornwall	−3·1	+2·6	+0·7	(16)

Source: J. Curtice and M. Steed, *Analysis of 1987 election*, in D. Butler and D. Kavanagh, *The British general election of 1987*, Basingstoke, Macmillan, 1988.

According to Curtice and Steed (1987), there was considerable geographical variation in the distribution of each party's share of the vote in the 1987 election. The UK did not cast a national verdict in favour of the Conservatives. The regional changes for the period 1983–87 are summarized in table 33. This shows that Labour's vote increased most sharply in north and west Britain, including Wales and Scotland, where both the Conservative and Alliance vote decreased. In the south and east of Britain, including the Midlands, Labour and the Conservatives marginally increased their share of the vote, whilst that of the Alliance fell. The Alliance vote fell particularly heavily in working-class constituencies in the north and west of Britain. This means that the Alliance suffered a serious setback in its attempt to erode Labour's share of the vote in its traditional heartlands. There is, therefore, 'clear evidence of a broad division between North/West Britain, consisting of Scotland, Wales and the North of England, in which Labour advanced strongly, and a contrasting area'. This is south and east Britain, including the Midlands, where the Conservatives did better than in 1983.[37]

Dealignment theses

A number of studies argue that voters have been increasingly reluctant to vote for the two major parties in recent elections and that people's occupational class provides an increasingly poor guide to their party choice when voting. It is generally agreed that between 1945 and 1964 voting preferences had two stable elements. First, people identified with and voted for one of the two major parties, the Conservatives or Labour. Second, white-collar households tended to vote Conservative and households headed by manual workers tended to vote Labour. Since then, it is argued, a dealignment in that pattern of voting has occurred. One form of dealignment is 'partisan' dealignment, the other is 'class' dealignment.

Partisan dealignment refers to the declining probability that individuals will remain loyal to a single political party in successive elections. Three kinds of evidence are said to illustrate the decline of political partisanship. The first is that since 1970 voters have steadily deserted the two main political parties in general elections. In elections between 1950 and 1970 over 90 per cent of the electorate voting chose either the Conservative or the Labour Parties. In all the following elections, including that of 1987, the two-party share of the poll fell to around 75 per cent. Since 1970, in other words, various other parties, such as the nationalists in Wales and Scotland, those in Northern Ireland and the former Alliance parties, have increased their electoral support at the expense of the Conservatives and Labour.

Second, whilst some of the increased support for third parties could have come from people who might otherwise have abstained, most was taken from the two major parties. Yet at the same time, there is little evidence of individuals becoming third-party partisans. For example, although votes for the nationalist parties increased proportionally in the mid-1970s, they fell away subsequently. Similarly, there is little evidence that people became Liberal or Alliance partisans. Liberal supporters appear to be fickle voters, not necessarily supporting the party at consecutive elections. According to Sarlvik and Crewe (1983), during the 1960s and 1970s only 30 per cent of those shifting their votes from a major party to the Liberals at one election voted Liberal at the next election. More recently, increased support for the Liberals and Alliance Parties in the 1980s has meant that a lot of people are shifting votes between elections, even if the degree of volatility does not seem to have increased substantially.

A third factor suggesting that partisan dealignment is taking place is the weakening of party attachment. One explanation is that there is disillusionment with the two main parties because of their failures in government. Another is that voters may be becoming more instrumental politically, choosing between parties on a 'what's in it for me?' basis. Alternatively, it may be that voters are more concerned with political issues which do appear to lend themselves to partisan solutions. Sarlvik and Crewe, for example, argue that the Labour Party has increasingly offered policies to the electorate of which its own supporters disapprove. They imply that Labour has been unpopular because of its traditional class politics. These include supporting the unions, nationalization and an expansion of the Welfare State. Such policies, they claim, have a diminishing appeal to the electorate.

Class dealignment refers to the declining probability that individuals vote for the party most closely associated with their social class and occupational status. Until the mid-1960s there was a strong correlation between occupational class and voting behaviour. Since then, two developments appear to have occurred. First, between 1964 and 1974, there was an increase in white-collar and professional support for the Labour Party, support which had traditionally gone to the Conservatives. This support seems to have been drawn especially from people working in the public sector. Second, since 1974, there has been a steady decline in the number of blue-collar manual workers, especially skilled ones, voting for the Labour Party. This has benefited both the

Conservatives since 1979 and the former Alliance Parties in 1983 and 1987.

Table 34

Support for political party, by occupational class, 1983 (%)

Occupational class	Conservative	Labour	Alliance	All the electorate
White-collar				
AB	26·7	7·8	19·2	19·0
C1	29·0	15·9	20·9	22·8
Manual, pensioners, unemployed				
C2	25.0	32·9	28·6	28·3
DE	19·3	43·4	31·3	29·9
Total	100·0	100·0	100·0	100·0

Source: Gallup Report No 275, July 1983.

Table 34 shows that in the 1983 election the Labour Party remained heavily dependent upon the support of manual workers, pensioners and the unemployed in groups C2, D and E. Over 75 per cent of its support came from these groups alone. The Conservative Party, in contrast, drew about a quarter of its support from white-collar workers in groups A and B. But it also found about a third of its support amongst skilled manual workers in group C. Support for the then Alliance Parties was almost an exact replication of the occupational structure, with 19 per cent support among groups A and B (19 per cent of the electorate), 21 per cent C1 (23 per cent), 29 per cent C2 (21 per cent) and 31 per cent D and E (30 per cent).

Interpreting dealignment

Some writers deny that class dealignment is happening, whilst accepting that some degree of partisan dealignment is taking place. They argue that a false impression is being given because most studies use inappropriate class categories. Heath and his colleagues (1985) suggest that the class dealignment thesis greatly exaggerates the degree of change in voting behaviour. They argue that it is change in the class structure and political change which are the important factors. They show that self-employed manual workers, and manual workers in supervisory positions, vote differently from other manual workers. Examining the voting behaviour of manual workers without authority, Heath and his colleagues show that in the 1983 election this group voted Labour in the same proportions as before. What happened was that this group was smaller than it had been previously, and in 1983 the Labour Party was electorally unpopular. Their conclusion is that 'whether for better or worse, Britain is still divided by class'. At the same time, 'the shape of the class structure has changed, with important implications for Labour'. They contend that 'Labour's decline, as well as the Alliance rise, have as much to do with political as with social sources of change'.[38]

As outlined earlier, one of the strongest electoral trends has been increasing regional differences in voting behaviour. Indeed, support for both the Conservative and the Labour Parties has steadily become more concentrated geographically since 1955. In essence, the Conservatives have obtained their support largely from southern and rural constituencies, whilst Labour has become concentrated in northern and urban ones. Liberal and former Alliance votes, in contrast, are very evenly dispersed across the country. There are three consequences. First, the number of marginal constituencies has reduced, as each major party consolidates its support in the constituencies it normally wins. Second, the nationalist parties have benefited from regional variations, since their support is regionally concentrated. Third, the centre parties such as the Liberal Democrats find it difficult to win seats under plurality voting, because their support is geographically dispersed.

The Implications for Management

Political parties provide the electorate with distinct choices in local, general and European elections. At every election, each political party publishes a manifesto outlining its policy programme, and what it proposes doing if elected to office. In a basically two-party system, and a 'first past the post' or plurality voting system, there is normally a clear winning party after general and local election campaigns. This gives the majority party immense power in carrying out its election pledges during its period of office. When there is broad political consensus on major policy issues, as between 1945 and 1975, political change, and its likely impact on corporate decisions and managerial actions, tends to be incrementalist over the lifetime of a Parliament—or of a local council. This is because, in these circumstances, the main political parties do not differ significantly in their key policy proposals. Political continuity is associated with incrementalist change in the policy process.

During periods of conviction politics, as in the 1980s, which political party is in office, especially at Westminster, does make a difference in terms of policy. There are likely to be major implications for management, in both the short and medium term. Changes in economic policy clearly affect an organization's marketing, production and financial planning and its business opportunities as a provider of goods or services in the market place. Changes in legislation affecting consumers, workers or product competition demand relevant response from managers. And changes in social policy can influence managerial decisions affecting resource allocation and demand for welfare provision by people in the community. Under these conditions, political discontinuity is associated with radical change in the policy process.

Given the party system and political structure prevailing in the UK, managements need to be alert to the strategies which can be used in influencing not only national government but also European Community institutions in the policy-making process. Very few organizations are overtly party political but some organizations, at different times, need to act politically to defend or extend their position as economic interest groups. Sometimes this is done on an individual, one-off basis. On other occasions it is done collectively, through such bodies as trade or business associations. These may be represented on permanent advisory or consultative committees of government departments or be invited to join *ad hoc* bodies of inquiry. Trade and business associations may also use full-time lobbyists, or employ MPs as consultants, to protect and advance their member organizations' interests in Parliament.

Because political power tends to be concentrated at central level in UK politics, organized pressure groups operate largely at that level. But local authorities influence the local environment, exercise regulatory powers over planning controls and similar activities and facilitate business development. In seeking to influence local authorities, managements lobby council members, approach council officers or operate through chambers of commerce. Further, since the late 1980s there have been increasing opportunities for local business people to become involved in governing polytechnics and colleges, in advisory and consultative committees and in training and education councils.

Decisions taken in the European Community also affect business and corporate decisions, and will do so more and more in the future. Managers need to be aware of the Community regulations and directives affecting their operations. They should also identify the funds available to their organization and the procedures for applying for financial support. Members of the European Parliament are an important source of information, as are the European Commission offices in the UK. As the political powers of the Community institutions increase, the need to develop strategies towards them, and links with these bodies, will become more necessary for corporate organizations. These strategies include establishing representation on relevant committees, contacts with key European decision-takers, and education and training programmes to update managers' understanding of European affairs.

This chapter has concentrated on the impact of parties and pressure groups on the political process in the UK. It seems likely, however, that as the country becomes more closely integrated economically with the European Community its national sovereignty will be weakened further. These trends have been accelerated by the growth of international economic interdependence, which has made it increasingly difficult for the interests of the medium-sized nation State to prevail in the economic sphere. There has also been a marked growth in the role of multinational companies, a deregulation of national capital markets and an increasingly globalized capital market. This makes it more difficult for States such as the UK, with open market economies, to operate economic policies out of line with the rest of the developed world. As Marquand argues, 'the globalisation of economic forces requires a corresponding globalisation of political institutions to cope with them . . . the nation-state . . . will have to share some of its power with supranational bodies'.[39]

An important demonstration of the increasing Europeanization of political decision-making, and its likely impact on management, is the proposal for a statute for a European company. The statute, which is linked with proposals for employee involvement, is designed to enable companies governed by the laws of different member States to choose a structure for co-operation and restructuring suited to the dimensions of the large internal market to be achieved in 1992. The latest proposal, put forward at the end of 1989, aims to free companies from the legal and practical constraints arising from the existence of twelve separate legal systems by offering them an optional structure based on Community law and independent national laws so far as they can be harmonized.

It is proposed that a European company may be set up by merger, by the formation of a holding company, or by the formation of a joint subsidiary. The structure of the European company envisages the option of either a single-tier board or a two-tier system with a management board and a supervisory board. The company will be treated in the same way as other companies governed by legislation of the member State in which they have registered offices. The involvement of employees in the European company provides three models of participation:

- Participation in determining the membership of the supervisory board,

- Participation through a staff representative body distinct from the governing bodies of the company,

- A form of participation to be established by collective agreement.

The management or administrative board and employee representatives will have to agree on the choice of model, since there can be no European company without employee participation, with all models conferring equivalent rights on employees.

These proposals and similar measures are clearly contentious, with the political parties having different views on the matter. They also indicate how the political interests of managers and business organizations need to be organized collectively and transnationally if they are to be protected and represented in the political process. This is increasingly likely to take place in the 1990s. Events will also be determined, of course, by the outcome of future elections at both European and national level.

References

1 BALL A. *British political parties*. Basingstoke, Macmillan, 1987. p 216.
2 *ibid*. p 3.
3 *ibid*. pp 4 and 5.
4 KING D S. *The new right*. Basingstoke, Macmillan, 1987. p 111f.
5 BELL D S (ed). *The Conservative government, 1979–84*. London, Croom Helm, 1985. p 3.
6 Gamble A. *The free economy and the strong state*, Basingstoke, Macmillan, 1988, p 29.
7 *ibid*. p 38.
8 *ibid*. pp 29–37.
9 SCRUTON R. *The meaning of conservatism*. Harmondsworth, Penguin, 1980. p 45.
10 WINTOUR P. 'Labour recruiters to woo the working class'. *The Guardian*. 17 January 1989. p 6.
11 LABOUR RESEARCH DEPARTMENT. 'The money that brought Thatcher to power.' *Labour Research* 77(12), December 1988. p 7.
12 WEBSTER D. *The labour party and the new left*. London, Fabian Society, 1981. p 1.
13 *ibid*. pp 2 and 4.
14 *ibid*. p 6f.
15 LABOUR PARTY. *Democratic socialist aims and values*. London, Labour Party, 1988. pp 1–3.
16 *ibid*. pp 4 and 5.
17 *ibid*. p 6f.
18 *ibid*. pp 8–11.
19 LABOUR PARTY. *Meet the challenge: make the change*. London, Labour Party, 1989. pp 5 and 6.
20 *ibid*. pp 9–54.
21 *ibid*. pp 55–88.
22 BUTLER D *and* KAVANAGH D. *The British general election of 1987*. Basingstoke, Macmillan, 1988. p 206.
23 TRADES UNION CONGRESS. *Report of the 119th annual Trades Union Congress*. London, TUC, 1988. p 482.
24 WINTOUR. *op cit*. p 6.
25 BALL. *op cit*. pp 28 and 120.
26 *ibid*. p 229.
27 WINTOUR *op cit*. p 6.
28 SOCIAL AND LIBERAL DEMOCRATS. *Our different vision*. London, SLD Federal Green Paper No. 7, 1989. pp 1 and 17.
29 *ibid*. pp 2–7.
30 *ibid*. pp 9 and 10.
31 *ibid*. p 11f.
32 *ibid*. p 12f.
33 *ibid*. pp 14–16.

34 BALL A R *and* MILLARD F. *Pressure politics in industrial societies.* Basingstoke, Macmillan, 1986. p 33f.
35 BUTLER *and* KAVANAGH. *op cit.* p 274f.
36 *ibid.* p 124.
37 CURTICE J *and* STEED M. *Analysis of 1987 elections* in *ibid.* p 320.
38 HEATH A, JOWELL R *and* CURTICE J. *How Britain votes.* Oxford, Pergammon, 1985, p 39.
39 MARQUAND D. 'Twelve into one will go.' *Marxism today.* April 1989. p 17.

9

Law and the Administration of Justice

In essence, the law is that body of rules, whether formally enacted or customary, which the State recognizes as binding on its citizens. It has also been described by Kahn-Freund (1977) 'as a technique for the regulation of social power'.[1] In this context, power is the ability to direct and affect the behaviour of others, ultimately by some sort of sanction. Besides social power, there is political and economic power. They tend to be interrelated and the sanctions for enforcing power may be either positive or negative. Positive sanctions reward people, negative ones threaten them. In any liberal society, naked power to determine rules and decisions, and to enforce them, by individuals, organizations or government, is insufficient to maintain social stability and social order. The power to act needs to be accepted as legitimate by those who are affected by such decisions, whether as property owners, employers, workers, consumers, citizens or in any of their other social roles. To be acceptable in democratic societies, the right of those with power to take decisions has to be recognized by those without positional or resource power, irrespective of any sanctions which the powerful may possess. In an ordered society ultimate power and the right to enforce it rest with those controlling the machinery and agencies of the State. It is contained, in other words, in the legislative, executive and judicial organs of government.

The major functions of governing are law-making, law application and law adjudication. In the liberal democratic State the concept of the 'rule of law' is fundamental. First, it reflects the preference of citizens for 'law and order' rather than anarchy, warfare or civil strife. It implies that conflicts and disputes between parties should be settled by peaceful and constitutional means rather than by the use of armed force, terrorism or other forms of physical coercion. Moreover, if the State is identified with force and coercive might, the rule of law lacks any moral authority or legitimacy. Second, the rule of law can also be interpreted as meaning that government itself must be conducted in accordance with the law and that the machinery of government must always operate through the law. In this way, the law acts as a buttress of democratic principles, since new governmental powers can be conferred on the executive and administrative authorities only by Parliament. Third, as the law develops, it should result in the rule of law reflecting changing social values, because the legal system exists in a wider social and economic context.

Law and Society

Harris (1984) argues that 'an understanding of the law cannot be acquired unless the subject-matter is examined in close relationship to the social, economic and political contexts in which it is created, maintained and implemented.' Law, far from being a social glue 'holding us all inside a boundary of legality . . . [is] but a part . . . of the overall *social structure*, having links and dependencies with other social elements and forces'. These social elements include:

- Political institutions, such as Parliament, political parties and pressure groups.
- Economic institutions, including employing organizations, trade associations and trade unions.
- Culture institutions such as literature, the arts, the press and television.

Some of these institutions and social groups are more important than others, some have more power than others, and some 'enjoy considerable prestige, whereas others may be thought of as less worthy'.[2]

The law, then, plays an important part in defining and regulating all kinds of social relationships. These include relations between individuals, between organizations, between individuals and organizations and between citizens and the State. Since laws are made, interpreted and applied by human beings, there are differing viewpoints about the nature of the law and the legal system in which the law operates. The social ambiguities inherent in the creation and application of law are summed up in the view that:

> Law may be regarded as a benign facilitating mechanism, making transactions possible between men [*sic*] and solving awkward problems as they arise; it may, alternatively, be seen as a mechanism of social control, regulating activities and interests in the name of either the community, a ruling class or the state. The state itself may be defined as either 'neutral arbiter' or 'interested party' in the solution of disputes and the balancing of interests. Again, law may be seen as an institution for the furtherance and protection of the welfare of everyone, or it may be seen, crudely, as an instrument of repression wielded by the dominant groups in society.[3]

Put simply, competing viewpoints about the relationship between law and society are essentially dichotomous. On the one side, society and the legal system are seen as reflections of a prevailing social consensus. On the other, they are seen as reflecting fundamental social conflict between competing groups. The former perceives the law to be protecting social values to which all subscribe, whilst the latter holds that the law is less than neutral, protecting some values and interests at the expense of others.

Developments in the law also reflect the historical, political and social contexts in which society evolves and changes. The emergence of a free labour market, for example, was a product of the industrial revolution. With the breakdown of the feudal agrarian system, by the mid-eighteenth century landless labourers moved to the expanding towns to become wage workers in the developing factory system. The growth of market capitalism and *laissez-faire* individualism led to the relationship between 'master' and 'servant' being based on a legal contract, despite the vast disparity of bargaining power between them. The contract of service was thus viewed as a legally binding agreement between the two parties in the employment relationship, containing agreed rights and obligations for each. Any breach of these legal rules entitled the aggrieved party, normally the master, to seek a legal remedy by bringing a civil action against the other for breach of contract. In line with the prevailing ideology of the period, there was relatively little State intervention to regulate the employment relationship.

The doctrine of *laissez-faire* assumed that all members of society, including masters and servants, were free and equal parties before the law and were able to regulate and arrange their affairs with one another, without constraints being placed upon them by third parties or the law. It also assumed that all individuals were equal in terms of their bargaining position and that, if people were left free to make their own decisions, competitive trade and industry would flourish and the national economy would thrive. In practice, of course, there were fundamental inequalities in terms of wealth, social position and bargaining power between most masters and servants. None the less, the employment contract, supposedly freely made between what later came to be known as employer and employee, was legally deemed to be made between two consenting parties of equal standing.

Given the early predominance of these ideas about freedom and equality of contract, it took many years before the State began to intervene to provide basic legal protections for individual employees in their contractual relations with employers. It was the infinite variability of the terms of employment contracts, coupled with the fact that in many cases employees could neither negotiate their terms nor readily ascertain the terms dictated by the employer, that led, over the years, to growing State intervention in regulating the employment relationship. This was done through a series of statutes. A number of social and political factors led to this development. They included:

- Changed philosophies about the role of the State in society.
- The reforming zeal of some politicians and campaigners.
- The absorption of working people into the democratic political process.
- The growth of union power and influence.

All these factors led slowly to the furthering of legislative intervention in the field of employment. The laws now existing provide the following:

- Information about the terms of the contract of employment.
- Legally enforceable employment protection rights for employees.

- Protective legislation regarding health and safety at work.
- Union membership rights.

It is not only in the field of employment and employment relations that the nineteenth-century emphasis on *laissez-faire* has given way to State and legal interventionism in the late twentieth century, although there has been a partial revival of *laissez-faire* ideas since the early 1980s. Slowly, *laissez-faire*, with its emphasis on State abstentionism, gave way to the idea that the State, through various legislative and other measures, should enter into economic affairs in an active and direct way. Yet prior to the Second World War economic ideas were dominated by the notions of free trade and freedom of competition. These carried with them the corollary that the economy was best left to regulate itself, unimpeded by any form of State intervention. But it was accompanied by the assumption that the State had a role to play in supporting that sort of economy. This supportive role was seen in the creation, often through law, of an economic environment conducive to trade, industry and business interests. It was also demonstrated by the various measures which were taken to protect the economic interests of the business community in preference to other interests.

Government support for the growth and consolidation of the industrial and commercial economy came from a number of sources. One was an imperialist foreign policy. Another came from the judiciary, which constructed a legal framework within which business affairs could operate smoothly and predictably. The legal notion of 'contract' was, and remains, the essence of the legal relationship between buyers and sellers in product, capital and labour markets. Indeed, the basic legal rules concerning contract stem almost wholly from cases determined by superior courts in the nineteenth century. The insistence of nineteenth-century judges on deciding cases, and creating legal contractual rules, using the juristic equivalent of *laissez-faire* economics—the notions of freedom and equality of contract— eventually led to legislative intervention in the twentieth century, especially in the areas of employee and consumer protection.

The nineteenth century also saw the development of legal rules relating to the form which business enterprises might take, and of the legal protections which particular types of enterprise enjoyed. The most common forms of business enterprise were, and still are, the limited company and the partnership. In the case of the limited company, for example, its most striking legal feature is its 'corporate personality'. Once created, the company is regarded in law as if it were a person, a legal entity in its own right, quite separate from the people owning and running it. The company thus has various legal rights and duties. They include owning and transferring property, entering into contracts, and suing or being sued. By treating the company as a legal person, having ownership of corporate assets, the law not only allows the relatively free use of those assets in the running and expansion of the business. It also provides significant protection for individual shareholders.

Another important aspect of the law with special relevance to economic activity is insurance. Every business venture has an element of risk, but there are some eventualities which can be anticipated and their effects mitigated. The attractiveness of insurance to business enterprises is clear. It is a means of protecting against losses arising from certain types of commercial or financial risk, thus providing a degree of security for the enterprise. But there are also certain statutory requirements relating to business insurance. The Employers' Liability (Compulsory Insurance) Act, 1969, for example, requires employers to take out insurance against claims by their employees who suffer illness or injury during the course of their employment. This protects not only the business enterprise but also employees, who, in the absence of such insurance, might find the employer unable to meet a claim for compensation.

From the analysis above, it may be inferred that the law relating to business enterprises and commercial relations is concerned predominantly with business property and the regulation and transfer of that property, in accordance with the dominant economic structure within which businesses operate. This should not be surprising, since, as Harris suggests, 'legal norms are invariably related to social and economic conditions prevailing at a given period'. It follows that 'the legal normative expressions of the relationship between the holder of property rights and the objects of those rights have their basis in social and economic practice'. Other property concepts such as ownership and possession, leases and mortgages, and contracts and trusts, are also legal normative reflections of the economic activities and demands of power interests at different periods.[4]

The legal systems of capitalist economies, therefore, inevitably exhibit a comprehensive set of legal rules and rights concerning private property, because private property is of such fundamental importance to these societies. Yet property is not treated in law as a homogeneous category. Because it has taken different forms and value at different times, each type of property has particular legal rules attached to it. The legal rules dealing with land, for instance, can be traced back to feudalism, whilst those relating to material objects such as manufactured goods, plant and machinery emerged during the development of early capitalism. Since a capitalist economy, such as that of the UK, depends upon the acquisition of private personal wealth, the legal system concerns itself to a large extent with the protection of that wealth, how it can be invested and consolidated, and how it can be transferred. Yet whilst the law purports to afford equality of treatment to everyone in society, regardless of social class, wealth or position, in practice it is primarily used for protecting and transferring property by only a small proportion of the total population.

Since the law is one of the most powerful carriers of dominant definitions of acceptable and unacceptable social behaviour, as well as being the most significant institution for settling disputes, it is important to understand the social background of its lawyer practitioners. The law embodies dominant social norms and values, and lawyers are engaged in their daily work in maintaining these values through their function of applying the law. Given these circumstances, it should not be surprising that, like all professional groups, the legal profession is predominantly middle-class in its origins and outlook. As Plowden (1970) writes:

> what distinguishes law . . . is its necessary connection with social structure. As long as British social structure is such that the traditional ruling class can still command some deference, the law, to be sure of respect, must partake of the style of that class. Until the thought of a High Court judge pronouncing a life sentence in a Birmingham accent no longer seems incongruous, High Court judges must speak with the tones of Oxbridge, and so must ambitious barristers, and so

must solicitors who do not wish to be thought inferior to barristers.[5]

This class homogeneity of lawyers contrasts vividly with the social positions of their actual and potential clients from lower-class backgrounds. With the traditional clientele of lawyers being drawn from the middle class, 'the danger is . . . that a legal profession [can] become captive to a class or group and promote its interests exclusively'.[6]

The middle and upper middle-class backgrounds of lawyers are even more marked amongst barristers than amongst solicitors, though some argue that class distinctions between the two branches of the legal profession are slowly breaking down. Research shows the predominance of professional and managerial backgrounds among lawyers, as indicated by fathers' occupations. It is the peculiarities of recruitment into the legal profession, and its unique position in the social structure, which tend to favour the middle-class aspiring lawyer. Further, the high cost of legal education, especially postgraduate training, is prohibitive for many potential recruits. Such considerations suggest that intending lawyers, whichever branch of the profession they choose, tend to come from a background which is financially secure and provides some form of independent income with which to supplement their training and early professional experience.

Since senior judges are appointed exclusively from the ranks of experienced and established barristers, 'it may be fairly said that members of the higher levels of the judiciary represent a distillation of those social class currents within the legal system'. The uniform social and educational background of senior judges, largely from an independent school and University of Oxford or Cambridge background, raises 'certain questions about the general social and political outlook of the judiciary as a whole'.[7] In analysing cases with a political element coming before judges, Griffith (1981) writes that:

> we find a remarkable consistency of approach in these cases concentrated in a fairly narrow part of the spectrum of political opinion. It spreads from that part of the centre which is shared by right-wing Labour, Liberal and 'progressive' Conservative opinion to that part of the right which is

associated with traditional Toryism—but not beyond the reaches of the far right.

Griffith concludes that UK judges cannot be politically neutral 'because they are placed in positions where they are required to make political choices which are sometimes presented to them'.[8] Lord Devlin (1978), in replying to this analysis, declares that too much is made by Griffith of the 'politics of the judiciary'. Their politics, he argues, 'are hardly more significant than those of the army, the navy, and the air force; they are as predictable as those of any institution where maturity is in command'.[9]

It would seem, then, that at the apex of the legal system there is a body of judges whose 'social class and educational background is likely to persuade them towards a conservative perhaps even reactionary outlook on the social world'. On the other hand, there is the rest of society, comprising groups and individuals with very heterogeneous beliefs, values and attitudes. In Harris's view, it is no answer for the judiciary to argue that changes in society and the law are the business of Parliament, not of the judges. 'The problems which critics of the judiciary raise are not merely *legal* problems.' They are at the heart of the political structure 'and any reforms which make far reaching changes will inevitably arise through pressure brought to bear on legal *and* political institutions in modern Britain'.[10]

The Categories and Sources of English Law

Because of its history and origins the English legal system differs from that of Scotland and that of western Europe. There are various ways of classifying English law, and its rules are derived from a variety of legal sources. This section explores the diversity of these legal categories and sources of the law to provide an analytical framework for understanding the complexities of the English legal system.

Classification

The basic distinction in English law is between criminal and civil law. As Williams (1973) writes, 'the law is divided into two great

branches, the criminal and the civil, and of these much the greater
is the civil'. The distinction between a crime and a civil wrong
does not rest on the nature of the wrongful act itself but on the
legal consequences that may follow it. 'If the wrongful act is
capable of being followed by what are criminal proceedings, that
means that it is regarded as a crime.' Where, on the other hand,
'it is capable of being followed by civil proceedings, that means
that is is regarded as a civil wrong'. Normally, criminal and civil
proceedings are easily distinguishable. They are brought in different courts, the procedures are different, the outcomes are different and the legal terminology is different. Crimes are divided into
indictable and summary offences. Indictable offences are the more
serious sorts of crime and are tried by judge and jury in the
higher courts, whilst summary offences are tried, often before
magistrates, in the lower courts.[11]

There are three main types of civil wrong:

- Breach of contract.
- Torts.
- Breach of trust.

A breach of contract occurs where a plaintiff brings an action
against a defendant who, it is claimed, has broken the terms of a
legally enforceable contract between them. Torts include wrongs
such as assault, battery, trespass, false imprisonment, defamation
of character, negligence or nuisance. Thus a tort 'is a civil wrong
independent of contract. It gives rise, that is to say, to an action
for damages irrespective of any agreement not to do the act
complained of.' A trust is an obligation enforced by the courts.
It occurs when a person, technically called a settlor, transfers
property to another person, called a trustee, on trust for someone
else, called a beneficiary. If a trust is breached the courts can
enforce it. More generally in civil cases, where proceedings result
in judgement for the plaintiff, the court may order the defendant
to do one of the following:

- Pay the plaintiff money.
- Do or not do something through an injunction.
- Perform a contract.

- Transfer property to the plaintiff.[12]

Another branch of civil law concerns the government of the State and its relationship to individual citizens. This is called constitutional and administrative law. Constitutional law is largely concerned with the organs of government, explaining where these bodies have come from and how they derive their constitutional power. The topics it deals with include: the royal prerogative; the functions of the executive, legislature and judiciary; the role of Cabinet government and that of the Prime Minister; and the position of the courts and the judiciary in the constitution. Administrative law is that branch of the law which focuses on the administrative agencies of the State, such as public corporations, delegated legislation and administrative tribunals. The essential difference between these two branches of the law is that constitutional law studies the organs of the State, whilst administrative law studies them in operation.

The law of property is concerned with the legal theory of the ownership, occupation and use of land. It also defines the various elements in property law, such as tenures and estates, 'fee simple' and 'fee tail', and easements and profits. 'Conveyancing' is the term given to the work of transferring legal title in property. In this area of the law, landlord and property law has grown very complex in recent years, because government has passed legislation affecting this relationship as part of housing policy.

Other than the distinctions between criminal law and civil law, alternative classifications include:

- Private law and public law.
- Substantive law and adjective law.
- Civil law and common law.
- Statute law and common law.
- Common law and equity.

Private law, for example, incorporates all the branches of law concerning cases where one individual is making a claim against another. It takes in contract, tort and family law. Public law concerns cases where the State is involved and the public has a direct interest in the outcome. It includes criminal, constitutional and administrative law and the law affecting welfare services and local government. Substantive law focuses on the legal principles established by the courts in particular branches of the law, whilst adjective law is concerned with the procedure used in those courts. The civil law and common law classification distinguishes between those legal systems, as on the continent of Europe, which are based on codes of law—civil law systems—and those, such as that of England, which are based on legal precedents and the interpretation of statute law—common law systems. The statute law and common law and the common law and equity classifications are considered in the next section.

Sources of the law

The main sources of English law are:

- Legislation.
- Common law.
- Equity.
- Custom.
- Books of authority.

Until the nineteenth century Parliament was primarily a deliberative body, and in practice parliamentary legislation, or statute law, was not a very productive source of law. With the rapid changes in society created by the industrial revolution, 'and with the growth of modern government, legislation has become the most productive source in fact, as well as the most important source in English legal theory'.[13] Although legislation is now the principal expression of public policy in legal form, the sources of that policy are varied. They include:

- The majority political party in the House of Commons.
- The departments of state, with their permanent civil servants.
- Public opinion, represented by pressure groups and the mass media.

Normally, the legislative process represents a continuous interaction between these forces. There is also the Law Commission, which acts as a major source of ideas for legal reform and plays an advisory role to Parliament or less controversial matters.

Parliament, or more exactly the monarch in Parliament, is traditionally defined as the supreme law-maker in the UK. Though judges make law, parliamentary legislation overrides the law which judges make in the courts. Before becoming an Act, a Bill is initiated in Parliament and proceeds through various stages of enactment. There are two types of Bill, public Bills dealing with matters affecting the public generally and private Bills dealing with limited or sectional interests. A public Bill may be introduced either by a Minister or by a member of Parliament, when it is known as a private member's Bill. Government Bills originate in various ways. These include:

- From the majority party's election manifesto.
- From national emergencies.
- From Government investigations.
- From recommendations of the Law Commission.

Private members' bills are normally the result of MPs being approached to support proposals put forward by pressure groups operating outside Parliament. In practice the amount of time allocated to private members' Bills is strictly limited and the majority of such Bills fail to reach the statute book.

As far as government Bills are concerned, the parliamentary process falls into three broad phases; first, a period of consultation takes place before a Bill is introduced; second, a Bill is debated and examined through the Houses of Commons and Lords; and, third, the Act is implemented after it has received the royal assent. Normally, preliminary consultation takes place amongst Ministers, civil service departments and outside pressure groups prior to a Bill being published. When wider public consultation is required, the government may publish consultative documents known as 'Green' or 'White' Papers.

Government Bills are introduced in either the Commons or the Lords. It is usual for controversial Bills to go through the Commons first, with only uncontroversial ones and Bills of an intricate nature being initiated in the Lords. Financial Bills and taxation

Bills can be introduced only through the Commons. In practice the sponsoring Minister presents the Bill to the Commons, where it receives a formal first reading, after which it is published. The Bill is given a second reading in the Commons, when a debate on its general principles and political merits takes place. On non-controversial issues a second reading may take place in committee, though any vote on the Bill has to be taken by the Commons as a whole. The Bill is then referred to a standing committee of the Commons or the Commons may refer it to a committee of the whole House. The object of the committee stage is to enable detailed scrutiny of the individual clauses of a Bill and to enable amendments to be made in committee.

When a Bill completes the committee stage, it is reported as amended to the whole House. At this report stage there may be further amendments, either on the proposal of the Minister or by the opposition. After a Bill has been considered in report, it receives its third reading. Only verbal amendments can be made at this stage, and debate is allowed only if at least six members of the Commons request it. When a government Bill has received its third reading in the Commons it goes to the Lords. Its procedural stages there are broadly similar to those in the Commons. Many Bills are approved by the Lords without further debate or amendment, but amendments can be made if they think it necessary. The passage of Bills through the Lords enables their drafting to be improved and new material to be introduced if necessary.

The Bill is returned to the Commons, where the Lords' amendments are approved or rejected. If no agreement is reached between the two Houses the Lords can delay non-financial Bills, but only for a year. At the end of that period they become law if they are again passed by the Commons. This limitation on the power of the Lords is based on the assumption that the Commons is the prime legislative authority in Parliament and that the role of the non-elected Lords is a revising and amending one, rather than rivalling that of the Commons. Parliament cannot legislate without the concurrence of all its constituent parts, since the assent of the monarch is required once a parliamentary Bill has passed through both Houses. Although this is a formality, a Bill does not become an Act of Parliament until it has received the royal assent.

In addition to the making of statutes by the parliamentary

procedure outlined above, Ministers can be given delegated legislative powers to make regulations. They need parliamentary approval before they can be enforced. This is done by presenting statutory instruments or orders before the House which require either affirmative or negative action. Some 3,000 pages of delegated legislation are added to the statute book each year.

Since the UK's admission to the European Economic Community, under the European Communities Act, 1972, the legal provisions contained in the relevant treaties have become part of the law of the UK, thus challenging the legislative sovereignty of Parliament. There is also provision for Community legislation to be incorporated into UK law. In addition to the various treaties themselves, the most important legal devices are regulations and directives. Community regulations automatically become legally binding on all member States, whilst directives must normally need to be specifically implemented. The member States have no power to question Community legislation, except through the European Court of Justice, and since it is implemented in the UK by subordinate legislation, or administrative circulars, such laws are not debated in Parliament in the same way as public or private Bills. There is, however, a special joint committee of the two Houses of Parliament which reviews European legislation, and it draws the attention of the House of Commons to any matters of importance. Its results are available for members of the public to read.

The common law originally meant the law that was not local, i.e. the law which was common to the whole of England. This may still be its meaning in particular contexts but it is not the usual meaning of the term. More usually the term signifies 'the law that is not the result of legislation, that is, the law created by the custom of the people and decisions of the judges'. Within narrow limits, popular custom creates law, as do the decisions of the courts, which are called precedents. The term 'common law' may also mean the law which is not equity. 'In other words it may mean the law developed by the old courts of common law as distinct from the system (technically called "equity") developed by the old Court of Chancery'.[14] In this sense the common law may even include statutory modifications of the common law. It will be appreciated, therefore, that the precise meaning of the phrase 'the common law' depends upon the particular context in which it is used. It is important to be clear about this, since a third meaning sometimes attributed to the term is law that is not foreign law. Used in this context, it contrasts English law, and that of other countries like the United States which have adopted it, with the Continental legal tradition, which is based on Roman law.

Judge-made common law, then, as developed through the doctrine of binding precedent, is one of the oldest and most fundamental features of the English legal system. The doctrine of precedent states that a decision made by a court in one case is binding on other courts in later cases involving similar facts. Precedent is the basis of the common law, and its essence is both its certainty and its flexibility. On the one hand, judicial decisions can be determined in accordance with previous cases. On the other, the possibility always exists for judicial pronouncements to be modified if the decision proves unjust, inadequate or out of date. Moreover, one of the peculiarities of common law is its ambiguity. For every precedent cited by one counsel in support of a client's case, another counsel proffers precedents of similar weight supporting the case of his or her client. Judicial discretion does, then, make a difference. As Twining and Miers (1982) argue:

> The exercise of discretion in choosing one particular formulation of the [rule of law] of a prior case involves basically the search for the most persuasive or cogent argument in its favour. While it is difficult to classify these reasons according to their acceptability or to the weight and priority that is attached to them, the status, acceptability, and permanence of decisions is in this country to a large degree controlled by judicial recognition of and adherence to a great number of constraints that operate on interpreters of precedent cases.[15]

Judges, in other words, select creatively from the mass of precedents cited and, by virtue of their different interpretations of precedent, their decisions can oscillate between the certainty and flexibility of the common law.

Judges also make decisions on the interpretation of statute law, since the doctrine of precedent also applies to statutory interpretation. The courts define their role in interpreting statutory provisions as applying the statute to the facts before them and giving effect to the intentions of Parliament, as expressed in that statute.

The courts have various techniques of interpretation. These are important, given the complex nature of modern statutes and their sometimes poor drafting. The three common-law techniques used are the 'literal rule', the 'golden rule' and the 'mischief rule'. The literal rule requires that words in statute are given their ordinary meaning. The golden rule aims that, in interpreting words literally, the courts ensure that no absurdity or inconsistency results. The mischief rule is the principle whereby the courts ask themselves what the 'mischief' is that the statute seeks to remedy. According to Harris statutory interpretation must be recognized as involving 'just as much a creative function . . . as does the interpretation of previous cases—and . . . judicial attitudes to public policy may enter into the deliberations of the court'.[16]

Equity is a particular branch of English law. It came into being in the Middle Ages when the courts of common law failed to give redress to individuals in certain types of cases. The disappointed litigants petitioned the king, who, through his Lord Chancellor, eventually set up a special court, the Court of Chancery, to deal with such petitions. Subsequently the rules applied by the Court of Chancery became equity, its most important branch being the law of trusts. In conflicts between the rules of common law and of equity, equity came to prevail. The system continued until 1875, when, as a result of the Judicature Act, 1873, the old courts of common law and the Court of Chancery were abolished. They were replaced by a single Supreme Court of Judicature, each branch of which had full power to administer both common law and equity.

Although the 1875 Act fused the administration of law and equity, it did not fuse law and equity themselves. Moreover, whilst it does not always matter whether a particular rule is law or equity, sometimes it does. A rule of equity means that it has to be read in the light of the whole complex of rules developed by the Lord Chancellor, and 'these rules do not necessarily apply if the rule in question is a rule of the common law'. In other words, to claim that a particular right is an equitable right means that all subsidiary rules of equity apply to it. On the other hand, saying that a particular right is a common-law right 'is shorthand for saying that it is to be interpreted in a common-law atmosphere, leaving out of account such equitable rules as apply only to equitable rights'. There is always the possibility that those relying on an equitable rule may find themselves outside its limits. But 'when this happens the contradictory common-law rule, which may generally seem to be a dead letter, becomes very much alive'.[17]

There are three generally accepted meanings of the term 'custom' in English law: general custom, mercantile custom and local custom. General custom is the common law built up on the basis of existing customs of the various regions of what was Anglo-Saxon England. It is now accepted that general custom is no longer a creative source of law, since it has been absorbed into legislation or case law. Internationally accepted legal customs are known as mercantile customs where they are accepted into the English legal system as part of its commercial law. As these customs develop, the law takes notice of the changes and they become formalized as laws. Local custom is the term used where people claim by virtue of a local custom, such as a right of way or the use of common land, that they have a legal claim which can be adjudicated by the courts. When the claim is accepted by the courts, the local custom is treated as local law.

The last sources of English law are the books of authority, largely the books of antiquity. Certain ancient textbooks fall into this category and are treated by the judges and the legal profession as universally accepted in each branch of the law to which they apply. Whether a book is accepted as authoritative depends on its professional reputation; there is no way of knowing this other than by a study of professional legal practice.

The Courts

The courts are the most obvious official means of resolving conflicts or disputes between parties in the modern world. Yet in practice relatively few of society's disputes end up in the courts. There are several factors militating against court hearings. They include the cost of litigation, the time it takes to get issues to court and the alternative methods of resolving or settling conflicts 'out of court'. The court system is nevertheless a central feature of the legal system. The decisions of the higher courts have great significance for the substance of law itself. Dominant social and political attitudes are communicated through judicial statements in the courts. 'And the courts of law are the ultimate arenas where disputes which cannot be settled any other way may be taken'.[18]

English courts are structured according to three sets of criteria. These are:

- Whether the court deals with civil or criminal matters.
- The extent of the court's jurisdiction.
- Whether the court is one of first instance or of appeal.

The division between civil and criminal matters is central to English law. Civil law comprises all legal rules not part of the criminal code, whilst criminal law covers offences such as murder, theft, crimes against public order, as well as many traffic offences. Private individuals or public bodies may alike be party to civil proceedings. The vast majority of criminal cases are brought by the Crown Prosecution Service under the Prosecution of Offenders Act, 1986, but there is no legal reason why private individuals may not initiate criminal prosecutions. In most instances there are distinctions between the aims and remedies associated with civil law and criminal law respectively. Civil law is concerned primarily with restitution or compensation, whilst criminal law is aimed at the apprehension and punishment of wrongdoers. These distinctions are firmly embedded in the court structure. The most important exception is the Queen's Bench Division of the High Court, which has both civil and some criminal jurisdiction.

In terms of civil jurisdiction, the county court, at the lowest rung of the civil court ladder, is limited in its powers in determining actions in contract and tort and other matters. In terms of hierarchy, county courts are courts of first instance, with both the Court of Appeal (Civil Division) and the House of Lords acting as appellate courts only. The three divisions of the High Court of Justice—Queen's Bench, Chancery and Family—deal in the main with first-instance trials. The Queen's Bench Division is concerned with contract and tort cases which cannot be dealt with in the county courts. The Chancery Division hears disputes over property, trusts, wills, revenue and company matters, whilst the Family Division hears divorce cases and other matrimonial matters.

It is through its appeal channels that the court structure is designed to ensure that justice is done in virtually all types of cases. In theory the doctrine of precedent requires that decisions of the higher courts are binding on all courts below them in the hierarchy. In practice, judges use interpretative devices to modify precedent. In this way the doctrine of precedent ensures that the law is kept up to date. The formal functions of the courts, claimed by jurists and legal writers, are then: 'the dispension of justice in dispute-solving, the maintenance of stability in the law through precedent, [and] the keeping of the law at least minimally in touch with the needs of a changing society'.[19] It is by these criteria that the court system can be evaluated.

The structure of the civil courts in England and Wales is outlined in figure 10. Since 1846 the county courts have provided a system for trying civil cases where a comparatively small amount of money is involved. There are some sixty county court circuits in England and Wales, with some 300 districts where a county court is held at least once a month. Each circuit has its own judge, though in the larger cities there may be more than one judge attached to the circuit. County court judges are assisted by a registrar, who is a solicitor, and a team of administrative staff. The jurisdiction of the county courts includes relatively small claims covering:

- Actions founded on contract and in tort.
- Actions concerning land.
- Equity matters.
- Probate disputes.
- The winding up of small companies.
- Bankruptcy matters.
- Undefended divorce petitions.
- Miscellaneous functions concerning adoption, guardianship and similar matters.

It is also open to the High Court to remit cases for trial to the county court where it thinks this course desirable.

As outlined above, the High Court of Justice is divided into three divisions: the Queen's Bench Division (QBD), the Chancery Division and the Family Division. There are a maximum of eighty High Court judges appointed to the three divisions, according to

Figure 10   The structure of the civil courts in England and Wales

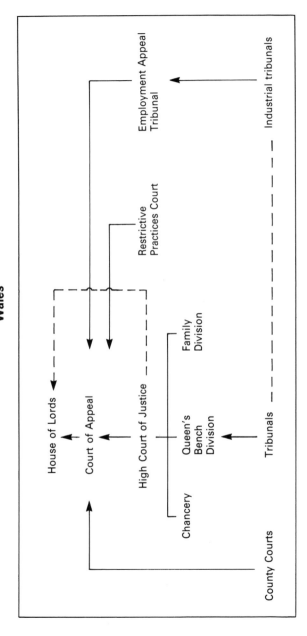

the pressure of work. The Queen's Bench is the largest division, and its jurisdiction is civil and criminal, original and appellate. In terms of its civil jurisdiction, the Queen's Bench Division covers all cases in contract and tort, whatever the value of the claim, though in practice it considers only claims above the county court limits. One branch within the Queen's Bench Division is the Commercial Court, which heard cases of a commercial nature, including insurance, banking and the interpretation of mercantile documents. The Queen's Bench Division also incorporates a separate Admiralty Court, with its own judge. Additionally, five High Court judges are appointed to hear cases in the Restrictive Practices Court, which examines agreements restricting prices or conditions for the supply of goods. Similar arrangements apply to the Employment Appeal Tribunal, which hears appeals from industrial tribunals. In its role as an appellate body the Queen's Bench Divisional Court exercises the supervisory jurisdiction of the High Court over inferior courts and tribunals, with the Family Divisional Court hearing appeals on family matters.

The Chancery Division of the High Court, as the direct descendant of the Lord Chancellor's equity jurisdiction, is substantially concerned with matters formerly belonging to the old Court of Chancery. Statute has also allocated responsibility to it for such important matters as the winding up of companies and revenue cases. Its jurisdiction includes:

- The execution of trusts.
- The redemption and foreclosure of mortgages.
- Partnership actions.
- Specific performance of contracts.
- Conveyancing and land matters.
- Patent and copyright actions.
- Revenue and taxation matters.
- Company matters.

Many of the cases coming before the Chancery Division are not disputes but proposed courses of action calling for judicial approval. One example is when arrangements need to be legally approved for altering a company's structure. The Chancery

Divisional Court hears certain income tax appeals and appeals from county courts in bankruptcy and land registration matters.

The Family Division retains jurisdiction in matrimonial cases formerly vested in the Probate, Divorce and Admiralty Division. It has also taken over jurisdiction, from the Chancery Division, of wardship proceedings and other matters concerning minors. Its legal responsibilities include:

- The granting of legal title.
- The hearing of complex divorce and matrimonial cases.
- Applications relating to adoption, the custody of minors and presumption of death.
- Hearing appeals on family law matters.

Appeals from any one of the three divisions of the High Court normally go to the Court of Appeal (Civil Division), though in a limited number of cases it is possible to leapfrog the Court of Appeal and go direct to the House of Lords under the Administration of Justice Act, 1969. The present jurisdiction of the court covers appeals from the High Court, including the divisional courts, the county courts, the Employment Appeal Tribunal and the Transport Tribunal. The Master of the Rolls is in practice the senior judge of the Court of Appeal, although the Lord Chancellor, ex-Lords Chancellor, the Lord Chief Justice, the Vice-Chancellor, the President of the Family Division and the Lords of Appeal in Ordinary are all members of the court.

The House of Lords in its judicial capacity is the final court of appeal in civil and criminal matters from all the courts in England, Wales and Northern Ireland, and in civil matters from courts in Scotland. In addition to the Lord Chancellor there are a maximum of eleven Lords of Appeal in ordinary to try such appeals. The court, for which a quorum is three, normally has five judges to hear an appeal. The cases always raise a point of law of general importance, and this is the sole ground for obtaining leave to appeal. Judgments of the House of Lords are always reported, because each one adds some new principle to the law or clarifies an existing principle. As the supreme court, the decisions of the House of Lords are binding on all lower courts, thus forming an important element as a source of law through the doctrine of judicial precedent.

In addition to the courts, there is an extensive tribunal system. Tribunals are quasi-legal bodies for deciding or adjudicating in disputes, normally after a decision has given rise to a disagreement. During the twentieth century tribunals have proliferated on a piecemeal basis, being established when and as necessary. Pliatzky (1980) identified sixty-seven 'tribunal systems' in the late 1970s. Various tribunal systems, which dispose of some 250,000 cases per year, have two main functions. One is resolving disputes between private individuals or between individuals and corporate bodies. The main areas here are employment and land and property. Industrial tribunals, for example, determine issues between employers and employees in matters such as unfair dismissal, redundancy payments and discrimination. Rent tribunals and rent assessment committees arbitrate between landlords and tenants and on other matters. The second function of tribunals is to resolve disputes between public bodies and private citizens such as social security appeal tribunals and income tax appeals.

The claimed advantages of tribunals are their specialization, accessibility, informality, flexibility, speed and low cost. On the other hand, there has been a tendency in recent years for tribunals to become more like courts. This is partly because of an increase in the use of legally qualified chairpersons and the use of legal representation by the parties. One result is a loss of some of their claimed advantages such as informality, flexibility and cheapness. Access to tribunals is seriously impaired by the non-availability of legal aid for most tribunal hearings. Delay is also a problem for some tribunals because of overloading and resource deficiencies.

Despite the powers of the courts and the existence of tribunals, there are still many areas of public activity which remain outside both. These are administrative decisions of government bodies which affect individuals and corporate bodies and where some injustice is felt to have occurred. Since 1976 in the case of central government, and 1974 in the case of local government and the National Health Service, commissioners have been appointed to hear complaints of maladministration. There are:

- One Parliamentary Commissioner who investigates complaints or grievances against central government departments.

- Three Health Commissioners.
- Five Local Government Commissioners, three for England and one each for Wales and Scotland.

The Implications for Management

The modern English legal system has evolved over many centuries and it embodies the social values of society's dominant elites. The law is also associated with certain 'general' standards of morality which may or may not be accepted in society at large. The law reflects moral values, and moral values affect the law. The socio-legal process is a complex one. Changes in the law are expected to reflect changing social values and standards of morality, whether through legislation or case law. In practice, however, there is often a time lag between what sections of society may accept as *de facto* new moral standards and norms of behaviour and what the law legitimizes *de jure* subsequently.

By this analysis, the morality of the business sector is rooted essentially in market values. These market values, in turn, are broadly reflected in the laws of the land as they affect relations between firms and their competitors, shareholders, suppliers, creditors, workers and customers. As the following chapter shows, managements need to be aware of the legal constraints within which their enterprises operate in all these contexts. Many business and commercial relationships are based on contract and good faith between the parties. The law also mirrors the importance of property relations in the business world. There is, too, a legally established framework within which business enterprises, in both the private and public sectors, are organized, conduct themselves and carry out the statutory requirements imposed on them. In this sense the law both facilitates business enterprise and constrains it.

Given the supportive legal framework within which modern business enterprises operate, it is somewhat surprising that, in practice, the business and commercial sectors are generally reluctant to use lawyers and the courts to resolve any legal disputes facing them. One reason is that the stability of business relationships may be impaired by using the courts. Another is the expense of litigation, especially where the dispute involves complex contractual documents, or a great deal of time in the courtroom dealing with the technical aspects of a business contract. Further, the basic common-law rules of contract have been largely superseded by specialized statutory provisions incorporating dispute prevention and settlement techniques.

It also appears that business contracts now almost always contain agreed means or procedures for solving certain problems. An expensive and protracted court action—where one of the parties is unable to fulfil the conditions of a contract, for example—can be avoided if the parties have a clause inserted in the contract which states what happens in these specified circumstances. The unforeseen circumstances may include strikes, the outbreak of war, fire, flood or natural catastrophe, or any other occurrence which is beyond the ability of the parties to control. Such a clause, a *force-majeure* clause, may provide that one or other of the parties may terminate the contract or, alternatively, that the delivery date should be extended during the period of the adverse circumstances.

Where a *force-majeure* clause is not used, there may be provision for third-party arbitration. Arbitration is intended to be an informal, private and speedy alternative to court hearings. The advantages of arbitration include:

• Flexibility.
• The parties are free to stipulate the identity of the arbitrator.
• The outcome is binding on all parties.

Arbitrators are under a duty to observe any agreed rules of procedure and to be objective in making their decisions. Arbitration can be invoked in a number of circumstances involved contractual disputes between business organizations. These include:

• Disputes of fact.
• Disputes of law.
• Disputes of both fact and law.

Consumers also have access to third-party intervention where they have complaints against a manufacturer or retailer. Some firms have introduced codes of practice, including conciliation or arbitration provisions, for consumer complaints. Conciliation procedures are not intended to operate by strict adherence to legal principles but to reach a satisfactory settlement. If they fail, the dispute is often referred to arbitration. This is carried out in accordance with the requirements of the Arbitration Acts and is quite separate from the small-claims procedure in county courts. Whatever kind of arbitration is used, and whoever acts as an arbitrator, the conduct and outcome of the arbitration process are subject to the overriding control of the law.

This may seem surprising but one reason is that there may be gaps in the contractual provision which neither party anticipated. The general law of arbitration can fill the gaps. Second, there is a basic principle in the law of contract which states that it is against public policy for any contractual terms to exclude the jurisdiction of the ordinary courts. Third, the legislation on arbitration contains specific provision concerning the involvement of the courts in arbitration matters.

Finally, managers need to be aware of the existence of relevant tribunals, their terms of reference and the remedies provided by them. This is especially so in the case of planning, land and industrial tribunals. Planning tribunals deal with appeals against planning and development decisions by local authorities; land tribunals are concerned with the valuation of land which is compulsorily acquired by public authorities; and industrial tribunals deal with claims by employees of unfair dismissal, discrimination or unequal pay for work of equal value against employers. Although managements are less likely to make use of the services of the various commissioners, public-sector managements need to know about citizen rights of access. They can then be alert to the types of administration action and behaviour—such as bias, turpitude or unjustifiable delay—which could give rise to complaints.

References

1   KAHN-FREUND O. *Labour and the law*. London, Stevens. 1977. p 3.
2   HARRIS P. *An introduction to law*. London, Weidenfeld & Nicolson, 1984. pp 9 and 10.
3   HARRIS P J *and* BUCKLE J D. 'Philosophies of law and the law teacher.' *The law teacher*. 1976. p 6.
4   HARRIS. *op cit.* p 99.

5 PLOWDEN W. 'Tomorrow's lawyers?' in ZANDER M (ed). *What's wrong with the law?* London, BBC, 1970, p 124.
6 FREEMAN M D A. *The legal structure.* London, Longman, 1974. p 116f.
7 HARRIS. *op cit.* p 341.
8 GRIFFITH J A G. *The politics of the judiciary.* London, Fontana, 1981. pp 34 and 230.
9 DEVLIN Lord. 'Judges, government and politics.' *Modern law review* 41, 1978. p 510.
10 HARRIS. *op cit.* p 365f.
11 WILLIAMS G. *Learning the law.* London, Stevens, 1973. pp 5–9.
12 *ibid.* p 15f.
13 FARRER J. *Introduction to legal method.* London, Sweet & Maxwell, 1977. p 88.
14 WILLIAMS. *op cit.* p 25.
15 TWINING W *and* MIERS D. *How to do things with rules.* London, Weidenfeld & Nicolson, 1982. p 291.
16 HARRIS. *op cit.* p 180.
17 WILLIAMS. *op cit.* p 27f.
18 HARRIS. *op cit.* p 142.
19 *ibid.* p 150.

10

Companies, People and the Law

Previous chapters have shown how modern business corporations in both the private and the public sector operate in interrelated social, economic and political environments. But organizations also undertake their activities as suppliers of goods or services, as users of scarce resources and, increasingly, as transnational organizations within a defined legal framework. Some of the activities of the corporate sector which the law seeks to regulate are its functions as:

- Unique business enterprises, each with its own legal personality.
- Providers of goods or services to consumers in the market place.
- Employers of human resources in the processes of wealth creation and welfare provision.

To some extent, therefore, the law acts as a counterbalancing force to the immense economic and social power inherent in the large-scale corporate enterprises of the late twentieth century. The impact of these legal counterbalances must not be exaggerated, however, since they often provide only a basic floor of protection for other organizations, consumers or workers. In practice, national law is a relatively blunt instrument for the effective regulation of market relationships and power relationships in the context of multinational businesses and international market forces. This is a weakness in the law, given the interests of small businesses, individual consumers and the workforce. According to Galbraith (1975), 'on no conclusion is [my research] more clear: left to themselves, economic forces do not work out for the best except for the powerful'.[1]

Within the legal framework, it is the contract between the

parties which remains the legal cornerstone of all transactions in business, consumer and employment affairs. Contract is the legal device facilitating the exchange of goods or services amongst individuals, groups and organizations in liberal democratic societies. A contract is a legally binding agreement between two parties whereby each party undertakes specific obligations, or enjoys specific rights, conferred by that agreement. The expression 'breach of contract' underlines the fact that the agreement is legally binding, and if one party fails to honour part of the bargain the other can sue and obtain a remedy through the courts. This chapter, in selectively exploring some of these legal intricacies, provides an introductory description of the law affecting organizations. But it is not claimed to be a detailed or definitive legal analysis of this complex part of the corporate environment.

Company Law

Modern companies, and the concept of corporate legal personality, were first created in law during the nineteenth century to facilitate business growth and commercial development. The nineteenth century also saw the extension of legal rules regulating the form which business enterprises could take and the legal protection which particular types of enterprise enjoyed. This was done through a series of Companies Acts which were periodically revised and codified to put companies on a distinctive legal standing. It is the Companies Acts which continue to provide the legal framework within which companies operate. As business corporations companies can own property, employ people, make contracts, sue and be sued. Today there are three types of company:

- Limited companies.
- Unlimited companies.
- Companies limited by guarantee.

Limited companies are companies limited by shares. Unlimited companies are companies whose members' liability is unlimited if the company is wound up. Companies limited by guarantee are companies whose members are required to pay up to a fixed amount if the company is wound up. Guarantee companies are formed for charitable organizations, where it is goodwill rather than working capital which is required from their members.

The most common type of company is the limited company, the company limited by shares. A limited company is financed by individuals or other organizations buying shares in it to provide its share capital. Those providing a company's share capital become members of the company. Under company law the company's ordinary shareholders have the power to elect directors to oversee the company's affairs, to dismiss directors and to share in corporate profits in the form of dividends. The amount of money capital paid to a company is called its paid-up capital. If a company is wound up, shareholders are entitled to receive an amount, proportionate to their shareholding, of any money left over after corporate debts have been fully paid. More importantly, shareholder liability for corporate debts is limited to the amount of their shareholding. Provided members of the company have fully paid the whole nominal value of their shares, there is no further financial liability on their part if, for whatever reasons, the company ceases to trade or operate.

A public company is a company whose shares are sold to the public, whilst a private company must not offer shares to the public. The legal requirements that a public company must satisfy include:

- A statement in the memorandum of association that it is a public company.
- Its name must end with the words 'Public Limited Company' (PLC).
- Its share capital must not be less than an authorized minimum of £50,000.
- At least 25 per cent of its shares must be paid up before allotment.

Further, a PLC cannot do business or exercise any borrowing powers unless the Registrar of Companies issues it with a certificate entitling it to do so. To obtain the certificate, the company must apply to the registrar in a legally prescribed form. These requirements include statements covering:

- The amount paid up on the alloted share capital of the company at the time of the application.
- The amount of the preliminary expenses of the company.
- Any sum or benefit paid to the promoter and the consideration for that payment of benefit.

Every company has a memorandum of association. This provides the following information:

- The name of the company.
- The location of its registered office.
- Its objects.
- A statement that the liability of its members is limited.
- The amount of nominal capital, with its division into shares of fixed amounts.

The memorandum must be signed by at least two subscribers. It is the memorandum which defines the company's legal personality and determines its external legal relationships. The legal regulations governing the names of companies require that the last word must be 'Limited' in the case of a private company or 'PLC' in the case of a public company. This is to ensure that all those having dealings with the company are aware of its legal standing. In the case of companies limited by guarantee, the Department of Trade (DoT) issues a licence allowing a company to be registered without the word 'limited' in its title. This is provided that the DoT is satisfied that the company's object is to promote commerce, art, science, religion, charity or any profession. Such companies must use their income to promote these objects and are legally prohibited from paying dividends to their members.

It is the objects clause which takes up the bulk of the memorandum of association. The main objects clause sets out the basic purpose of incorporation, followed by a number of subsidiary clauses giving the company power to buy land, borrow money, acquire other businesses and do anything which is necessary to carry out its main objective. The form used by company formation agencies usually has a set of standardized objects clauses, leaving only the main objects clause to be specifically designed for the individual company. If a company does anything outside the scope of its objects the action is *ultra vires*, beyond its powers, and is void in law, thus preventing its members from taking action to render it valid. The purpose of this part of the law is to protect corporate shareholders, who normally invest in a company which they expect to succeed. The objects clause may only be altered for certain limited purposes by passing a special resolution at a general meeting.

A company limited by shares also has a set of articles of association. These govern the management of the internal affairs of the company. Unless it registers a different set of articles with its memorandum, a company is automatically governed by the model set of articles incorporated in the Companies Act, 1948, although the Companies Act, 1985, empowers the Secretary of State to make regulations which can be easily amended, without the passing of a new Companies Act. A company may alter or add to its articles by passing a special resolution at a general meeting. This is subject to its memorandum of association and the provisions of the Companies Act. The articles constitute a contract between the company and its members, though the Companies Act permits a company to alter its articles against a member's will. This is provided that the alteration is made *bona fide* in the interests of the company as a whole. A company's articles may not be altered, however, if doing so would:

• Exceed the powers conferred by the memorandum or be in conflict with it.

• Be inconsistent with the Companies Act or any other statute.

• Increase the liability of existing members, unless they have given their written consent.

The members of a company are its shareholders. Legally, they have to agree to be members and to have their names entered in the company's register of members. Any person having the capacity to make a contract may be a member of a company, including aliens, bankrupts, registered companies and minors.

Membership ceases when the names of members are validly removed from the company register. This is done when members either transfer all their shareholdings to someone else or transmit them to an executor or trustee. This takes place in the case of death or bankruptcy respectively. Every company must have a register of members. This shows:

- The name and address of each member.
- The number of shares held.
- The amount paid or agreed to be considered as paid on the shares.
- The date when each member was entered on the register.
- The date when a person ceased to be a member.

Companies having more than fifty members are required to have their register in the form of an index. Alternatively there must be a separate index containing sufficient information to enable any member's acccount to be found in the register. In all cases, the company register must be open to inspection for at least two hours on every business day.

Company shares are issued in different classes, each having particular legal rights. These vary and include the right to share in corporate profits, to participate in company affairs and to claim a share of surplus assets on the winding up of the company. Basically, ordinary shares are the equity or risk capital. They entitle the holder to a share of the company's profits, through dividends, where the company's directors think them justifiable. If a business prospers, its ordinary shares rise in value; if it fails to do so, its shares decline in value. Ordinary shareholders are also entitled to take part in company affairs by voting at general meetings.

Preference shares provide their holders with the right to receive a fixed dividend on the nominal value of their shares annually, if the company makes sufficient profit. But there are no further rights to participation, unless shares are designated as participating preference shares. This is because the risk of not receiving a dividend is less than it is for ordinary shareholders. Preference shareholders are therefore normally denied the right to vote at general meetings. They normally carry full voting rights only in special circumstances. Preferential rights may be extended to the division of a company's assets on winding up, with preference shareholders having the right to repayment of their capital first. To counterbalance this, they are not usually entitled to a share of any surplus assets the company has on being wound up.

The Companies Act requires every public company to maintain a register of interests in shares at its registered office or at a place where the register of members is kept. Any parties acquiring an interest of a 'notifiable percentage' of issued shares that carry the right to vote at a general meeting are required to notify the company in writing within five days of their having done so. The current notifiable percentage is 5 per cent, though this may be varied by statutory instrument. The company must enter in the register the parties' names, addresses, the ways in which the interests were acquired, and the number and class of shares involved. Notification and a record in the register are then required of any changes in the interest, up to and including the time when it falls below the 5 per cent level. Any parties failing to notify a notifiable interest are guilty of an offence and are liable to imprisonment, a fine or both. The Act also deals with the 'concert party'. This is a group of persons acquiring small quantities of shares with the intention of later combining their holdings. Those acting in concert are required to disclose their agreement to the company and to keep each other informed.

Every registered public company must have at least two directors; public companies registered before 1 November 1929, and private companies, must have at least one director. Directors are not employees or servants of the company, although they may hold office in addition to a directorship. In law, directors are agents of the company. When directors make a contract on behalf of a company, it is the company which is liable for it, not the directors. This is provided that the directors do not exceed the power conferred on them by the company's memorandum and articles of association. Company directors occupy a fiduciary position in relation to the members of the company and its employees. Where directors make a contract with a company of which they are directors, on their own behalf, the company may rescind the contract and require the directors to surrender any profit made from it. Directors are therefore required to declare their interests in any matter under discussion. With certain limited exceptions, loans to directors are prohibited and, in the case of public companies, can constitute a criminal offence.

Anyone may become a company director, including a company. The only exceptions are beneficed clergy, undischarged bankrupts, persons disqualified by the courts and certain persons involved in managing insolvent companies. Certain information about its directors must be made availabe by every company. This information includes:

- A register of directors.
- A register of directors' interests in shares and debentures.
- Particulars of directors' service contracts.

The register of directors must show, among other things, any other directorships held, other than those of wholly owned subsidiaries, whilst the register of directors' interests must include those of spouses and infant children. The approval of the general meeting is required for determining most contracts for the services of directors and for substantial property transactions between directors and the company.

The Elements of Contract Law

'The contract is, in essence, an exchange of promises.' Sometimes the agreement refers to a promise to be fulfilled by one party in the future. This is called an *executory* contract. More usually, in everyday contracts, 'the exchange is instantaneous and the contract completed straight away (as in the case of ordinary purchases in shops): these are called *executed* contracts'. The law of contract, as developed by the judges, paralleled the development of social and economic *laissez-faire* in the nineteenth century. This held that the affairs of business, manufacturing, trade and employment were best left to the individuals concerned, with a minimum of State intervention or parliamentary legislation. The legal counterparts of this individualist philosophy were the twin assumptions of freedom and equality of contract. In a free market economy keen competition is crucial, and the attitude of judges and legislators 'was that it was up to the individuals concerned to strike the best bargains they could negotiate. It was certainly not up to the court or Parliament to repair bad bargains.'²

Today there are six essential elements in a valid contract. These are:

- Offer and unconditional acceptance.
- Genuine agreement between the parties.
- Intention to create legal relations.
- Capacity of the parties.
- Legality and possibility.
- Consideration and form.

An offer, for instance, must state all the terms of the offer, be communicated to the offeree and be distinguished from an invitation to treat. It must not be vague and can be terminated before it is accepted by revocation, lapse of time, rejection or death. Acceptance must be unconditional or else it is regarded as a counter-offer. Acceptance, in turn, must be communicated to the offeror, though it can be implied from the party's conduct, and it has to be made within a reasonable or stipulated time.

In the determination of a valid contract, there must be genuine agreement and consent between the parties, and a number of factors can affect this. Misrepresentation, for example, may be either fraudulent or innocent. Where fraudulent misrepresentation occurs, the aggrieved party may avoid the contract with or without seeking damages. Alternatively the aggrieved party can affirm the contract and seek damages. With innocent misrepresentation, the main remedy is to avoid the contract, though damages may be awarded even after performance has taken place. Similarly, fraud, if proved, allows the injured party to avoid the contract, with or without seeking damages. Mistake involves the subject matter of the contract or the identity of the parties. If the mistake is fundamental the contract is normally rendered void in law. Duress and undue influence also affect the genuineness of consent. Duress is actual or threatened violence against or the imprisonment of the party concerned and, at common law, any contract induced by duress is void. Undue influence is where a party is coerced and precluded from the exercise of free judgement. Contracts induced by undue influence are voidable at the courts' discretion.

There are two presumptions regarding intention to create legal relations. In social or domestic agreements the courts hold that there is normally no intention to create legal relations. In business agreements, by contrast, the courts presume that there is such an intention. This presumption is rebutted, however, if there is express provision to that effect between the parties.

It is essential that the parties to a contract have the proper capacity to make one. The contractual capacity of contracting parties is affected by a number of factors. For their own protection, for example, minors have limited contractual capacity. As a general rule, minors can enforce contracts against other people but cannot, with certain exceptions, have contracts enforced against them. The main exceptions are contracts for necessaries, contracts for minors' benefit and voidable contracts. Thus if goods are deemed necessaries, minors are obliged to pay a reasonable price for them, not necessarily the contract price. Contracts for minors' benefit include educational, service or apprenticeship contracts, provided it can be shown that the fundamental purpose of such contracts is to the minor's ultimate benefit. By statute, certain contracts are void and cannot be enforced against a minor. These include contracts for repaying money debts or money loans and contracts for goods supplied or to be supplied, other than necessaries.

Contracts with persons of unsound mind are generally valid but there are a number of exceptions. First, if the contracting party is aware of the other party's mental disability the contract is voidable at the discretion of the mentally unsound person. The onus of proof lies with any persons claiming insanity. They must prove that their disabilities prevented them from understanding the consequences of the transaction and that the other party knew this. Second, where the property of the mentally ill has been placed under the courts' control, any contract involving the disposal of the property does not bind the patient. Contracts are also voidable if individuals who were drunk at the time of making a contract can prove that they were temporarily incapacitated owing to intoxication and that the other party was aware of it. Although bankrupts are not devoid of contractual capacity, certain limitations are placed upon them. It is an offence for undischarged bankrupts, for example, to obtain credit beyond a limited amount without disclosing their position.

The contractual capacity of a limited company is governed by its memorandum and articles of association, with a company's capacity to contract being found in the objects clause. This specifies in detail the business that the company is empowered to conduct. Any lawful transaction decided by the directors is deemed to be within the capacity of the company and within the ostensible authority of the directors. Outsiders are protected only when they deal with a company in good faith. There is a presumption that good faith exists, with the onus on the company to rebut it. This can be done by showing that the outsider had actual knowledge that the transaction was outside the scope of the objects of the company or the ostensible authority of the directors. The presumption is difficult to rebut in practice, since outsiders are expressly relieved of any obligation to inspect and investigate the capacity of the company or the authority of the company's directors to make contracts.

Another feature of contract law is that, at the time of its formation, the contract should be capable of being performed. Where it is reasonable to do so, however, future difficulties should be anticipated and provided for. A contract which is illegal at its formation is devoid of legal effect. Where a contract is legal when made and subsequently becomes illegal, because of a change in the law, such a contract will normally be discharged on the ground of frustration. Contracts may be illegal because they are forbidden by statute or by common law. Examples of contracts contrary to statute would include gaming or wagering contracts, which are subject to various Acts passed after 1845 such as the Moneylenders Acts, 1900 and 1927, or the Trading with the Enemy Act, 1939. Examples of contracts which are contrary to common law include contracts for immoral purposes, interfering with the course of justice, in restraint of trade, or defrauding the Inland Revenue.

The general rule in English law is that unless something of value is given in exchange for a promise or undertaking the promise cannot be enforced against the promissor. Consideration or form, therefore, may be regarded as the element of the bargain in a contract and, at its simplest, involves a *quid pro quo* between the parties. There are a number of legal rules relating to consideration, though there are many exceptions owing to case-law decisions. The main ones are that:

- Every simple contract has to be supported by a consideration, which must be legal.
- The consideration must move from the person to whom the promise is made. This rule is connected with the legal doctrine of privity of contract, which basically means that only those who are parties to the contract acquire rights and obligations under it.
- The consideration must be something beyond the promissor's existing obligations to the promisee.
- The consideration must not be in the past. This means that a promise made in return for some past benefit or service is normally unenforceable at law. Where it can be shown that services were rendered at the express or implied request of the promissor, however, the courts take the view that this is sufficient consideration to support a subsequent promise to pay.
- The consideration must be real, though it need not be adequate, since it is up to the parties to make their own bargain.

The following remedies are available for breach of contract:

- An action for damages.
- A claim for *quantum meruit*.
- An application for a decree of specific performance.
- An application for an injunction.

An award of damages by the courts is intended to be compensatory, not punitive. If a legal right has been infringed, but no actual loss has resulted, the courts normally award nominal damages only. Further, injured parties are expected to take all reasonable steps to mitigate the extent of any damage and are unable to claim compensation for losses due to their own failure to act in a reasonable way after the breach occurred. A distinction is drawn between liquidated and unliquidated damages. The former are damages agreed upon by the parties at the time of entering into the contract. Only the fact that a breach has occurred needs to be proved and no proof of loss is required. To be enforceable by the courts, liquidated damages must be shown to be a genuine pre-estimate of loss and not a penalty inserted as a threat of punishment in the event of a breach of contract. Where the courts conclude that the prearranged sum is in fact a penalty, it will not be awarded.

A number of legal rules are applied by the courts to determine whether a penalty is involved. These include:

- Where the words used by the parties are not conclusive.

- Where a single sum is payable as damages for any one of several breaches, varying in gravity.

- Where the sum involved is extravagant.

The essence of a penalty is a payment to frighten defaulters into carrying out their side of the bargain, whilst the essence of liquidated damages is a genuine pre-estimate of the likely loss in case of a default. Where a penalty is deemed to be involved, the courts award unliquidated damages, based on normal principles, instead. Unliquidated damages are awarded by the courts where no damages are provided for in the contract itself. Here proof of loss is required.

Quantum meruit is a claim based on reasonable remuneration and is distinct from a claim for compensation for loss which is based on an action for damages. The following are the circumstances where a claim based on *quantum meruit* is appropriate:

- Work has been carried out under a contract which subsequently turns out to be void and damages cannot be awarded for the breach of a void contract.

- Substantial performance of the contract has been carried out.

- There was an express or implied contract to render services, with no agreement to remuneration.

- The original contract has been replaced by a new implied contract.

A claim for *quantum meruit*, in short, offers an alternative course of action to plaintiffs who might otherwise seek damages.

Awards for specific performance were formerly available only in courts of equity but are now available in any court. However, the courts exercise discretion according to the following principles:

- Action must commence within a reasonable time, since 'delay defeats equity'.

- The plaintiff's conduct is also taken into account by the courts, with those going to equity needing to have 'clean hands'.

- Specific performance is never granted in the following circumstances: where damages are an adequate and appropriate remedy; where the contract is one for personal services; where the courts are not able to supervise the contract; where a promise is not supported by consideration; where undue hardship would be caused to the defendant; or where the contract is not binding on both parties.

Injunctions are another equitable remedy which the courts may award in cases where damages are neither an adequate nor an appropriate remedy. At their simplest, injunctions are court orders restraining an actual or contemplated breach of contract. There are several forms of injunction, such as interlocutory, prohibitory, perpetual and mandatory. They are governed by the same guiding principles as in the paragraph above.

Fair Trading and the Law

Companies and other business enterprises now have to deal with a spectrum of law covering fair trading and fair competition. This branch of the law has grown piecemeal, especially in the post-war period, and falls into two broad categories: restrictive trade practices legislation and consumer protection legislation. The intrusion of public law into private sales and marketing, for example, which was once the preserve of commercial law, is one of the striking legal developments of the twentieth century. Whilst early legislation was aimed largely at the honest trader, today its main aim is to protect the consumer. This change of object is related to legal, political and economic factors. The largest single influence has been an increase in social awareness in the twentieth century, resulting in a corresponding concern for regulating consumer markets by legislation. A second factor is the considerable development of manufacturing and marketing techniques which afford advantage to producers. The third factor is the inadequacy of civil law as a remedy, especially given its cost and the relative ignorance of consumers regarding their legal rights.

Restrictive trade practices

Legislation against restrictions on trade arose from changing government attitudes to business arrangements after the Second World War. Prior to the war, trading monopolies and restrictive practices were generally tolerated and even encouraged as a means of protecting industry and employment. A different philosophy developed subsequently. It supported the view that the economy is better stimulated by competition than by protectionism. Hence, over the years, Parliament has passed legislation aimed at prohibiting a wide range of restrictive or collusive practices and at controlling monopolies and mergers.

Legislation to limit restrictive practices and monopolies was first passed in the 1940s and 1950s. These Acts were limited in their scope and effectiveness. The most important pieces of legislation covering these areas are:

- The Fair Trading Act, 1973.
- The Restrictive Trade Practices Act, 1976.
- The Resale Prices Act, 1976.
- The Competition Act, 1980.

The Fair Trading Act, for example, extends the restrictive trade practices legislation to restrictive agreements covering services, as well as to goods, and to information agreements. It also transfers the functions of the Registrar of Restrictive Trading Agreements to the Director General of Fair Trading, which was a new role created by the Act. The Act repeals and replaces the provisions of earlier legislation on monopolies and mergers, renaming the Monopolies and Restrictive Practices Commission the Monopolies and Mergers Commission (MMC). In addition, the Director General of Fair Trading is given certain responsibilities for administering the law on monopolies and mergers.

The Restrictive Trade Practices Act covers restrictive agreements on goods, services and information. A restrictive agreement is one between two or more persons on:

- Prices charged or to be charged.
- Terms of supply or purchase.
- Recommended prices.
- Quantities and descriptions of goods.
- Manufacturing processes.
- Persons or areas to be supplied.

For an agreement to be deemed 'restrictive', there must be acceptance of a negative obligation restricting a right which would otherwise exist. Such negative obligations must be accepted by at least two parties. Certain defined terms and conditions are disregarded by the Act, and certain types of agreement are exempt from its provisions. Where an agreement is caught by the Act, it is normally referred to the Restrictive Practices Court by the Director General of Fair Trading. In these circumstances there is a statutory presumption that the agreement is contrary to the public interest and, unless the court is persuaded otherwise, the agreement will be declared void in respect of its restrictive provisions.

In order to justify an agreement before the court, the parties must show, first, that it is within one of the eight 'gateways' provided in the Restrictive Trade Practices Act for satisfying the court that the agreement is permitted. The gateways are:

- Protection of the public from injury.
- Specific and substantial benefit to the public.
- The necessity to counteract competitive activity.
- Necessity in dealing with a third party enjoying a monopoly position.
- Protection of employment.
- Benefit to export earnings.

- Necessity of another restriction already found in the public interest.

- No material adverse effect on competition.

Second, the parties must satisfy a further provision that the agreement is not unreasonable, having regard to the 'balance' between the circumstances pleaded before the court and any detriment to the public. This double test—that of the gateway and of balancing provisions—is a difficult one to pass in practice.

The Competition Act adds to the Director General's powers to police restrictive practices. It empowers the Director General to conduct preliminary investigations into courses of action appearing to constitute anti-competitive practices. Where it is decides that a practice is anti-competitive, assurances may be sought from the parties. If undertakings fail to provide the Director General with appropriate assurances, a 'competition reference' may be made to the Monopolies and Mergers Commission to investigate whether a particular course of dealing is against the public interest. The Act also enables the Commission to investigate certain public bodies and the prices of major public concerns.

The Resale Prices Act consolidates earlier legislation. It prohibits resale price maintenance, in the sense of enforcing minimum retail prices, unless their enforcement is justified before the court. Terms of contract requiring minimum resale prices are rendered void in contracts for the sale or supply of goods between suppliers and dealers. The Act also prohibits the withholding of supplies as a means of coercing dealers to maintain minimum resale prices. The only means of exempting specific goods from the Act are on application to the Restrictive Practices Court. The grounds for exemption are that:

- The quality of the goods would otherwise be reduced.

- The number of retail outlets would otherwise be reduced.

- Prices in the long term would generally rise.

- Goods would be retailed in circumstances likely to cause a danger to health through misuse.

- Any necessary services would cease to be provided or would be substantially curtailed to the detriment of the public.

The law relating to monopolies and mergers is principally consolidated in the Fair Trading Act. Both the Secretary of State and
the Director General of Fair Trading have powers to refer matters
to the Monopolies Commission. These matters fall into four
categories:

- Monopolies in the supply of goods or services or the export
  of goods, with a monopoly being a market share of 25 per
  cent or more.

- Mergers where the merger creates a group with 25 per cent
  or more of the market, or adds market share to such an
  existing monopoly, or the acquired assets are valued at £15
  million or more.

- General references.

- Preferences on restrictive labour practices.

The Monopolies and Mergers Commission may be charged with
simply preparing a factual report or be asked to make recommendations for action. The latter may be persuasive, but the power
to adopt remedies rests solely with the Secretary of State.

The enforcement of legislation against restrictive trade practices
lies mainly in the hands of the Secretary of State, the Director
General of Fair Trading, the Monopolies and Mergers Commission, the Restrictive Practices Court and the European Commission. The Secretary of State, for example, has powers under
the Restrictive Trade Practices Act to apply legislation to certain
agreements, to exempt other agreements and to instruct the Director General not to take proceedings against certain registered
agreements. The Secretary of State can also institute inquiries
by the Monopolies and Mergers Commission and make orders
following a report. The Director General has a number of roles:
acting as registrar of restrictive and information agreements;
making monopoly references to the Commission; investigating
anti-competitive practices; and acting as the competent authority
in the UK regarding the European Commission. The Monopolies
and Mergers Commission reports on references made to it requiring factual reports or requests for recommendations. The Restrictive Practices Court, which has both lay and judicial members,
decides on questions of fact by majority, with no appeal.

The Corporate Environment

Questions of law are decided by the court's judicial members, with appeals going to the Court of Appeal.

Consumer protection

'One of the most potentially valuable forms of protection to the consumer was introduced by the Fair Trading Act 1973.'[3] The legal protection provided to consumers under the Act is threefold.

- The Act creates a watchdog or Ombudsman for consumer affairs, the Director General of Fair Trading.
- The Act creates a mechanism for facilitating consumer protection whereby the Secretary of State is able to define new offences operating against the interests of consumers.
- A part of the Act provides particular protection against the abuses of 'pyramid selling'.

The Director General has five functions under the Act. The first is protecting the economic interests of consumers. This means keeping under review and collecting information on commercial activities in the UK, especially those relating to the supply of goods or services to consumers. The second function is receiving and collating evidence of those commercial activities which appear adversely to affect the general interests of consumers. Third, the Director General has the duty of advising the Secretary of State on matters concerning the above and of making recommendations of action to be taken to protect consumer interests. Fourth, the Director General can seek orders from the Restrictive Practices Court against persons who persistently maintain a course of conduct which is either detrimental to the interests of consumers or regarded as unfair to them. A course of conduct is regarded as unfair to consumers if it contravenes the criminal law or a civil obligation. This enables the Director General to deal with suppliers of goods and services who persistently contravene consumer protection legislation. Before referring the matter to the Court the Director General must try to obtain a satisfactory written assurance that the course of conduct will cease. Fifth, if the matter proceeds to the Court, 'any judgment given in civil proceedings which includes a breach of contract or breach of duty shall be sufficient evidence of proceedings'.[4]

The machinery for consumer protection established under the Act involves several stages. These are:

- A reference by the Director General to the advisory committee provided by the Act.
- The recommendation of the Director General to the Secretary of State.
- The consideration and report of the advisory committee.
- An order by the Secretary of State in furthering the advisory committee's report.

In determining whether to refer a consumer trade practice to the advisory committee, the Director General includes any practice in connection with the supply of goods or services. These can relate to:

- The terms or conditions of sale or supply.
- The manner in which those terms are communicated to the customer.
- The promotion of the goods or services.
- The methods of selling in dealing with customers.
- The method of packing or supplying the goods.
- The methods of demanding or securing payment for the goods or services.

All these matters are scrutinized by the Director General in determining whether to proceed with the matter on the grounds that it adversely affects the economic interests of consumers.

The central feature of pyramid selling is that the distribution of goods and services is done through a tiered pyramid of central and local selling points. People joining such schemes as distributors are usually promised large profits from two sources. One is from promoting the product; the other is from commission for introducing new distributors who assist in the distribution process. For this reason, people can be induced to make large payments when joining a scheme. This sort of scheme has led, in some cases, to abuse and hardship. Section 120 of the Fair Trading Act, 1973, provides that if any participant — or invited prospective participant—in a pyramid selling scheme makes any payment to, or for, the benefit of the promoter to the advantage of a participant in the scheme and:

> is induced to make that payment by reason that the prospect is held out to him [*sic*] of receiving payments or other benefits in respect of the introduction of other persons who become participants in the trading scheme, then any person to whom or for whose benefit that payment is made, shall be guilty of an offence.

The legislation provides for imprisonment of up to three months, even on summary conviction, either as an alternative or in addition to a fine.[5]

The Act has a number of advantages for consumers. First, it provides an experienced and centralized machinery for combating unfair trading practices. Second, abuses are dealt with as they arise by the flexibility of statutory instruments, without recourse to new or amending legislation. Third, the existence of the Act provides a statutory deterrent against unfair trading practices. Fourth, local enforcement of the Act is delegated to local authority Departments of Weights and Measures or consumer protection units. These organizations have detailed experience of enforcing the Trade Description Acts, 1968 and 1972, as well as the Weights and Measures Act, 1963. Fifth, consumers have the knowledge that, whilst they may be reluctant to sue, the State can prosecute on their behalf, and the courts can award compensation where it is applicable under the Powers of Criminal Courts Act, 1973.

The Trade Descriptions Act, 1968, provides that any manufacturers or traders who, in the course of business, apply false trade descriptions to goods, or supply goods to which a false trade description has been applied, commit an offence. For all practical purposes, goods can be regarded as having a false trade description applied to them when they are described in terms which lead people to consider buying them, or making a purchase, when they would not have done so had the terms been different and more accurate. The Act also contains provisions about statements of price by the sellers of goods and about inaccurate descriptions of any services offered. There are provisions, too, applying to false trade descriptions used in selling business services, and covering the wording of competitions and promotions which are used to boost the sale of goods.

Part of the Act is amended by the Consumer Protection Act, 1987. The latter introduces new provisions prohibiting misleading indications on prices. These apply to most businesses, including services, and are designed to protect consumers from inaccurate statements about prices. A code of practice for traders is linked with the 1987 Act and gives detailed guidelines about what is and what is not allowed. Any infringement of the code of practice is strong evidence that there has been a breach of the Consumer Protection Act.

The Trade Descriptions Act, 1972, applied to situations in which goods manufactured overseas were marketed in the UK under a 'United Kingdom name or mark'. Its purpose was to prevent intending buyers from wrongly inferring that the use of such a name or mark indicated that the product was of UK origin. It was an offence under the Act to fail to show the country of origin prominently, when goods of foreign origin were marked with a UK name. However, the Trades Descriptions (Origin Marking) Miscellaneous Goods Order, 1981, which required origin marking on certain specified goods wherever they were made, including the UK, was withdrawn after protests from the European Economic Community. After that decision the Trade Descriptions Act, 1972, was repealed and replaced by the Consumer Protection Act, 1987. Legislation also makes it an offence to sell goods or services by relying on the inertia of selected customers. With goods, this normally means supplying them so that the selected customer has the choice of sending them back or keeping them and paying for them. With services, it normally means providing the selected customer with a note indicating that payment should be made for an offered service and that the service will be provided unless the receiver of the note takes action to reject the offer.

The main civil law statute setting out the basic terms and conditions which any buyers, businesses or consumers are entitled to expect from business sellers of goods is the Sale of Goods Act, 1979. This incorporates revisions made by the Supply of Goods (Implied Terms) Act, 1973, and the Unfair Contract Terms Act, 1977. The Supply of Goods and Services Act, 1983, codifies all existing common-law rights regarding contracts for the supply of a service. It also gives statutory authority to the rights of the consumer by implying certain terms into every contract for the supply of a service. These are that:

- The service will be carried out with reasonable care and skill.
- The service will be carried out at a reasonable price, unless a price has already been agreed.
- The service will be carried out within a reasonable time, unless the time has already been agreed by the parties.

Since the passing of this Act the law relating to the supply of goods and services has been placed on a similar footing to the law affecting the sale of goods.

Essentially it is the Sale of Goods Act, 1893, which is codified in existing legislation covering the sale of goods. The 1893 Act has substantially stood the test of time and is based on the assumption that every transaction under which goods or services are supplied and paid for is in law a contract. It is also assumed that, with very few exceptions, the absence of a document specifying the terms and conditions of the contract is irrelevant for any purpose other than showing that the agreement between the seller and the buyer was on the particular occasion in unusual terms. The principal usual terms, derived from the Act, are that the seller has the full right to provide the buyer with the goods; that if sold by description or sample the goods conform to the description or sample; that the goods are of 'merchantable quality'; and in certain circumstances that the goods go beyond that 'quality' by being suitable for the purpose which the buyer had in mind when purchasing them.

The changes made in the Sale of Goods (Implied Terms) Act, 1973, and the Unfair Contract Terms Act, 1977, are of fundamental importance in this area of the law. In broad terms, the effect of the 1973 and 1977 legislation is to make void any attempt by businesses to take away the consumers' statutory rights. Businesses can no longer use so-called 'exclusion' clauses to avoid the consequences of supplying goods which do not comply with the implied warrantees on quality contained in the 1893 Act. The 1973 Act specifies a number of conditions which are implied in every consumer contract for the sale of goods. In commercial and non-consumer contracts it is still permissible for the implied conditions established by the Act, or arising through implication, to be excluded. But the exclusion is valid only where the courts decide that it is fair and reasonable.

The effects of the 1973 Act on guarantees applying to consumer contracts are, first, that the seller is always liable for the quality of the product when it is sold and, if the product fails, it must be replaced or repaired free of charge by the seller. Second, the seller may be liable for consequential loss if a fault in the product results in harm to the buyer or the buyer's property. Third, the buyer has the right to bring a claim against the seller at any time up to six years from the date of purchase. In a dispute it is for the courts to decide how long a product or a component ought to last.

The Unfair Contract Terms Act makes far-reaching changes in the law of contract and tort. Virtually all types of contract are affected by it, including sale of goods, hire-purchase, services, manufacturers' guarantees, and so on. The Act applies not only between businesses and consumers but also between businesses and businesses. It deals with exemption clauses and any clause where a party seeks to limit or avoid liability for non-performance. The Act also protects consumers from unscrupulous indemnity clauses. These are clauses where traders require consumers to indemnify them against loss or to permit them to substitute manifestly different goods or services from those for which they had bargained.

Consumer credit is largely regulated by the Consumer Credit Act, 1974. The purpose of this complex piece of legislation is to provide a comprehensive legal code to govern consumer credit and consumer hire purchase, and effective means to secure its enforcement. The Act provides general terms covering different types of financial transaction. The object is to classify the various forms of such transactions and make it easier to apply uniform rules to them. The Act is a valuable instrument protecting consumers. The range of techniques goes far beyond most other forms of consumer legislation. Its two most striking features are, first, the creation of a central enforcement mechanism based on a licensing system controlled by the Director General of Fair Trading. 'The second is the remarkable power conferred on the court to intervene in the agreement between the debtor and the creditor.' Debtors are given the right to cancel the agreement, or to terminate it, despite the fact that they are unable to prove misrepresentation or illegality. Debtors may also apply to the courts to reopen the agreement if it is deemed to be extortionate for the debtor, and under this power the courts may alter the terms of the agreement or indeed cancel it altogether.[6]

Employment Protection Legislation

The relationship between employers and employees, which governs the terms and conditions of employment, the execution of work and collective bargaining between them, is both complex and of vital economic significance to both parties and to society generally. It is important to the community at large that employer-employee relations are relatively harmonious and mutual, whilst social considerations demand that employees should not be exploited commercially by being underpaid or exposed to unnecessary dangers in carrying out their tasks. The legal relationship between the two parties has evolved over the centuries by the application of common-law rules on contract, tort and crime in various employment situations. Since the complex and special needs of employers and employees are not always adequately met by the application of broad common-law principles, statutory provisions have been created to establish a detailed framework of legal rules affecting them. These are aimed at regulating and controlling the conflicting demands of employers, employees and society as a whole, in the labour market and in the place of work.

Basically, employment or labour law covers three main areas:

- Individual employment relations, especially the law focusing on the contract of employment and the job protection rights of employees.
- Collective employment relations, especially the law affecting trade unions, collective bargaining and industrial conflict.
- Health and safety at work, such as the Factory Acts and the law of industrial injuries.

Given the wide scope of labour law, and the terms of reference of this book, this section concentrates on the nature of the contract of employment and the employment protection rights of individual employees.

The contract of employment

In law employees are individuals working under a 'contract of service' for an employer, for wages or a salary. This contrasts with the self-employed, who work under a 'contract for services' for fees, commission or similar payments. Since the nineteenth century the working relationship between employers and employees has been legally embodied in the contract of employment. This is an arrangement whereby an employee agrees to work for an employer who agrees, in turn, to pay for the work done. The formation of the contract is according to the general law of contract. Apart from merchant seafarers and apprentices, who are covered by special provisions, the contract may be oral or in writing or both. Until fairly recently it was usual to find only a few terms of the contract specified, such as rates of pay and hours of work. Today, as can be seen in figure 11, the employment contract contains a variety of terms and conditions, derived from several sources. These have developed from the law, collective bargaining, managerial rules and custom and practice over the years.

According to O'Higgins (1976), 'the express terms [of the contract] pose few problems'.[7] These are the terms of the contract, which are spelled out, either in writing or verbally, and normally include the following:

- The date of starting work.
- The terms of payment.
- The hours.
- Holiday entitlement.
- Holiday pay.
- Sickness pay.
- Grievance and disciplinary procedures.
- The pension, and so on.

Some of these terms may be expressly incorporated in the contract

Figure 11   Sources of the contract of employment

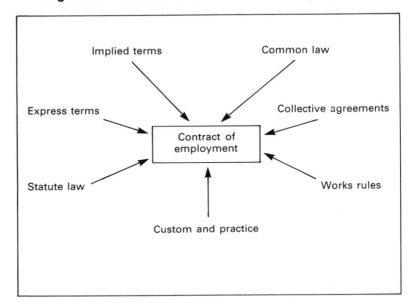

of employment by reference to documents such as collective agreements, works rules or employee handbooks. Express terms take precedence over all other sources of the contract, apart from statutorily implied terms. Under current employment legislation, employers are required to provide employees with a written statement of the main terms and conditions of their contract within thirteen weeks of commencing work. This contractual statement is not the contract of employment itself but is normally the best evidence of its express terms.

The implied terms of the contract are those inferred by the courts. Both employers and employees have certain common-law duties which are implied in the contract of employment. In the case of the employer, there is the duty to provide agreed pay, to take reasonable care of the employee's safety, to co-operate with the employee, and not to expose the employee to grave danger of health or person. On the employees' part, there is the duty to give honest and faithful service, to use reasonable skill and care when working, and to obey all lawful and reasonable instructions given by the employer or its agents. The latter is sometimes known as the duty of co-operation and provides the basis of the employer's common-law powers of discipline.

A collective agreement or particular terms of it may be incorporated into individual contracts of employment, either by express words or by implication. It is quite common in the individual contract to find words stating that the employee's pay and hours of work are to be determined in accordance with the relevant collective agreement. Even where no express words are used, and the normal practice is to pay wages and provide conditions negotiated with union representatives, there is no difficulty in implying a term that pay and conditions are to be provided in accordance with the collective agreement. This normally applies to union members and non-unionists working for the same employer.

Works rules, or those incorporated in an employee handbook, also become terms of the contract of employment. Like collective agreements, these employment rules may be incorporated into the contract, either expressly or by implication. Where employees sign a document saying that such rules form part of their contract, they become express terms and the signatories are bound by them. Works rules and those in employee handbooks may also become part of the contract by being prominently displayed in the workplace or where they are proved to be local custom in the establishment. Moreover, as Lewis (1983) indicates, works rules offer an advantage to employers. 'Whereas a collective agreement can only be altered with the consent of the parties to it, management can lawfully change the content of the works rules at any time.'[8]

A custom or practice may be implied as a term of the contract of employment if it is 'reasonable, certain and notorious'. To be reasonable, it must be approved of by the judges. To be certain, it must be precisely defined. And to be notorious, it must be well known. Not every custom and practice, therefore, can be considered as part of the contract of employment. In reality 'many practices are followed by employers as management policy and not because they accept that they are obliged to behave in that way'.[9]

Statutory employment rights

Since the 1970s employees have been provided with a series of statutory employment rights which effectively supersede and extend their rights at common law within the contract of employment. Generally the enforcement of these statutory rights is kept separate from enforcing any common-law rights. Cases determining whether the statutory right of employees not to be 'unfairly' dismissed by their employers has been infringed, for example, are normally heard in industrial tribunals. Cases determining infringement of the common-law right not to be 'wrongfully' dismissed, in contrast, are heard in the civil courts. Unfair dismissal occurs when employees are dismissed for an insufficient reason under the law, and without due process. Wrongful dismissal is where employees are dismissed, in breach of their contract of employment, without due notice or payment in lieu of notice.

The legislation currently providing employment protection and related rights for employees is largely incorporated in:

- The Equal Pay Act, 1970.
- The Trade Union and Labour Relations Act, 1974.
- The Sex Discrimination Act, 1975.
- The Race Relations Act, 1976.
- The Employment Protection (Consolidation) Act, 1978.
- The Employment Acts, 1980 and 1988.
- The Trade Union Act, 1984.
- The Wages Act, 1986.

The major statutory employment rights of individuals are outlined below.

The right to a written statement of the main terms of employment. Within thirteen weeks of starting work, employees are entitled to a written statement from their employer setting out the main terms of their employment. To qualify for this, they must work for sixteen or more hours a week, or less than eight where they have had five years of continuous employment. The information which is provided includes:

- The identity of the parties.
- The date when employment began.
- Job title.
- Pay, and method of calculating it.
- Intervals of payment.
- Hours of work.
- Holidays and holiday pay.
- Sick pay.
- Period of notice.
- Periods of continuous employment.
- Pension scheme.
- Details of grievance and disciplinary procedures.

In providing the statement the employer can refer employees to supporting documents, such as collective agreements, containing the information.

The right to an itemized pay statement. Employees are entitled to receive an itemized pay statement at regular intervals from their employers, setting out their gross pay, net pay and the amounts and reasons for any deductions.

The right to a guarantee payment. After one month's service employees are entitled to receive a fixed payment, reviewed annually by the Secretary of State for Employment, for up to five days in any three-months period in which they would normally work but do not do so because their employer is unable to provide work for them.

The right to payments due to medical suspension. Employees with at least one month's service are entitled to receive a week's pay for each week of suspension from work on medical grounds. This provision is subject to a maximum of twenty-six weeks' pay.

The right to equal pay. When employed by the same or an associated employer, men and women have the right to equal treatment in respect of their terms and conditions of employment. The legislation works by inserting an equality clause in the contract of employment. This means that there should be equality of treatment where a man and a woman are employed on 'like work', on 'work rated as equivalent' or on work which is of equal value.

After the European Commission had decided that the British
Equal Pay Act was deficient in meeting the requirements of European Community standards in 1982, an amending statutory instrument was issued in 1983. This means that equal pay can be claimed
even when the jobs are completely different, provided that the
demands made, such as effort, skill or decision-making, are of
equal value.

> However, the whole remuneration package has to be con-
> sidered, not just pay . . . The Act does not apply solely to
> pay. It extends to other terms. It also applies to both men
> and women. The comparator has to be in the 'same employ-
> ment' as the claimant.[10]

The right to payments in the event of employer insolvency.
Where an employer becomes insolvent, employees have the right
to certain payments as preferential debts. They include any unpaid
items such as wages and salaries, guarantee payments, medical
suspension pay, accrued holiday pay and statutory sick pay. Certain other debts may be claimed, including notice pay, unfair
dismissal awards and statutory redundancy pay.

The right to restrictions on deductions from pay. Deductions
from workers' pay by employers may not be made unless they are
authorized by statute, by the workers' contract or by the workers
themselves, in advance, and in writing. Nor can contractual
changes be used to authorize changes retrospectively. The payments from which deductions cannot be made include wages,
salaries, holiday pay, bonuses and statutory payments. Benefits
in kind, pensions and redundancy payments, however, are
specifically excluded. Deductions from workers' pay in the retail
trade for cash shortages, or stock deficiencies, are limited to 10
per cent of gross wages on any pay day, though there is no limit
on termination of employment. Further, 'the repeal of the Truck
Acts means that manual workers no longer have a statutory right
to be paid in cash. The issue will be subject entirely to matters of
employment contracts and union-employer negotiation.'[11]

The rights of expectant mothers. Pregnant employees have the
right not normally to be dismissed because of their pregnancy
and to reasonable time off work for antenatal care. Additionally,
women who have worked for two years continuously with an
employer for sixteen or more hours per week are entitled to

maternity leave, maternity pay and to return to work after their confinement. The right to return to work applies till the end of the period of twenty-nine weeks, beginning with the week in which the child is born. The woman must inform the employer of her intention to return to work and this must be done, in writing, at least twenty-one days before maternity absence. The employer has the right to send a written request within forty-nine days from the notified date of the beginning of confinement, asking for confirmation of a woman's intention to return. The employer must explain that failure to give written confirmation within fourteen days results in the loss of the right to return. She must in any case notify the employer, in writing, of her proposed return to work at least twenty-one days beforehand.

The right not to be dismissed or to have action taken short of dismissal because of trade union membership or activities. Employers may not dismiss, or take action short of dismissal, against employees who are members of an independent trade union or take part in union activities. Nor are employers allowed to take action against their employees to compel them to join a union, whether it is independent or not.

The right not to be discriminated against on the grounds of sex, marital status or race. It is unlawful for employers to discriminate against individuals on the grounds of their sex, marital status, colour, race, nationality or ethnic origin. Discrimination can be direct, indirect or by victimization. Direct discrimination is where one person is treated less favourably than another on one of the prohibited grounds. Indirect discrimination is applying a 'require-ment or condition' to one group which is or would be applied equally to another but which is such that the proportion of one group complying with it is considerably smaller than the pro-portion outside that group who can comply. Victimization is treat-ing persons less favourably because they have used the anti-discrimination legislation, or are suspected of having used it, or have properly alleged breaches of it. Both the Sex Discrimination and Race Relations Acts permit discrimination, however, where it is a 'genuine occupational qualification'.

The right to a minimum period of notice. Employees with at least one month's service are entitled to at least one week's notice of the termination of their contract of employment. The period increases to two weeks' notice after two years' service and then goes up by one week for each additional completed year of service, subject to a maximum of twelve weeks. The minimum notice which has to be given by an employee to an employer is one week and does not increase with length of employment.

The right to time off without pay for public duties. Employees holding certain public offices, such as justices of the peace and local councillors, are entitled to reasonable time off without pay, irrespective of their length of service.

The right to transfer employment with a change of ownership. The Transfer of Undertakings Regulations, 1981, reverse the common-law position that a change in ownership of an enterprise automatically results in the termination of contracts of employment. These regulations expressly state that the contract of employment continues. The regulations apply where there is a legal change of owner but do not include changes in control arising from changes in share ownership alone.

The right to a redundancy payment and time off work in redundancy situations. Employees dismissed by reason of redundancy may be entitled to statutory redundancy payments. They must have been employed by the employer, or an associated employer, for at least two years continuously and be under sixty-five in the case of men and under sixty in that of women. The amount of payment depends on the employee's age, length of service and weekly pay. Employees lose any right to a redundancy payment where the employer offers suitable alternative employment and the employees unreasonably refuse it. Employees declared redundant are entitled to time off with pay to look for work and to make arrangements for training for any future employment.

The right not to be unfairly dismissed. Most employees who work for sixteen or more hours a week, and who have been employed for at least two years continuously, have the right not to be unfairly dismissed, though where the dismissal is by reason of race, sex or trade union membership there is no continuous employment qualification. To justify dismissing an employee lawfully the employer has to have a fair reason and act reasonably in carrying it out. Where employees think they have been dismissed unfairly they have the right to take their claim to an industrial tribunal. If a claim is upheld the tribunal has the power to recommend re-engagement or reinstatement or to award compensation. Compensation, which is awarded against the employer, can consist of a basic award plus a compensatory award, based on the applicant's net loss as a result of the dismissal.

Dismissal is always unfair unless it is on account of:

- The capability or qualifications of the employee.
- Employee misconduct.
- Employee redundancy.
- The contravention of a statutory duty.
- 'Some other substantial reason'.

Dismissal is always automatically unfair where it is on the grounds of:

- Proposed or actual trade union membership or activity.
- Proposed or actual non-membership of a union.
- Unfair selection for redundancy.
- Pregnancy.

In addition to having a fair reason for dismissing an employee, employers must be able to demonstrate that they have carried out the dismissal in a reasonable way if they are to avoid claims for unfair dismissal at an industrial tribunal. A main test of reasonableness is whether the dismissal was carried out in accordance with the code of practice on disciplinary procedure, issued by the Advisory Conciliation and Arbitration Service, and relevant case law. This means, in practice, that any disciplinary action is expected to:

- Follow proper procedure, including a reasonable investigation of the circumstances.
- Be consistent in the application of disciplinary measures.
- Be appropriate for the situation.
- Take account of any mitigating circumstances.

The right to a written statement of the reasons for dismissal. Employees with a minimum of six months' service are entitled, on request, to receive a written statement from their employer giving the reasons for their dismissal.

The Implications for Management

Given the vast amount of company, fair trading and employment law with which organizations have to comply, it is necessary for top management in each case to accept responsibility for ensuring that the enterprise they lead meets the minimum standards required. Under the Companies Act, for example, all companies are required to send details of their affairs to the Registrar of Companies through an annual return. This is to ensure that the general public has access to a great deal of information about the activities and management of companies. The sort of information provided by each company concerns its membership, management and capitalization. Thus the matters incorporated in the annual return include the following:

- A list of the company's members, with names, addresses, number of shares held and number of shares transferred.
- A list of persons ceasing to be members.
- The address where the register of members is kept.
- Details of the share capital of the company.
- Details of the company's indebtedness.
- The information required to be in the register of directors.

Certain documents have to be attached to the annual report, giving details of the company's activities during the year. These are:

- Certified copies of every balance sheet and profit and loss account laid before the general meeting.
- Certified copies of the auditors' reports on the balance sheets.
- Certified copies of the directors' reports accompanying the balance sheets.

In addition, every private company must file a certificate with its annual return stating that it has not issued an offer to the public inviting them to subscribe for its shares or debentures.

Companies are normally reluctant to call on lawyers and the courts to resolve any contractual disputes arising between them. As outlined in the previous chapter, this is partly because of the expense of litigation. It is also because of the need to maintain good working relations between companies and to avoid undermining them by using the courts to resolve business disputes. For these reasons, business contracts almost invariably contain agreed methods or resolving specified problems when they arise. Where this fails, arbitration can be used. Arbitrators act impartially and provide a relatively informal method of enabling companies and organizations to resolve any contractual difficulties between them. Nevertheless, the conduct and outcome of any arbitration proceedings are subject to the overriding control of the law.

Legal control of arbitration proceedings is necessary because, first, however detailed the contractual specifications, there may well be gaps in the provisions which neither party has anticipated. Second, there is a general principle, under the law of contract, that it is against public policy for any contractual term to exclude the jurisdiction of the ordinary courts. Third, legislation relating to arbitration contains provisions concerning the courts' involvement in arbitration matters in the last resort. However, any legal appeal against an arbitration award going to court requires the consent of all the parties or the leave of the courts. The latter is not granted unless the question of law at issue substantially affects the rights of the parties to the arbitration arrangements.

In the area of fair trading, it is not the role of the Director General to take action on behalf of any individual consumer, but the Office does have power to act against individual firms. Under the Fair Trading Act, 1973, the Director General is required to have regard to any complaints received from consumers or other persons. The Act says that where the Director General has reason to believe that an organization, or person, has adopted and is persisting in a course of conduct detrimental and unfair to the interests of consumers, satisfactory written assurances may be demanded from the business declaring that it will cease to operate in that way. If the business declines to give such an assurance, or gives it but fails to implement it, the Director General may bring proceedings before the Restrictive Practices Court or any other appropriate court. Any breach of such court orders is punishable as an offence.

The Office of Fair Trading (OFT) requires quite a number of such undertakings to be given. They arise from reports received from members of the public and the local authorities. They also arise from note being taken of repeated appearances of traders and companies in the courts on charges under legislation aimed at protecting consumers. Particulars of undertakings given by firms are normally published in the press and details are incorporated in the annual report of the Director General of Fair Trading. The Fair Trading Act includes among the duties of the Director General that of encouraging trade associations and similar bodies to establish codes of practice for their members. These contain guidance in safeguarding and promoting the interests of consumers. Many trade associations for individual industries in the consumer goods and services fields have been at the receiving end of this encouragement since the Act came into operation.

It is an essential element of fair trading that no party to a transaction willingly permits another party to bind itself by contract under an important and relevant misunderstanding. If the misunderstanding has been created or allowed to persist, there is fraud, and the contract can be rescinded. But there are occasions when misunderstanding results from an inadvertent failure to pass information over or from lack of knowledge of what would be a material fact at the time. On these occasions there is 'innocent misrepresentation'. The law about innocent misrepresentation has developed over the years to restore fairness in such situations. Companies need to be aware that it provides remedies for situations which arise when transactions are completed but otherwise would not have done had those involved known all the material facts at the time.

Management also needs to recognize that although legislation is the main source of law on the sale of goods, it is not the only one. There are at least four other areas of law to which aggrieved parties can have recourse. One is the common law relating to the sale of goods, particularly where the Sale of Goods Act is ambiguous or does not cover the particular point. Second, the ordinary principles of contract may apply, for example, in relation to the formation of the contract. Third, the law of tort remains very important, largely because manufacturers' liability is based principally on the tort of negligence. Fourth, certain other statutes affect the law on the sale of goods, as in hire-purchase cases.

The common law continues to be an important source of the law relating to consumer credit, too. First, the common law applies to all those agreements which are outside the financial limits of the Consumer Credit Act, 1974. The Act applies only to agreements up to a certain amount, and the debtor must not be a corporation, thus resulting in a number of agreements remaining outside its scope. Second, the Act is intended to codify and rationalize those areas of law where there are anomalies. It is not intended to displace principles applicable to the ordinary law of contract. The areas where the common law continues to be a source of consumer credit law include:

- Matters arising in the formation of the contract.
- Where it implies certain conditions in consumer credit contracts.
- Where third-party rights are affected by common-law remedies.

With the extension of employment legislation since the 1970s, employees now have a wide range of employment protection and related rights which, if infringed, may be upheld in industrial tribunals. One implication is that management needs to know its obligations under the legislation and ensure that subordinate managers do not flout employee rights under statute law. This requires the development of effective personnel and employee relations policies by top management, embodying at least the minimum standards of protection provided by the law. These in turn need to be regularly monitored and evaluated by management to make sure that they are being implemented fairly and effectively. These policies then need to be adapted and modified in the light of experience and practice. Personnel departments have a vital role in the creation, implementation and evaluation of such policy.

Of all the legislative provisions aimed at promoting greater job security for individual employees, one of the most significant is that providing them with the right not to be unfairly dismissed. If employers are to minimize the risk of being taken to an industrial tribunal for claims of unfair dismissal, they need properly designed and administered disciplinary and dismissal procedures. Subordinate managers need to be trained in using and applying them. In this way, consistency and equity for employees and legal protection for employers can be achieved in the disciplinary process.

It is also necessary for employers and management to exercise greater care in recruiting, selecting and appraising employees than was probably the case in the past. When there was no employment protection legislation, employers and managers could take risks in recruitment and selection on the grounds that they could readily dismiss unsuitable employees. Today managers need to be more professional when engaging people so that they have some confidence that new employees are suitable for the job for which they have been selected. Properly monitored induction and probationary periods are part of this process. As a result, employee recruitment and selection now take longer, and are more costly in real terms, than they were in the past. Another implication is that more managerial attention is being devoted to human resource planning, human resource management and human resource development than in the past. This is especially the case in organizations where the effective managing of people is seen as a necessary condition of employee efficiency and corporate success.

It is clear from the preceding outline of the law that the legal context in which the corporate sector operates is very complex and highly specialized. Managements need not only appropriate legal advice but also to ensure that subordinate managers are aware of their legal duties and responsibilities. This means in practice that managers need to have training and development in various aspects of the law. These include its basic principles as well as specialist areas such as marketing, consumer and employment law. Whilst larger organizations in both the private and public sectors employ their own legal specialists, smaller enterprises are more likely to need legal advice on an *ad hoc* basis. One way of obtaining it is by membership of an appropriate employers' or trade association. Managerial updating of legal matters can be done through regular scanning of trade journals and law reports and by attending seminars and workshops.

References

1 GALBRAITH J. *Economics and the public purpose.* Harmondsworth, Penguin, 1975. p 3.
2 HARRIS P. *An introduction to law.* London, Weidenfeld & Nicolson, 1984. pp 250 and 262.
3 BALL B *and* ROSE F W. *Principles of business law.* London, Sweet & Maxwell, 1979. p 233.
4 *ibid.* p 234.
5 THE FAIR TRADING ACT 1973. (c 41). Section 120.
6 BALL *and* ROSE. *op cit.* p 155.
7 O'HIGGINS P. *Workers' rights.* London, Arrow, 1976. p 28.
8 LEWIS D. *Essentials of employment law.* London, Institute of Personnel Management, 1983. p 20.
9 O'HIGGINS. *op cit.* p 31.
10 LEWIS P. 'Other individual rights' in TOWERS B. (ed). *A handbook of industrial relations practice.* London, Kogan Page, 1987. p 341.
11 *ibid.* p 335.

Epilogue

This book has attempted to describe and analyse the complex external environment in which modern organizations, both private and public, operate in the late twentieth century. The task has been carried out by identifying the multiplicity of external contexts impinging on corporate decision-taking and some of the main implications for management and its subordinates. The following have been examined:

- The demographic and social structure.
- The economic background and the impact of market forces and government policy on corporate decisions.
- The framework within which political decisions are made and implemented.
- The nature and forms of the law within which the corporate sector operates.

Although the book focuses on the corporate environment in the UK, an emerging feature of the times is the steadily increasing importance of the international context. This is especially the case in terms of the economy, with the emergence of a new-style global economy dominated by large transnational organizations, fast-reacting finance capital markets and international markets for commodities, services and scarce managerial skills. Owing to these international forces, a major characteristic of the corporate environment is economic instability and market turbulence. Indeed, the UK economy has become increasingly open, subject to foreign competition and market-centred, especially since the 1970s. From being relatively protected, insular and static, it is now exposed, accessible and dynamic, certainly in comparison with the immediate post-war period. It is consequently more vulnerable to import penetration, corporate take-overs by foreign-based firms and the loss of export markets, where UK companies are unable to compete with overseas producers. All these economic developments are of growing significance to corporate decision-takers and their managerial subordinates, as well as to the customers and clients for their goods and services.

One reaction to the globalizing of the economy has been the creation of regional trading areas such as that of the European Community. One of its aims is to provide an 'internal' economic market enabling the business corporations of its member States to compete on fair and equal terms with one another, whilst excluding those of non-member States, which face tariff barriers for their products and services. This regionalization of economic markets, though protecting the trading and national interests of the nation States within the 'clubs', by definition discriminates against those sometimes poorer, less developed countries excluded from them. Moreover, the existence of economic groupings such as the European Community could even intensify competition in the world economy, in the medium term, amongst these concentrated centres of economic power. And this will certainly not benefit the poorer nations. Whatever happens in the longer term, however, one of the immediate challenges facing UK companies in the 1990s is how they are going to adapt to the demands of the single European market as the economies of the member States become ever more integrated and interrelated.

The emergence of the global economy and of the regional economies with their epicentres in western Europe, North America and the Far East is coinciding with the growth of environmental pressure groups, some of them internationally based. They want more socially responsible production processes, the elimination of industrial pollution and the maintenance of the eco-system. The growth of environmentalism is an external pressure facing all kinds of organizations. These range from agricultural and extractive-based ones to those in manufacturing, distribution and the public services. What the environmentalists want is for the corporate sector to be more ecologically aware. The demands being made include:

- Conserving resources.
- Saving energy.

- Eliminating non-eco-friendly products.
- Protecting the countryside, the rivers and the seas.
- Cleaning up the cities and other aspects of the physical environment.
- Slowing down growth rates.

All these demands of the environmentalist lobby carry economic and financial costs for the corporate sector, as well as for workers and consumers. And it is a lobby that will increase in importance, rather than diminish.

In contradistinction to the global economy, and in parallel with the regionalization of economic interests, there is the shrinking of the nation State. In west Europe, its political manifestation is embodied in the existence of the European Community. Increasingly each of its member States is relinquishing its national sovereignty and, in the process, is party to the gestation of a transcendent Community sovereignty which is eventually likely to override that of each of the constituent member States. Political power centres cannot long be divorced from economic power centres, so some form of political union is probable at a future date. This development is going to put growing pressure on management in the corporate sector to take account of these supranational political changes, and consequent policy outputs, in its decision-making role.

Another feature of the international setting is the breakdown of superpower hegemony. On the one side, there is the United States of America, increasingly beset by economic difficulties which are reflected in its budget deficits, trade imbalances and changing economic infrastructure. On the other side, there is the break-up of the east European power bloc, centred on Soviet Russia, with demands there for economic reform, political democracy and open societies. Whilst this is potentially destabilizing in terms of the international balance of power, it provides economic opportunities and economic choices alike for the Western economies, including that of the USA. For the UK, with its post-war 'special relationship' with the USA, the dilemma is particularly stark. Do its businesses and politicians continue with this special relationship, based as it is on a common language, a mass culture and recent history, or do they definitively turn towards Europe—

including eastern Eurcpe— with its polyglot languages, elitist culture and shared historical tradition? How this dilemma is eventually determined has immense implications not only for the corporate sector but also for the UK population as workers, consumers and citizens.

Another feature of the times is continuous and exponential social and technological change. It is somewhat paradoxical that whilst economic and political forces are developing in centrifugal directions, and pulling outwards, social and technological changes are essentially centripetal and pulling inwards. To some extent advanced capitalist societies like the UK are becoming more atomized than in the past, with the majority of individuals having rising expectations about what they expect from life and the ways in which they can optimize their life chances. With growing affluence, more social and geographical mobility, and higher educational standards for many people, the late twentieth century is in essence an individualist society, not a communitarian one. This raises problems for the corporate sector as an employer, since it requires skilled, committed and flexible employees to do the complex range of job tasks demanded by modern business enterprises. With people wanting autonomy, choice and personal freedom in their private as well as their working lives, there is pressure on employers to create organizational structures and corporate cultures conducive to these values. Yet given the co-operative and collectivist nature of the work process, it is not easy to achieve in practice.

The advent of cheap, reliable and small-scale micro-electronic technologies is also decentralizing many working and job relationships. Virtually all sectors of the economy, with very few exceptions, are now using these technologies, created by the development of the microprocessor and the microcomputer. Few products, services or working processes are unaffected by the new computer-based technologies. In a sense the production, distribution and consumption of goods and services have become democratized through the application of micro-electronics. Such technologies create new demands for specialist job skills, work aptitudes and forms of organization. All these factors place additional responsibilities on managements in terms of organizational structuring, research and development, investment planning, training costs, and the recruitment and retention of staff.

Economic and political affairs in the late twentieth century, therefore, are becoming more internationalized and globalized, whilst in some respects social relations are more fragmented and diffused, certainly in comparison with other periods. There is the emergence of transnationalism and supranationalism on the one hand, and of the atomization and segmentation of society on the other. The main features of transnationalism are economic, corporate and market-based, with supranationalism being political, democratic and based on citizenship rights. Societal atomization and segmentation, in contrast, are epitomized by the reassertion of individualist and market liberal values amongst many of the population. The developing corporate environment is thus divaricated, dynamic and transitory. Self-developing managers need to update their knowledge of it continuously, thus enabling them to respond effectively to the social, economic, political and legal challenges facing them.

Bibliography

ABERCROMBIE, N. and WARDE, A. *Contemporary British society*, London, Heinemann, 1988.

ACKOFF,R. *A concept of corporate planning*, New York, Wiley, 1970.

ALLEN, M. (ed.) *The Times 1000, 1987–88*, London, Times Books, 1989.

ARMSTRONG, G. 'Commitment through employee relations', paper presented to Institute of Personnel Management National Conference, 22 October 1987.

ARON, R. *Eighteen lectures on industrial society*, London, Weidenfeld & Nicolson, 1961.

BACON, R. and ELTIS, W. *Britain's economic problem*, London, Macmillan, 1976.

BAINS, M. (chairman), *The new local authorities : management and structure*, London, HMSO, 1972.

BALL, A. *Modern politics and government*, London, Macmillan, 1983.

BALL, A. *British political parties*, Basingstoke, Macmillan, 1987.

BALL, A. R. and MILLARD, F. *Pressure politics in industrial societies*, Basingstoke, Macmillan, 1986.

BALL, B. and ROSE, F. W. *Principles of business law*, London, Sweet & Maxwell, 1979.

BARRETT, M. *Women's oppression today*, London, Verso, 1980.

BELL, D. *The end of ideology*, New York, Free Press, 1960.

BELL, D. *The coming of post-industrial society*, London, Heinemann, 1973.

BELL, D. S. (ed.) *The Conservative government, 1979–84*, London, Croom Helm, 1985.

BENN, T. *Arguments for socialism*, Harmondsworth, Penguin, 1980.

BLACK, J. *The economics of modern Britain*, Oxford, Robertson, 1985.

BLAU, P. and SCOTT, W. R. *Formal organizations*, London, Routledge & Kegan Paul, 1963.

BLAUNER, R. *Alienation and freedom*, Chicago, University of Chicago Press, 1964.

BORRITZ, G. J. *Commercial law*, London, Butterworth, 1986.

BROOK, L., JOWELL, R. and WITHERSPOON, S. 'Recent trends in social attitudes', *Social trends* 19, London, HMSO, 1989.

BROOKE, P. 'The Conservative revolution', in CONSERVATIVE PARTY, *The first ten years*, London, CPC, 1989.

BROWN, C. *Black and white Britain*, London, PSI, 1984.

BUTLER, D. *and* KAVANAGH, D. *The British general election of 1987*, Basingstoke, Macmillan, 1988.

CENTRAL STATISTICAL OFFICE, *Social trends* 19, London, HMSO, 1989.

CENTRAL STATISTICAL OFFICE, *UK balance of payments*, London, HMSO, 1989.

COMMISSION FOR RACIAL EQUALITY, *Ethnic minorities in Britain*, London, CRE, 1985.

COMMISSION OF THE EUROPEAN COMMUNITIES, *European file : the big European market—a trump card for the economy and employment*, London, 1988.

CONSERVATIVE PARTY, *The first ten years*, London, CPC, 1989.

COSER, L. A. *The functions of social conflict*, London, Routledge, 1965.

CRICK, B. *In defence of politics*, Harmondsworth, Penguin, 1964.

CROSSMAN, R. H. S. Introduction to *The English constitution* by Walter Bagehot, London, Fontana, 1963.

CURTICE, J. *and* STEED, M. *Analysis of 1987 election*, in D. BUTLER *and* D. KAVANAGH. *The British general election of 1987*, Basingstoke, Macmillan, 1988.

CURWEN, P. J. *Public enterprise*, Brighton, Wheatsheaf, 1986.

DAHRENDORF, R. *Class and class conflict in industrial society*, London, Routledge, 1959.

DAHRENDORF, R. *On Britain*, London, BBC, 1982.

DAVIDSON, M. J. *and* COOPER, C. *Women managers*, Sheffield, MSC, 1983.

DAVIDSON, M. J. *and* COOPER, C. 'The pressures on women managers', *Management Decision* 4, 1987.

DEAL, T. E. *and* KENNEDY, A. A. *Corporate cultures*, Reading, Mass, Addison-Wesley, 1982.

DEARLOVE, J. *and* SAUNDERS, P. *Introduction to British politics*, Cambridge, Polity Press, 1984.

DEPARTMENT OF EMPLOYMENT. *Employment Gazette.* March 1988, London, HMSO.

DEPARTMENT OF HEALTH. *Working for patients*, London, HMSO, 1989.

DEVLIN, Lord. 'Judges, government and politics', *Modern law review*, 41, 1978.

DONALDSON, P. *Economics of the real world*, Harmondsworth, Penguin, 1986.

DRUCKER, H., *et al. Developments in British politics* 2, London, Macmillan, 1966.

DRUCKER, P. *Technology, management and society*, London, Heinemann, 1970.

DRUCKER, P. *The new realities*, London, Heinemann, 1989.

DUNLEAVY, P. *and* O'LEARY, B. *Theories of the state*, Basingstoke, Macmillan, 1987.

EQUAL OPPORTUNITIES COMMISSION. *Guidelines for equal opportunities employers*, London, EOC (no date).

ETZIONI, A. *A comparative analysis of complex organizations*, New York, Free Press, 1975.

EUROPEAN COMMUNITIES (No. 3/87). *Trade union information bulletin*, Brussels, Commission of the European Communities, 1987.

FARNHAM, D. *Personnel in context*, London, IPM, 1986.

FARRER, J. *Introduction to legal method*, London, Sweet & Maxwell, 1977.

FLORENCE, P. S. *Ownership, control and success of large corporations*, London, Sweet & Maxwell, 1961.

FORTE, Lord. 'The lady at No. 10 means business', in CONSERVATIVE PARTY, *The first ten years*, London, CPC, 1989.

FOX, A. *Royal Commission on trade unions and employers' associations research paper. Industrial sociology and industrial relations*, London, HMSO, 1966.

FREEMAN, M. D. A. *The legal structure*, London, Longman, 1974.

FRIEDMAN, M. *The counter-revolution in monetary theory*, London, Institute of Economic Affairs, 1970.

FRIEDMAN, M. *and* SCHWARTZ, A. *A monetary history of the United States*, Princeton, Princeton University Press, 1963.

GALBRAITH, J. *The new industrial state*, Harmondsworth, Penguin, 1967.

GALBRAITH, J. *Economics and the public purpose*, Harmondsworth, Penguin, 1975.

GAMBLE, A. *The free economy and the strong state*, Basingstoke, Macmillan, 1988.

GIDDENS, A. *Sociology*, Cambridge, Polity Press, 1989.

GRIFFITH, J. A. G. *The politics of the judiciary*, London, Fontana, 1981.

GROSSMAN, G. *Economic systems*, Englewood Cliffs, Prentice Hall, 1967.

HACKMAN, F. (ed.) *UK national accounts*, London, HMSO, 1989.

HALSEY, A. H. *Change in Britain*, Oxford, Oxford University Press, 1986.

HALSEY, A. H. 'Social trends since world war II', *Social trends* 17, London, HMSO, 1987.

HANDY, C. *Understanding organizations*, Harmondsworth, Penguin, 1985.

HANNAH, L. *and* KAY, J. A. *Concentration in modern industry: theory, measurement and the UK experience*, London, Macmillan, 1977.

HARRIS, P. *An introduction to law*, London, Weidenfeld & Nicolson, 1984.

HARRIS, P. J. *and* BUCKLE, J. D. 'Philosophies of law and the law teacher', *The law teacher*, 1976.

HASKEY, J. 'The ethnic minority population of Great Britain', *Population trends* 54, winter 1988.

HEATH, A., JOWELL, R. *and* CURTICE, J. *How Britain votes*, Oxford, Pergammon, 1985.

HEPPLE, B. 'The race relations acts and the process of change', *New community* XIV, autumn 1987.

HIRSCH, F. *Social limits to growth*, London, Routledge, 1976.

HOBBES, T. *Leviathan*, Oxford, Blackwell, 1946 (originally published 1651).

HOLMES, P. 'The Thatcher government's overall economic performance',

320   *The Corporate Environment*

in D. BELL (ed.) *The Conservative government, 1979–84*, London, Croom Helm, 1985.

HUSBAND, C. (ed.), *'Race' in Britain*, London, Hutchinson, 1987.

JENKINS, K., CAINES, K. *and* JACKSON, A. *Improving management in government : the next steps*, London, HMSO, 1988.

JOWELL, R., WITHERSPOON, S. *and* BROOK, L. (eds.), *British social attitudes: the fifth report*, Aldershot, Gower, 1986.

KAHN-FREUND, O. *Labour and the law*, London, Stevens, 1977.

KERR, C., *et al. Industrialism and industrial man*, Harmondsworth, Penguin, 1973.

KEYNES, J. M. *The general theory of employment, interest and money*, London, Macmillan, 1936.

KING, D. S. *The new right*, Basingstoke, Macmillan, 1987.

KLEIN, G. *The elements of banking*, London, Methuen, 1986.

LABOUR PARTY. *Democratic socialist aims and values*, London, Labour Party, 1988.

LABOUR PARTY. *Meet the challenge: make the change*, London, Labour Party, 1989.

LABOUR RESEARCH DEPARTMENT. *Labour Research* 44, 1987.

LABOUR RESEARCH DEPARTMENT. 'The money that brought Thatcher to power', *Labour research* 77(12), December 1988.

LANGE, O. *Essays on economic planning*, London, Statistical Publishing Society, 1967.

LANGE, O. *and* TAYLOR, M. *On the economic theory of socialism*, London, McGraw Hill, 1964.

LAWSON, N. 'We're growing to win the league', in CONSERVATIVE PARTY, *The first ten years*, London, CPC, 1989.

LEFTWICH, A. *What is politics?* Oxford, Blackwell, 1984.

LESTER, A. 'Anti-discrimination legislation in Great Britain', *New community* XIV, autumn 1987.

LEWIS, D. *Essentials of employment law*, London, IPM, 1983.

LEWIS, P. 'Other individual rights', in B. TOWERS (ed.), *A handbook of industrial relations practice*, London, Kogan Page, 1987.

LIPSEY, R. G. *Positive economics*, London, Weidenfeld & Nicolson, 1983.

LITTLEJOHN, J. *Social stratification*, London, Allen & Unwin, 1972.

LOCKE, J. *An essay concerning the true original, extent and end of civil government*, London, Oxford University Press, 1947 (originally published 1690).

MACINNES, D. *Thatcherism at work*, Milton Keynes, Open University Press, 1987.

MARQUAND, D. 'Twelve into one will go', *Marxism today*, April 1989.

MARRIS, R. *The economic theory of managerial capitalism*, London, Macmillan, 1964.

MARSHALL, T. H. *Citizenship and social class*, Cambridge, Cambridge University Press, 1950.

MARTIN, J. *and* ROBERTS, C. *Women and employment : a lifetime perspective*, London, HMSO, 1984.

Bibliography 321

MILL, J. S. *Utilitarianism, liberty, representative government*, London, Dent, 1972 (originally published 1851).

MINFORD, P. 'Keeping faith with the future', in CONSERVATIVE PARTY, *The first ten years*, London, CPC, 1989.

MISHAN, E. J. *The economic growth debate*. London, Allen & Unwin, 1977.

MORI, *British public opinion: general election, 1987*, London, MORI, 1987.

MORSE, G. (ed.) *Charlesworth's company law*, London, Stevens, 1987.

MOYLE, J. *The pattern of ordinary share ownership*, Cambridge, Cambridge University Press, 1971.

NAISBITT, J. *Megatrends: ten new directions transforming our lives*, London, Macdonald, 1984.

NOËL, E. *Working together: the institutions of the European Community*, Luxembourg, Office of the European Communities, 1989.

O'HIGGINS, P. *Workers' rights*, London, Arrow, 1976.

ORGANIZATION FOR ECONOMIC CO-OPERATION AND DEVELOPMENT. *Quarterly labour force statistics*, Paris OECD, 1989.

PACEY, P. *The culture of technology*, Oxford, Blackwell, 1983.

PAINE, T. *The Rights of man*, Harmondsworth, Penguin, 1984 (originally published 1791).

PLIATZKY, L. *Report on non-departmental bodies*, London, HMSO, 1980.

PLOWDEN, W. 'Tomorrow's lawyers?' in M. ZANDER (ed.), *What's wrong with the law?*, London, BBC, 1970.

ROBINSON, D. *Monetarism and the labour market*, Oxford, Oxford University press, 1986.

ROSE, R. *Politics in England*, Basingstoke, Macmillan, 1989.

ROUSSEAU, J. J. *The social contract*, Oxford, Clarendon, 1972 (originally published 1776).

ROYAL COMMISSION ON THE NATIONAL HEALTH SERVICE. *Report*, London, HMSO, 1979.

SARLVIK, B. *and* CREWE, I. *Decade of dealignment*, Cambridge, Cambridge University Press, 1983.

SCASE, R. 'Women managers', *Management today*, March 1987.

SCHEIN, V. 'The relationship between sex role stereotyping and requisite management characteristics', *Journal of applied psychology* 57, 1973.

SCOTT, J. *Corporations, classes and capitalism*, London, Hutchinson, 1979.

SCOTT, J. *Capitalist property and financial power*, Brighton, Wheatsheaf, 1986.

SCRUTON, R. *The meaning of conservatism*, Harmondsworth, Penguin, 1980.

SMITH, A. *The wealth of nations*, Oxford, Clarendon, 1976 (originally published 1776).

SMITH, D. *The rise and fall of monetarism*, Harmondsworth, Penguin, 1987.

SOCIAL AND LIBERAL DEMOCRATS. *Our different vision*. London, SLD Federation Green Paper No. 7, 1989.

SPENCER, A. *and* PODMORE, D. (eds.) *In a man's world*, London, Tavistock, 1987.

SPENDER, D. *Men's studies modified*, Oxford, Pergamon, 1981.

SPENDER, D. *Invisible women*, London, Writers and Readers, 1989.

THOMASON, G. *A textbook of personnel management*, London, IPM, 1975.

THOMASON, G. *A textbook of personnel management*, London, IPM, 1981.

TONGE, R. *Feminist perspectives*, London, Allen & Unwin, 1989.

TOWERS, B. (ed.) *A handbook of industrial relations practice*, London, Kogan Page/IPM, 1987.

TRADES UNION CONGRESS. *Report of 119th annual Trades Union Congress, 1987*, London, TUC, 1988

TWINING, W. *and* MIERS, D. *How to do things with rules*, London, Weidenfeld & Nicolson, 1982.

VICKERS, G. *Freedom in a rocking boat*, Harmondsworth, Allen Lane, 1970.

WEBSTER, D. *The labour party and the new left*, London, Fabian Society, 1981.

WIDDICOMBE, D. *The report of the committee of inquiry into local authority business*, London, HMSO, 1986.

WILLIAMS, G. *Learning the law*, London, Stevens, 1973.

WINTOUR, P. 'Labour recruiters to woo the working class', *Guardian*, 17 January 1989.

WOODWARD, J. *Industrial organization: theory and practice*, London, Oxford University Press, 1965.

WOODWARD, J. (ed.) *Industrial organization: behaviour and control*, London, Oxford University Press, 1970.

WRIGHT MILLS, C. *The power elite*, New York, Oxford University Press, 1956.

ZANDER, M. (ed.) *What's wrong with the law?*, London, BBC, 1970.

Index